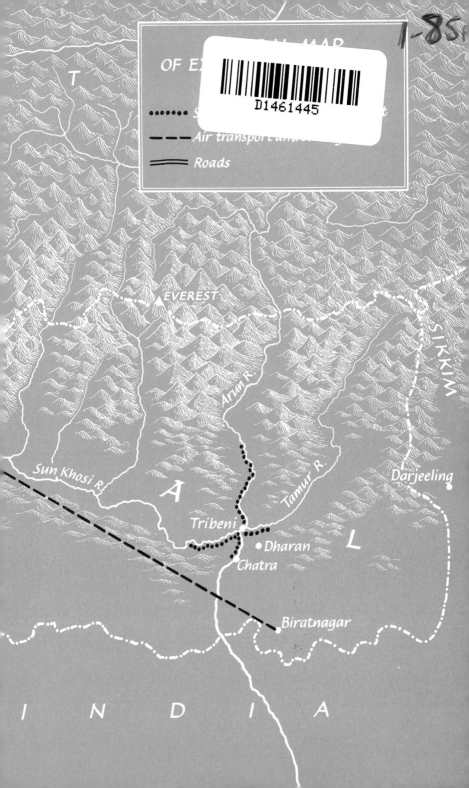

1-85

OF E... ...L MAP

D1461445

········ S...

– – – Air transport and ...

═══ Roads

T

EVEREST

Arum R.

SIKKIM

Sun Khosi R.

A

Tamur R.

Darjeeling

Tribeni

Dharan

Chatra

L

Biratnagar

I N D I A

Andrew Cowan.

The Great Himalayan Passage

The Lost World of Quintana-Roo
Tiger for Breakfast
Mustang
Lords and Lamas
Cavaliers of Kham

THE GREAT HIMALAYAN PASSAGE

Across the Himalayas by hovercraft

Michel Peissel

Collins
St James's Place, London, 1974

William Collins Sons & Co Ltd
London · Glasgow · Sydney · Auckland
Toronto · Johannesburg

First published 1974
© 1974 Michel Peissel
ISBN 0 00 211841 6

Set in Monotype Imprint
Made and printed in Great Britain by
William Collins Sons & Co Ltd Glasgow

To Olivier and Jocelyn, that they may always remember the words of Bertrand Russell that: 'Much of what is greatest in human achievement involves some element of intoxication, some sweeping away of prudence by passion.'

Contents

Illustrations

Acknowledgments

We are particularly grateful to His Majesty the King of Nepal for the privilege of having been allowed to travel along the great rivers of his country.

As to our enterprise itself, it would not have been possible without the constant and kind assistance of a great many people, to whose help a few words of formal acknowledgment can never do justice. Our thanks go first to Field-Marshal Surendra, B. Shaha, Colonel Charles Wylie, and Mr Robert Trillo, whose vital role in our expedition is, I hope, evident throughout this book.

To the generosity of Mr Elmar Brenninkmeyer and Sir William Collins we owe the opportunity to travel from dream to reality. To Michael Pinder, John Trueluck and their friends we are grateful for the work they did on our machines. Our thanks also go to Mr J. A. Billing of Anglesey, who coached us in mechanics, and to Joe Skladzien and Bob Hobman, who helped us prepare for the journey.

We are also grateful for the kind assistance in Nepal of His Excellency Mr T. O'Brien, CMG, the British Ambassador, Brigadier E. D. Smith, DSO, MBE, Colonel J. Roberts, OBE, Mr and Mrs Weatherall, Captain Willshire, Mr Everatt, and Chuck McDougal. Last I would like to thank Charles Clasen for his help with my manuscript.

As for Michael Alexander, I trust this book will make it clear he is to blame for everything that happened – and thus shares whatever merit this expedition may have.

M.P.

THIS is an account of an expedition by hover-craft across the Himalayas and an adventure into the frontiers of a new technology. It is the story of how the jungles of the Indian plains and the cold tundra of the Tibetan highlands are united by the flow of mighty rivers whose secret courses have never before been travelled; an account of a marginal world, better known for its peaks yet better understood from its rivers, which cut a direct route from snowfield to swamp land, from the pastures of yaks to those of the rhino. It is also the story of all who share the river's fate, the tale of vanishing cultures and receding horizons, a quest for the unknown in a world often thought to be without mystery.

1 *Dreams on Hot Air*

At 5.30 a.m. on June 9th, 1972, witnessed by six small children in rags, I stood with Michael Alexander at 8500 feet on the banks of the sacred Kali Gandaki river at Tukutcha. It was freezing cold. To the south, the towering mass of the Dhaula-ghiri range glistened in the morning sun, while ahead of us rose the almost sheer face of Annapurna towering 18,000 feet above the dull roaring waters of the river which here cuts through the deepest gorge in the world.

To the children present we must have seemed a strange pair. Both over six feet tall, we were clad in amazing garments – rubber mud-boots, bright orange and blue waterproof trousers and jackets, fur hats and skintight diver's shoes. At our feet was our monster, an orange and grey hovercraft, the first machine the children had ever seen apart from the distant out-line of an occasional passing helicopter or plane.

There was no wind. The time had come to set off. My stomach fluttered with fear and excitement, for this was the day I had looked forward to for so long. Two hours later, covered with spray, fighting the river's roaring waters, I emerged from the gorge on to the northern face of the Him-alayas. That morning both Michael Alexander and I successfully completed what had seemed an impossible dream: we had crossed the Himalayas in a hovercraft. This was the end of a three-month struggle up rivers never before navigated, large stretches of which had never been seen by foreigners. That morning I like to think that in a small way something had changed in the world.

It all began in October 1970 when, belatedly, I became ac-quainted with hovercraft. It was a surprise encounter, based on the sudden realization that, while I was lamenting the fact that I had been born too late to partake of the Wright brothers' adventure, or to pioneer the steam engine or the automobile, and had even missed out on the rocket to the moon, I was in fact sitting idle while somewhere engineers were developing a new and amazing means of transport. Here I felt lurked an adventure worthy of my heroes the Lindberghs and the Bleriots, and all those pioneers with hats and goggles whom I had watched with envy as they jogged around in black and white on ancient films. In the hovercraft, I thought, might lie the key to some of my dreams.

Like any traveller, I always felt that I had some stake in everything that moved, and having experienced so many forms of transport I could hardly be indifferent to something new. The hovercraft, I learned, was invented in 1958 by the British engineer Christopher Cockerell, based on the elementary fact (known for centuries) that air blown under an object can lift it. Like all great inventions, it is simple, and when I realized this I suddenly felt that one day it would surely be seen as one of man's great discoveries.

Man has always sought to improve his mobility, trying to overcome gravity and friction, the arch-enemies of displacement. He invented the wheel: but even a wheel was not much use over rough terrain. Someone then invented the train which ran on tracks. Later the creation of expensive paved roads brought cars. But neither railroads nor cars could run everywhere, especially in mountainous terrain where gravity is a worse obstacle than friction. Planes and helicopters have smoothed out mountains, but they are not a good means of seeing things and landing still remains a delicate operation. However, in 1958, with rockets going into outer space and the moon but a step away, many believed that most of the answers to transport had been found.

Not so Christopher Cockerell, who that same year was using his wife's hairdryer and two coffee tins to design the first hovercraft. By blowing air into the tins he caused them to rise and slide about on a cushion of air. Friction had at last dis-

appeared from surface transport, but of course, like everything
new, it was something which people at first refused to take
seriously; in fact, few do even today.

Although a hovercraft can travel over land and water, mud
and snow, and needs no roads or airfields, it does have its
shortcomings; it cannot negotiate large obstacles, and has great
difficulty going uphill. The latter problem is only a matter of
power; negotiating obstacles was another matter. A Frenchman,
the engineer Jean Bertin, put a skirt on the hovercraft and this
suddenly allowed it to fly a little higher and pass over obstacles
up to six feet in height. But six feet is not very high, and
a hovercraft with skirts that deep was a monstrous,
heavy machine; skirts, it seemed, were not the answer to everything.

It then occurred to me that if you cannot fly over an obstacle
you can always bounce over it, and thus a small hovercraft
might be made to bounce over big rocks. I realized that all I
needed was a bouncing hovercraft.

Why I needed one was another story. Since 1959 I had
travelled over 3500 miles on foot and muleback across remote
areas of India, Nepal and Bhutan. These weary marches, made
in the course of five expeditions to the Himalayas, had led me
to reflect how strange it was that we could travel by rocket to
the moon but that we still had no practical mechanical means
of penetrating those mountain regions, where the yak and the
human foot still ruled unrivalled. That is when I began thinking
about hovercraft, and recalled the sacred Kali Gandaki, and
how this river eventually opens a direct road through the
Himalayas, cutting its way between two of the world's highest
peaks before rushing on to the sea. What if I could follow
its foaming course, and ride up its waters from India to
Tibet? Such a thought seemed sheer madness, an impossible
feat.

Or was it?

The less I knew about hovercraft, the wilder were my ideas.
Since hovercraft do not in theory touch either the ground or
water, I could see no reason why they should not shoot up

rapids, bouncing on their air cushions over rocks and up water-falls. If this were possible, in a few hours one could travel a distance it would take days to travel on foot. Roads, I knew, had long ago proved a failure in the Himalayas; they were expensive to build, and the very few that existed were constantly made impassable by monsoon rains and winter snow. Thousands of workers were required to keep these rare roads open in the Indian, Nepalese and Bhutanese Himalayas. Now, in my enthusiasm, I saw transport transformed not only in the Himalayas but elsewhere. If I could shoot up through the Himalayas in a hovercraft, it would be child's play to travel on the sluggish rivers of other lands. Thus every country could acquire nationwide networks of highways overnight, since every river, even dry ones, was also potentially a road. Whole new areas would be opened up to exploration, and vast inaccessible regions would suddenly come within reach.

Such was my dream. The strategic and economic implications were also tremendous, of course, but I was not primarily motivated by economic considerations. The real reason for my wild enthusiasm was rooted in my love and fascination for the Himalayas. Since 1959, in the course of several expeditions, I had spent a total of three years wandering the remote, rugged trails that make their way between the great peaks towards the Tibetan highlands. There I had left my heart, for I had found in the wild ranges a world whose overpowering dimensions spoke to the soul. For thirteen years I had come to consider these regions my second home. Katmandu and Nepal might now be listed in the files of every travel agency, but I knew well that the land still retained its mysteries.

I realized how little was known of the Himalayas when I first measured on foot the true dimension of that continent that stretches from Afghanistan to Burma. Then in 1964 I had the privilege of becoming the first foreigner to reside in and explore Mustang, an ancient Tibetan realm, today part of Nepal, located one hundred miles north of Annapurna. I realized again the absence of exact geographical knowledge in 1968, when I crossed on foot the secret valleys of the far eastern Himalayas of Bhutan. I had to learn to speak Tibetan. I yearned now to return, and perhaps discover other secret valleys and visit more uncharted areas.

I was well aware that the Himalayas were not just the refuge of mystics and sages, but the home of the greatest variety of peoples and tribes to inhabit any one area of Asia. Hidden in the inaccessible folds of the Himalayas is also an infinite variety of animals, reptiles, insects and plants, reflecting the range of climates between the sweltering plains of India and the high glacial tundra of Tibet.

Confined to the few trails that exist, I had only been able to scratch the surface of the land's variety and take a glance at its marvels. Over forty different tribes in the Himalayas have been recorded, many unstudied and never or rarely visited; how many more might yet thrive unrecorded no one could tell. Among the many mysteries of the Himalayas there was one I particularly wanted to solve, and that was to find out who had built the staggering cliff cities that I had sighted on my journey to Mustang, vast skyscraper-like networks of caves dug out by some long-forgotten race into the cliffs that bordered the upper valley of the Kali Gandaki.

Still, I knew that I would never have either the time or the physical energy to travel more than a small section of their vast extent, so long as I was limited to slow progress along the narrow trails. I felt travelling by hovercraft could provide the means of opening up many of these otherwise inaccessible regions to scientific investigation. This is what I was now determined to prove.

However childish my enthusiasm appeared, I was aware of the obstacles confronting me – not only technical ones, such as developing a new craft capable of going up rapids, but also the dangers inherent in pioneering a new technique for shooting up some of the most violent rivers in the world, rivers that had never even been accurately mapped. In addition, there were intricate problems of a logistical and diplomatic nature. So great were the difficulties that, rather than feel discouraged, I resolved to devote all my energies to overcoming them.

So much for my motives. The adventure's practical beginnings date from one grey afternoon in London when, seated on a comfortable couch, I decided to share my idea. Michael Alexander lay sprawled in an armchair before me. Between us on a glass table a skull stared across the room at stuffed birds. These were perched on the edge of an eighteenth-century painting, hanging on the wall of one of the most original flats I have ever seen. No less exotic was Michael Alexander, its owner. Hero in World War II at the age of 23, a prisoner at Colditz, he had since then spent most of his life seeking adventures. These included discovering and identifying the city of Firozkoh, the eleventh-century summer capital of the Ghorid Kings of Afghanistan, organizing the first guided safaris on the Duke of Bedford's estate, setting up a fashionable London restaurant and kidnapping a friend from the Foreign Legion. He has written five books. He is also a director of *Animals*, a magazine on wildlife. Handsome and energetic, some six foot two in height, he was then 52, and said to be a difficult man. Casually, I said: 'Wouldn't it be fantastic to cross the Himalayas in a hovercraft?' Michael did not stir. After a long silence, he snapped, 'Someone's already had a go, and it proved quite impossible.' We had an argument. I crossed the room and picked up the phone; and it all began. Slowly, inevitably, I was dragged into having to live up to my words, and proving Michael wrong. I was ringing Colonel Charles Wylie. A Gurkha officer, he had been the brilliant organizing secretary and one of the key members of the successful 1953 Everest expedition, a friend whom I felt would surely set Michael right. 'No,' said the surprised voice on the phone, 'no one has yet crossed the Himalayas in a hovercraft, but Hillary and some friends took a jet boat to Nepal and travelled up part of the Sun Khosi river. One of the boats overturned and two people were nearly drowned.' Had Charles Wylie stopped there, said good night and hung up (for it was past ten) everything would still have been all right, but he added: 'If you are really interested in hovercraft, why don't you call Christopher Cox. He's a keen climber – you met at the Alpine Club the other day.

He happens to be secretary of the U.K. Hovercraft Society.'

The wheels began to turn. I accepted an invitation to lunch with Christopher Cox the following afternoon, quite unworried by the fact that I had never yet seen a real hovercraft. Christopher was mostly keen on hearing about my Himalayan travels; as to hovercraft and my wild plan, he preferred to leave the matter to experts, and suggested that I contact Robert Trillo, one of England's most brilliant hovercraft engineers, for many years Christopher Cockerell's personal assistant.

Unabashed, I called Trillo on the phone. A little bewildered, he suggested I write. The next day I left Michael to life in Belgravia and flew to my home in Spain, unaware that I had had my last peaceful hour for a long time to come.

In Spain I began building a model hovercraft, based on what I imagined them to be like, since I had still not seen one and had only the vaguest idea of how they really worked. I bought some glue, dismantled my son's Japanese electric cars – which had never worked – and then, an amiable omen, I found a free gift propeller in a tin of Spanish biscuits.

A latecomer to the tool bench, a notorious bungler since childhood of balsa wood kits, I still marvel today at my achievement, for what I did was to reinvent (quite unnecessarily) the hovercraft. I made a skirt to my own design out of a plastic bag, and stuck it on the polystyrene foam lid of a packing crate. To my surprise, it worked. My small hovercraft would skid all over my house, cutting in from carpet to floorboards at the end of a wire I had connected to the elusive poles of a battery.

I was delighted and, rushing outside, had my hovercraft skitter down the rocky street straight towards a puddle, over which it proceeded with great ease. Some of the local fishermen stared in sad sympathy at my apparent madness, quite unaware that I was demonstrating for the first time in this little Spanish village one of the revolutionary inventions.

I worked all day and dreamed all night of new hovercraft, and I built six working models before actually laying eyes on a book which explained how the real ones worked, and which arrived only with Robert Trillo's reply to my first letter.

In my letter I had outlined my idea, which was based on the simple observation that rivers, even the fastest and most dangerous, have only a slight gradient – so slight that if a car could run up a rapid river it would hardly notice it was going uphill. The truth of this statement had struck me when I realized that the Rhône, which I had always taken for a relatively fast river, was only 168 metres above sea-level at Lyon, which is over 200 km from the sea – a rise of only some six feet per mile. The same calculation showed that rougher rivers were climbed equally slowly. This was vital, because I had just learned that hovercraft at best could only climb a gradient of one in ten – a limitation which seemed to spell the immediate failure of my project, since everyone assured me that Himalayan rivers were considerably steeper than that. To Robert Trillo, I outlined what I believed to be the maximum gradients of the Himalayan rivers, describing from memory what I thought to be the maximum height of the turbulent waves of the rapids we should have to climb.

On receiving this information, Robert Trillo, far from pouring cold water on my plans, set about locating a machine that might suit our purpose. Altogether he contacted eight hovercraft manufacturers in Canada, the United States, France and England. Interested in a possible sale, most of them replied hopefully that, although they had never tried their craft on rapids, they were confident I would find them adequate. One manufacturer did add that his machine had been tried up fast water on the St Lawrence under St Catherine's Bridge in Montreal. Several suggested that I try out their craft. Eager to see a real hovercraft at last, I rushed to England, where I stayed with Michael. He seemed as gloomy as ever, going through piles of books on Tchaikovsky, having been commissioned to write a biography of the great musician. But although his attitude to my project had not noticeably changed over the past month, his curiosity had been aroused sufficiently for him to accompany me for the first trials.

Any goodwill Michael might have shown was soon drowned in the sand-pit of the Heathrow Water Ski Club. Dressed for the City, he had insisted on having a ride on a hovercraft which a young salesman eagerly declared could go anywhere and do anything. Anything, that is, except make it back to the grassy banks of the Heathrow sand-pit, thus obliging Michael to wade ankle deep in mud in order to get out of a craft that all morning had shown considerable talent for breaking down! Even when operative, the machine had failed to climb up a very slight bank. To add insult to injury, the salesman nearly drove away with Michael's favourite hat, and, not surprisingly, he now viewed my project with an increasingly jaundiced eye. This first trial also shattered my own enthusiasm. Now that I had seen a real hovercraft, I began to have doubts. But I refused to admit this, and decided to try out another machine.

Reluctantly, Michael drove me up to Peterborough, a town set in flat country with not so much as a peak or a distant hill, the only high points being dozens of huge factory chimneys sadly pointing to a rainy sky. Looking at another cumbersome machine, travelling over another pond in another sand-pit, I began to wonder whether, since I had a knack with yaks, I should not stick to more time-honoured means of transport. Indeed, my project seemed to be running aground, for I now learned that none of these machines could be flown out to India or transported to the great Himalayan rivers, since their rigid superstructure could not be dismantled. Short of my chartering a flying Hercules, they could only travel by boat. As for going up rapids, that was no problem so long as there were no rocks above ten inches in height and no waves of more than one foot deep.

I should have given up all hope had we not suddenly been presented by the sales manager of Hover-Air Ltd with a strange little machine. 'I thought you might be interested in this little one as a kind of auxiliary craft,' he said casually.

Thus we were introduced to a minute inflated rubber dinghy with two fans run by engines so small they could have been carried in the palm of one's hand. To my surprise, Michael was the first to react favourably at the sight of the proto-type that was now unloaded from the roof of a Land-Rover.

I also felt that here might lie the answer to our problem.

For an hour we watched John Trueluck, the company's test pilot, roar about the sand-pit on his $8' \times 5'$ flying rubber dinghy, to the noise of what sounded like a dozen jets at take-off. That night, back in London, I called Robert Trillo. What we needed, I now felt certain, was an inflatable hovercraft. Could he come up to Peterborough, see the machine we had found, and give us his opinion?

Leaving his serious work, Robert agreed to come up the following week. On the train to Peterborough he initiated me into some of the finer points of hovercraft, explaining exactly how they worked, and how, with little or no contact with land or water, they are extremely difficult to steer, being subject to the slightest wind. I also became familiar with such strange technical terms as 'bag-skirt', 'finger-skirt', and 'going over hump'. 'Going over hump' for a hovercraft is approximately what breaking the sound barrier is for a plane. The hump is a wave of water created by the air escaping under the craft. This air which lifts the craft creates a hollow depression in the water. To get the hovercraft going fast you have to push it out of this depression, which for a while travels underneath the craft, forming a sort of bow wave. Until you climb over this wave, the craft is doomed to drag along slowly. 'Hump speed' is the speed at which a craft goes over the hump and moves fast enough not to dent the water any more. I said 'yes' to all these explanations, though I was not sure whether I had understood them all.

That evening, going back to London, I felt reassured. Strange calculations in the dining-car made Robert Trillo come out with the verdict that the prototype we had seen was in fact a remarkable little machine. Its very light, inflatable hull gave it a very good rating in terms of power to weight, and this was enough for me to forget momentarily that the craft could only go over obstacles six inches high and had had trouble moving over thick grass.

Would it be possible, I wondered, to have a similar but larger craft made, with more power and higher skirts? Robert

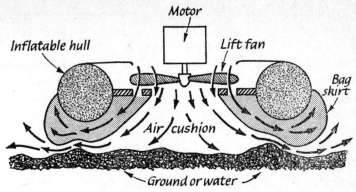

Compressed air flowing from tips of fan filled up the rubber bag under our craft – rest of air is trapped between the bags of our skirt. This cushion of air forces the craft up while a little escapes under the skirt which it stops from touching the ground. The bag-skirt material will mould to the shape of nearly all obstacles yet without touching the obstacles.

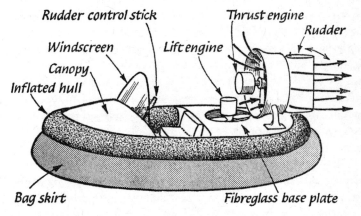

Thrust engine and fan push the craft forward; a pivoting rudder commanded by a stick in front of seat can be made to deflect air and thus turn the craft. As craft does not touch ground (see above) it needs only a little power to advance.

HOW HOVERCRAFT WORK

Trillo was willing to make one, but pointed out that not only would it be expensive, but there would be no guarantee that it would serve my purpose. I thought I detected in his remark a certain scepticism about my whole project. I must admit that, seen from the flat landscape of Peterborough, and on the edges of a stagnant pond, the Himalayas seemed very high and very far away. As for the monstrous rapids up which I planned to ride, they were surely out of all proportion to even the largest craft we had seen.

Michael had little to offer except sound advice, as usual. 'Why don't you get the small one and try it out, and then you will know what needs doing to it.' I had not thought of that. Next morning I was on the phone talking to Hover-Air Ltd. The voice at the other end was disheartening. No, they did not plan to go into production for a long time, six months or more; the craft they had was only a prototype, an idea they had been playing with. Of course I did not suspect the company was going into liquidation, which explained its reluctance to tie up more funds in a new machine, even if it was to go to the Himalayas. But I quite rightly suspected that they thought me slightly mad, so I resolved to return a third time to Peterborough, try out the machine myself, and talk them into making one specially for me in a hurry.

Thus I came to drive a hovercraft for the first time. As the machine was too small to allow for an instructor, I was sent off on my own in a flurry of spray and to the screech of the two little seven horse-power motors originally designed for a power saw. The noise was so loud that I promptly forgot which lever was which, as I skated all over the pond, like some aquatic fly, heading for what looked like the meanest and fastest-approaching cliff I have ever seen. In a panic I cut both engines and flopped to a watery halt. Starting up again, I made it painfully back to the low bank where the test pilot and the sales manager were waiting anxiously.

Short though this trial run had been, it was enough to convince me that riding a small hovercraft was an experience never to be forgotten. Passing from land to water without so much as a bump gives one the impression of flying, while on turning one feels as if one is skidding on ice in a runaway car on some frozen Canadian lake. It is not an experience to be universally recommended, but it is certainly one to be remembered.

Somehow I managed to persuade the company to speed up production of another prototype. By working overtime, they agreed that they could deliver it to me by the middle of June. All was going well except that my wife, back in Spain, saw no necessity to spend my last penny on a machine that had not even been properly tested.

I expounded to her the finer points of my plan; how with a hovercraft that could travel up Himalayan gorges I could see more of the Himalayas in three months than I could ever hope to see in ten years of successive expeditions on foot. Furthermore, I could penetrate unexplored terrain, which might lead to fascinating discoveries – not to mention opening up the Himalayas, and mountains in general, to a new form of transport. Just think of what an achievement it would be to cross the entire Himalayas by boat! Why, it would be one of the achievements of the century! My wife, like Michael, was not impressed. But it was too late in any case; my enthusiasm had passed the point of no return.

Every day I became more convinced that I should devote all my time to this new project. With Michael's help, I wrote an outline, grandly entitled *International Himalayan Hovercraft Expedition*. Our objective, I declared roundly, was 'the exploration of the great gorges and valleys of the headwaters of the major Himalayan rivers of either Bhutan, Nepal and India, with special attention to comparative ecology and settlement patterns.' 'An investigation and study of the Himalayan valley cliff dwellings will also be carried out,' I wrote, so that 'the use of the hovercraft for rapid penetration into regions so far inaccessible to all vehicles will allow the expedition to cover in a few months territory yet unvisited that would otherwise take several years to investigate.'

The expedition was placed under the supervision of Colonel

Charles Wylie, while Robert Trillo consented to act as technical adviser to our project. The next four pages of the outline almost convinced me that it was feasible. My major problem in the immediate future was finding the necessary funds to set up our expedition. To travel in the remotest corners of the Himalayas on foot is, as I well know, a very expensive proposition. To fly out two or three hovercraft specially designed for penetrating unchartered gorges and secret valleys miles from a mechanic or petrol station was something close to a military operation, and beyond my limited means.

Michael by now had agreed to go ahead with me on the project, but declared he could not allocate any money to the venture. Money being such a bore, I refused to worry about it, trusting that nobody could fail to see in our project one of the most adventurous schemes of the century. I felt certain large manufacturers would come forward with donations. To begin with, the petrol companies, then the manufacturers of hover-craft engines, and those who would build our new larger hover-craft. For I still planned to have an entirely new craft built on the basis of what we could learn from the little machine I had bought. If billions were being spent to gather a few rocks on the moon, I felt certain that someone might find a few thousand pounds to back a venture that I believed was surely more exciting, and eventually could prove more significant, than crossing the Atlantic in a sailing boat, for instance, or driving across the Sahara on a tricycle.

Now followed three months of intense propaganda and daily interviews with the managers and directors of large firms in England, France and Spain. Everyone, it seemed, was most interested in our project . . . until the mention of finance, whereupon they would stand up, wish us luck, and apologize. I almost began to believe that European industry was on the brink of bankruptcy. Or was it that everyone thought I was mad – a possibility that Michael would inevitably raise from time to time. Yet although he continued to play Devil's Advocate 'for my own good' – or so he said – he later admitted when I was away that he too had begun to be obsessed by those magic words, 'Himalayas' and 'Hovercraft'. In London his flat now became our expedition headquarters.

Under a portrait of Ludwig II, the mad king of Bavaria (an omen?), and staring at the human skull (another omen?) we spent hours elaborating our strategy. Inevitably our requests for help from businesses, universities, rich friends and foundations ended up with the same reply, 'We are sorry, but . . .'

Then came the letter stating that my machine would be ready in a week, and could I come and collect it from Peterborough. A hovercraft expedition without a hovercraft was one thing. With a hovercraft it became quite another matter.

On June 28th I flew to London in the company of a young long-haired friend by the name of Joe. He was our new-found mechanic, guitar in one hand and spanner in the other. We were now ready for the trials – a mad four months during which Joe, his guitar, Michael and I, and a bevy of beautiful young ladies, were kept busy hovering all over England, France and Spain.

The machine was tested for the first time on the stately lawns of Osbaston Hall, Leicester. Champagne flowed while the machine ran painfully round the lawns sucking in all the cut grass until it choked to a halt. The second day my belt buckle got into the left propeller and everything came to a sudden end in a grinding of plastic blades. Not for nothing, it seemed, had the manufacturers called it 'Hovernaut'. Two days later, repaired by our guitarist, the hovernaut sat in the waiting-room of one of my publishers in London while the receptionist had mild fits over her carpet being soiled, and the press was prematurely called to look over our little machine. Few came, although the *Daily Express* headed an article in its society column in large letters, 'Explorer Michel takes easy way into unknown.' Nobody appeared to take us seriously. Michael, notorious for abandoning his car, doors open, in the middle of Piccadilly, suffered the indignity of being photographed as he put sixpence in a parking meter beside the hovercraft. This dismal shot was then reproduced around the world. After leaving Heinemann's lobby, the hovercraft was transferred to

The hovercraft in London. Below: the police disapproved of our first trials on the Cher, especially when we shot the rapids under the château of Chenonceau.

Pagodas are said to have originated in Nepal. Here, the skyline of Bhadgaon, one of the seven towns in the Katmandu valley.

the roof of Michael's car and parked in a mews, where, to bolster my confidence, I set about painting 'Himalayan Hover-craft Expedition' on the door – just to help make our project seem real.

I soon realized I had acquired a little monster and, like all monsters, it began to attract attention. Our arrival with the incongruous machine perched on the roof of the car drew large crowds of curious onlookers. 'Look, there's a hydrofoil!' some would say, 'Look at that funny machine!' In London, an old gentleman came up to us. 'I beg your pardon, is that your thing sitting up there?' 'Yes,' I said, slightly exasperated. The old man then rattled on quite excited. He at least fully appreciated what lay in store for us, 'going to the Himalayas with this!' He added, 'I was in India in 1922 at the time of the first Everest disaster.' I could see in his eyes a gleam of envy and a spark of enthusiasm. Some people, after all, did appreciate that we were pioneers. The younger generation, on the other hand, did not so much as bat an eyelid. 'Oh,' they would say, 'it's just a hovercraft.' They had read about them in magazines. Their goal was beyond the moon.

Soon I discovered that my monster was a legal anomaly as well. When I decided to take it to France, I was informed that hovercraft were considered strategic machines, and that to export one I needed to obtain clearance from the War Office. However unstrategic the baby hovercraft looked, we had to get the documents. At Dover we boarded another hovercraft, the ferry. Our little machine looked silly lying beside the massive *Princess Margaret* whose skirts rose 15 feet high. The pilot of the ferry came down to see our craft and invited us to sit in his cabin, a room clustered with dials. We had a chat about going over hump, and he wished us luck. I also thought I saw a smile on his face.

There was no smile on the face of the French customs officer. 'What is it?' he kept repeating. 'A boat, a car, or a plane?' 'Nothing,' I answered, 'I mean, it's neither.' 'Have you a *triptique*? A driver's or pilot's licence? A boat permit? Some-thing at least?' 'No,' I had to answer. 'But surely you have something?' 'It's an *aéroglisseur*,' I explained lamely, 'a British *aéroglisseur*.' The man did not understand except that, being British, it was suspect. 'You must have some sort of document.' I showed him the bill. That was not good enough. As there was no legislation on hovercraft, in France or anywhere else except in England, no one knew what they were. We only cleared customs when I managed to prove that 'it' was a machine, just a machine, a machine being a thing with an engine. Our engines being so small, we did not have to pay customs, and thus at last we sped towards Paris, the 'machine' rocking about on the roof, the propeller turning in the wind, and Joe strumming his guitar.

'*Oh! Regardez, un Oouvercraff!*' At red lights excited crowds gathered. In Paris the press came to the Plaza, but they wanted a picture in front of the Eiffel Tower, so they got a picture in front of the Eiffel Tower. We then sped south, Michael's car radiator boiling over. All of us were keen on trying the thing out. By this time 'all' meant not only Michael, Joe and myself, but two other friends as well – an unnecessarily large crew of enthusiasts, but all with faith, the essential prerequisite for those first weeks, when everything went wrong.

To start with, there was nowhere we could try out the machine. Requests to borrow public or private lakes ended with refusals, since lake owners imagined ours to be some gigantic monstrous machine. We felt sorry for the little hovercraft, but pity soon turned to anger when we had no sooner secured a lake than it started breaking down. First the tail fell off, then the engine stopped and Michael was obliged to swim ashore towing the hovercraft. My father-in-law, a fervent Bugatti fan in the days when cars were cars (before electric starters), and no doubt considering also his daughter's future more than my safety, declared he had trouble visualizing us in the Himalayas. I was almost inclined to agree. Nevertheless, the hovercraft worked long enough to allow me to round up some of his cows in what will no doubt go down among cowboys as the first Hoverrodeo. The cows did not mind, while we emerged spattered with dung.

So much for games. We now had to get down to work and begin our first serious trials. How serious was another matter. I had decided upon a run down one of the unnavigable portions of the Cher river. With Joe and yet a new friend, Olivia, in charge of first aid and food, we set off.

No sooner had we arrived on the deserted banks of the Cher than a man popped up and ordered us off. Boats, we were told, were strictly forbidden, as the river was officially unnavigable. 'But,' I protested, 'we don't even touch the water!' To no avail. From then on our trials were enhanced by the thrill of illegality. We stealthily advanced on the river farther north, sending scouts ahead to make sure there were no witnesses.

I shall never forget my first river journey. For all I could tell, the Cher might have been the Amazon. For thousands of years nothing had disturbed its banks, where trees leaned lazily into the water. Between its sandy shores I advanced over a crystal carpet in a landscape never yet disturbed by man. As in a dream, I drifted over lilies, reeds, weeds and mud, down little gullies of foam and along dark tree-lined channels. Every yard revealed a new and varied perspective of water and shore, of sun and shade, as I coasted down the most beautiful virgin scenery I had ever seen. Save for the roar of the engine, it was like sliding in a dream, the river unwinding smoothly before me as if in a film, or as if I were a dragonfly gliding between the colourful banks of an aquatic paradise.

Turning a bend, I came upon a fisherman. Startled by the noise, he suddenly realized that where he stood there was not enough water for a boat to pass, so he made frantic motions for me to stop. I took no notice, steered the craft up a sand-bank out of the river and drove around him on dry land before hitting the water again. As I did so I turned round: the fisherman in amazement had dropped his rod. Such are the origins of stories about flying saucers. I was laughing to myself when suddenly I realized I was about to go over the edge of a small dam. Hovercraft have no brakes. To stop suddenly one deflates the cushion and the machine becomes an ordinary boat. I did this and managed to coast ashore in time.

From there we drove the hovercraft to Chenonceau, the well-known château of the Loire with its famous ballroom spanning the river – which is, incidentally, the river Cher just before it joins the Loire. Here I frightened some 200 tourists in a daring dash under one of the arches, much to the fury of the local authorities. Joe took a photograph, and we rushed off to the Loire itself.

On the Cher I had been able to familiarize myself with steering, a difficult process since one had to turn ahead of the bends as the machine would skid for yards before actually responding. This required a good deal of skill, especially since at water level the bends could only be seen at the last minute.

On the Loire Joe tried the machine for speed. Suddenly, with a great bang, the thrust propeller exploded, shattering into a thousand slivers that cut the fibreglass rudder casing to shreds. The machine was a partial wreck. With considerable trouble, Olivia, Joe and I hauled the hovercraft up a steep embankment and loaded it back on the car. Our French trials were over. Now we headed for Spain.

2 *Testing Times*

'Trouble, trouble, trouble, that's all it will give you,' a friend prophesied. That is all I got in the weeks that followed. Everything went wrong. After proving in the sea that it could tackle waves of considerable size, the engine broke down. Once it was repaired, I headed for the Muga, a little river that flows down from the Pyrenees. With Michael as witness two hundred yards from where I started, I hit the sharp branches of a tree. The impact was followed by a bang, and the hovercraft collapsed beneath me with one of its four inflatable sections torn. It took a full week of repairs before I was ready again – ready for the most pathetic fiasco of my life.

It is a film I hate to turn on in the little private cinema in my head. If I close my eyes, I can still see every incident clearly in black and white. Bañolas, the 1971 International Water-Ski Olympics, a crystal-blue mountain lake. (The first part of the film is in colour.) Thirty thousand people, most with binoculars, sitting in grandstands. A festive mood, Coca-Cola bottles everywhere. Athletes from all over the world in fancy gear, carrying water skis negligently on their shoulders, pretty, suntanned girls; business-like sports editors; a press room equipped with teletypes, and large American TV crews monitoring the event on an international hook-up by satellite. The film then turns to a dull black and white. I am there, standing by my little machine, looking at last like my heroes, a combination of Lindbergh and the Wright brothers. I dwarf my minute monster, which is held together by several pieces of tape. A swoosh, and past goes the last water-skier in the finals. Great applause. A man signals that my turn has come. Just as I lean over to start the two engines I hear over the microphones:

'For the first time in Spain a miniature hoveRRRRR – ' then the engines drown the commentator's voice. Surprised by the roar, people crane their necks. I am hidden in the little cove behind the grandstand. I jump in, push down the lift throttle, the hovercraft rises, I shoot down the beach, hit the water and skid fifty yards, well within view of the far end of the grandstand. All 60,000 eyes are on me, except for those of the commentator and the glass eyes of the television cameras. The cameras scan and scan an empty lake. Nothing appears on the screen – for good reason. Just as I am about to come into view, my rear engine stops dead. I cut my lift, stand up awkwardly and try to restart the engine. Amidst deathly silence I hear the announcer repeat, 'For the first time in Spain . . . for the first time in Spain a hovercraft,' and then, as he impatiently waits, he adds more details about the craft, about my project. 'Yes, across the Himalayas, believe it or not . . . A hovercraft for the first time in Spain.' I continue to pull, getting more and more nervous. The engine coughs, I pull again and again, frantic, panic-stricken, all eyes upon me. Then I fall down. The rope has broken. 'For the first time in Spain – have you got the name right?' the commentator continues, while he alone of all the spectators is unable to see me paddle slowly, ever so slowly, back to shore. Here the film ends, but not my shame and frustration. I wanted to drown, to disappear, but there I was stuck with my horrible machine. I very nearly lost faith. The next day, against my will, I was talked into trying again. This time everything went well. But the memory remains . . .

More breakdowns and trials followed. The trials were quite satisfactory and I experienced the thrill of going up my first rapids – small, yet rapids nevertheless – a twenty-mile ride over gravel and beds of boulders and up little steps of bubbling water in the river Fluvia. I had now learned to control the craft a little better, and it went over obstacles greater than its alleged clearance height with amazing ease.

In September, exceptional floods hit the coast of Spain. The little Muga broke its banks, and the highway was swept away when the water level rose 30 feet overnight. Several people lost their lives. It was still raining when, with a friend from Cadaqués, Bob Cordukes, I decided to take the hovercraft out. It was a gamble, but I had to know if my craft could manage turbulent fast water, for all my trials so far had not taken me on anything resembling the white pounding rivers I had occasionally seen at the bottom of Himalayan gorges.

The Muga was unrecognizable. Three hundred yards wide, it swooshed along carrying an ill-assorted cargo of dead sheep, wooden barrels, trees and logs. Nervously I got the engines to start and set off. In a few minutes all my theories were confirmed. The craft slid down the bank over the rushing water. For a second, the current brushing against the bottom of the skirt pulled me downstream, but then as if by a miracle the craft headed up against the water. Indifferent to waves and current, it raced over the thundering mass of the flood. I was amazed. I was just about to write all this to Michael that evening when a cable arrived: *Hover-Air liquidating in two days imperative you come to sale. Michael.*

Leaving the floods, I flew back to London. There Michael greeted me, together with Piers Weld-Forester, who conveniently owned a haulage firm. He was also a racing driver, and our journey to Peterborough was quickly done. I had little time to make up my mind. This was possibly the only chance we should get to have another small inflatable hovercraft. Should we plan on using this model? If so, we needed two or three more. Or should we get a bigger and better one? At last we decided to buy more small ones, planning to modify them later.

A liquidation sale is a sad sight. Here, in what had been the factory of Hover-Air Ltd, was a pile of hovercraft and equipment looking as if they were ownerless dogs about to be sold. Hundreds of people had flocked for the kill, to buy for a few pounds what a week before had been worth a thousand. The company engineers roamed about like demobilized soldiers, seeing their dreams crumble and their work squandered by the cruel demands of finance.

The sale was interpreted by many as an evil omen for hovercraft in general, as Hover-Air was the third company to go into liquidation that year. There were six hovercraft like mine for sale. Regardless of price, I had to purchase at least two – an awkward imperative at an auction. My expedition was at stake, yet my wallet was no thicker than before; in fact, less so. The sale began. One by one the larger two seater craft were sold off to wealthy local farmers. What could they want with a hovercraft? I wondered, eyeing them suspiciously as potential rivals.

Then came the turn of the 'Hovernauts'. I was the only client to have tried one, yet the word had spread already that these machines were possibly more versatile than any other craft on the market. Would I be outbid?

Ready to bid against us was a small group of ill-assorted aficionados, fanatics regularly constituted (as always in England) into a Hovercraft Club, with its own rules and regulations and even possessing its own journal. These young men were eyed with scorn by such persons as Robert Trillo and the real professionals; yet they in turn looked at Michael and me as if we were motor-boats breaking into a regatta. Already our plans had been the subject of their weekly news sheet, and there was considerable talk of our project behind our backs.

Ostentatiously parked in front of the factory was Michael's friend's massive truck, the longest I had ever seen, a true warehouse on wheels. Wearing a black fur coat and hat, Michael cut a sinister figure, while I was dressed in what looked like the uniform of a chauffeur of some Hispano Suiza in an old film. We hoped we looked like Mr Rolls and Mr Royce in for a kill. At any rate, we tried to keep up the pretence that our wallets were as thick as Michael's furs, and that I (the evil foreigner) possessed several obscure numbered accounts in Switzerland. The farmers looked at us in defiance; the members of the Hoverclub, equally apprehensive, eyed us with irony.

The critical moment came. The auctioneer rattled on too long about the merits of the hovernaut, and the prices began to rise. I managed to get the first craft for nearly half the price I had paid for the prototype. Then the bids soared for the second, and I eventually got the third, while the others went for increasingly higher prices to the company's ex-employees – a comforting fact, for they had the best reason to know how good the machine actually was.

On the second day of the auction, once the tension had gone, I became acquainted with Michael Pinder and Jim Kent, two king-pins of the British Hovercraft Club. They volunteered some useful advice over buying spare parts, and by the end of the sale we were deep into their world. 'Not a bad bunch,' agreed Michael, who detested clubs, especially of the sporting kind, having time only for the Zoological Society of London and the Royal Geographical Society, of both of which he is a Fellow. Of course, it was difficult for us to keep up with the fanatics. Indeed, it required considerable resourcefulness on our part to conceal the fact that, even if we were about to accomplish the hovercraft feat of the year, we were a trifle more ignorant of mechanical matters than their latest new member.

'Only on the backs of llamas can Mr Peissel ever hope to reach an altitude over 3000 feet with his machine.' This was the kindest of seven remarks written of us by Mr John Vass, the 'hovercraft correspondent' of the *Daily Express*, as if to prove our project unfeasible. An influential member of the hovercraft fraternity, his comments were convincing, if not altogether polite. 'Well, what shall we do?' I said to Michael. 'We have been challenged!'

'To begin with,' said Michael, looking at the letter, 'Mr Vass should be reminded that Himalayan Lamas have two legs and only one "l", unlike the four-legged, double "l" llamas of Peru. At least on this count Mr Vass is wrong. Secondly, Mr Vass is rude; this is also a mistake. As for his predictions, the best thing we can do is prove them wrong as well.'

We had our own doubts about how our craft would perform at high altitudes. It seemed no one had yet taken such machines to any great height. Time had come for us to modify our original craft to face the most rugged conditions.

A week later I was dragging our hovercraft to Andorra at 4000 feet and looking for water. Finding none, I pushed on over the border into France up to 6620 feet, on the snow-bordered and windswept shores of the Lac des Bouillouses. It was now November, and the lake was freezing hard. In a shower of icy spray I slithered down the snow and hit the water. At first the hovercraft operated well; then, losing momentum, fell under hump. No matter how hard I tried, I could not get over hump again, since the craft was slowly becoming coated with ice and the carburettors froze up. Perhaps Mr Vass was right. Our machine did seem underpowered at 6620 feet, especially in such poor conditions. Yet later that day on another lake at only 5000 feet it operated reasonably well.

In the meantime Robert Trillo was at work with his slide-rule, and produced a neat little report on how we could modify our engines to gain sufficient additional power (in theory) to be able to travel up to 10,000 feet. We hoped Mr Vass was soon going to have to eat his words – and correct his spelling. His opinions had also done little to help us solve our money problems, for which it seemed we did need the prayers of Lamas. Yet what was money, compared to the other major problem we had to overcome – for instance, that of obtaining permits to go to the Himalayas in the first place?

Anyone who had ever organized an expedition to the Himalayas knows that half the trouble is getting there, or rather obtaining permission to go there. Fifteen hundred miles of the Himalayas border on Chinese-occupied Tibet. Quite naturally, none of the border countries to the south is keen on seeing mountaineers roam about a sensitive frontier, many sections of which are still ill-defined and constitute disputed territory. Bhutan itself is virtually a forbidden land, while the Himalayan border regions of India are sealed off by the 'Inner Line', a strategic frontier set some thirty miles from the Tibetan border and into which few or no foreigners are allowed to travel. In Nepal this same 'Inner Line' is replaced by 'restricted areas', also forbidden to foreigners.

It was evident that, if a climber had to wait six months to obtain permits to scale an innocent peak, it would be even more difficult to visit these sensitive areas with three hovercraft considered by the British War Office as 'strategic items'. We had already seen our machines banned from the placid banks of the river Cher, so there was no telling what welcome they would receive in India or Nepal, not to mention Bhutan. Over the past thirteen years I had on six occasions secured permits to cross into the forbidden Himalayan frontier areas. I was thus well acquainted with all the problems this involved, and could recall how it had taken me ten years to secure an entry permit to Bhutan and six months to be allowed to go to Mustang, not to mention weeks of waiting in Delhi, including an interview with Mrs Gandhi, only to be refused on several occasions travel permits into the Western Himalayas of Kashmir.

I had not dared mention all this to Michael, since I knew his inevitable reaction would be to call off the whole project before we made complete fools of ourselves. All I could do was recall what had so often been repeated to me as a child, 'Where there's a will there's a way.' What way I was not sure. I discussed the matter with Colonel Wylie, and thus I came to learn that General Surendra Shaha – today a Field-Marshal – was in London. This was fortunate, as I knew him well. For nearly ten years he had been Commander-in-Chief of the Nepalese Army, and was therefore exactly the person to help us. I then learned from Charles Wylie that he had himself recently retired as Commander-in-Chief, but, if this sounded like bad news, I was immediately cheered on discovering that he was now 'Chairman of the Remote Area Development Committee' of Nepal. In other words, he was the person most concerned with exactly those areas we planned to visit.

I immediately got in touch with the General. The Gurkha soldiers of Nepal won such a reputation for courage and ferocity that the British, who fought them in 1814, later incorporated Nepalese soldiers as mercenaries in their own army. Since then, Gurkhas have reaped Victoria Crosses by the dozen on the battlefields of Flanders, Borneo, North Africa and Burma. To have been Commander-in-Chief of the Nepalese Army was thus no small achievement, and suggested courage and excellence in all the martial arts. Anyone might have been surprised, as I was, to discover that General Surendra Shaha was in fact a poet. Short and stocky, and with a twinkle in his eye, he was officially in London because of the health of his wife, the brilliant daughter of Nepal's fabled man of letters, His Highness Field-Marshal Kaiser Jung Bhadur Shramsher Rana, known as the Nepalese Voltaire. The General was also on a secret mission, one that not even the most brilliant intelligence officer could have guessed: he was planning to publish a love story he had written, and to find a producer for the musical play he had composed. I was familiar with operatic generals, but I had yet to meet a general who wrote operas!

Our negotiations opened with a dialogue in which I attempted to illustrate the merits of hovercraft and the implications of our expedition, while the General expanded on the beauty of Nepalese love songs and the delicacy of sentiment of his heroine, a little captive bird from the harems of his forefathers.

The Orient is often a mystery to Westerners, and there was no telling what went on in General Surendra Shaha's mind as we exchanged views on our pet projects: his books, his love of music, his musical play; my more prosaic dreams of shooting up the Kali Gandaki, Narayani, the Sapt and the Sun Khosi, not to mention the Indrawati and the fearful Arun river.

Weeks later, in early December, we sat discussing these matters once again over a whisky, one eye on the television screen, when a newscaster suddenly announced: 'War has broken out in Bengal. India has declared war on Pakistan, and the subcontinent is under martial law.' My heart sank. This was the death warrant of our project, for we should have to cross India to reach the Himalayas. When would the conflict end? What were its implications? I was in the right company to receive sound advice, opera or no opera. General Surendra was one of the key figures of Asian politics. We eyed the television set for a while in silence. The next day we learned that Nepal was now isolated and all communications with Katmandu were cut. We were in deep waters.

Our project was now bedevilled by two conflicting imperatives: the uncertain ending of the war and the time limit set by

the monsoon. It was essential we reached the Himalayas well
before the monsoon rains in June, and it was now December.
The best season for our expedition was March, April and May.
If we were to go at all, we should have to be off by February,
in just over a month's time.

It was out of the question to go to the Indian Himalayas,
for Pakistani troops were being massed on the Kashmir border.
India would not allow us into Bhutan either, whose frontiers
were only thirty miles from East Pakistan and separated from
it by a strip of Assam which was currently the centre of Indian
military operations. All we could do was pray for the war to
come to a hasty end, or hope that in spite of the hostilities
Nepal would be able to open a new link with the outside world
and let us in.

In face of these setbacks we were obliged to carry on as if
nothing had happened. The General, who was waiting for the
fighting to die down in India in order to return to Nepal,
promised he would take up the matter of our expedition with
the Prime Minister in person, and then advise us on the best
way of getting our machines out to Nepal – no easy task, since
these strategic items would now have to pass through a country
at war.

In the meantime Michael Pinder got to work on Trillo's
plans for increasing the power of our machines, and prepared
with John Trueluck, the former test pilot of Hover-Air Ltd, to
make new thrust units and stronger steering equipment that –
hopefully – would allow our craft to operate at 10,000 feet
above sea-level.

Ten days before Christmas, forgetting all these problems, I
prepared with a smile to face the French press and television
on the banks of the Seine. My plan was to give such a startling
demonstration of our machine's abilities that someone, at least,
would be moved to help finance our project because now, two
months before our planned departure date, I had only a few
pounds left.

The barge of the Touring Club de France, moored alongside
the Quai de la Concorde had been rented, printed invitations

had been sent out, and drinks were to be served after the demonstration, scheduled for 10 a.m. on December 16th. All was set, except that two of the hovercraft were in Southampton and the third was still in Spain. My wife was to drive this up to Paris, which she faithfully did. Arriving at 3 p.m. the day before the trials, she explained that at 70 m.p.h. somewhere near Narbonne a gust of wind had ripped the hovercraft off the roof of the car and it had crashed upside down on the road. 'I think I found all the pieces,' she said. 'They're in the boot.' And so they were.

It was too late to call off the press conference, and it seemed that I was heading for another Bañolas, the only difference being that no one this time would have the pleasure of seeing me paddle ashore. For a moment I considered jumping into the Seine in front of the press. On second thoughts I appealed to Michael on the phone. I was all nerves; he, unperturbed, calmly replied that he would take the next ferry with one of the new craft. 'I'll be on the Seine at 10 a.m.' he said, 'if all goes well.'

At five to ten the reporters were all stamping up and down the dock in the cold, and there was no machine in sight. I was running around wondering whether suicide by drowning was painful. Michael's ferry from Southampton had been due in Le Havre at 7 a.m. That is, if he had managed the previous day to obtain in two hours a permit to export our 'strategic' craft; if he had been able to book a passage; and if the French customs had allowed him in with our unclassifiable 'machine'. If?

Despite the cold, the pressmen were keen with anticipation. There were reporters who had just come back from Cape Kennedy, the aristocracy of French technical correspondents, all sceptical about the whole mad-sounding idea as outlined on their invitation cards: *Traverser l'Himalaya en Aéroglisseur.* No one believed it possible – that was why they had come.

At 10 a.m. sharp, the large dark-green bonnet of a vast car appeared at the top of the ramp leading to the quay. Resplendent on its roof was 002, our second craft. Slowly it pulled up alongside the Touring Club barge. Out came Michael in his black fur coat and black fur hat, elegant, calm, and *très britan-*

nique with his greyish hair, then out of the other door leaped a beautiful young lady clad in a leopardskin coat. It looked like a *concours d'élégance*. All that was missing was a dog.

The press were impressed, and nobody noticed that I had nearly fainted with relief. Our gathering now took on that intensity characteristic of great events in the pioneer days of the automobile or the plane. Michael looked his part – *L'anglais excentrique*. I, hair in the wind, pale and thin, moved around like Professor Picard. This was hover or bust.

Up and down the river I hovered, under the famous bridges, past the Louvre, back towards the Eiffel Tower, in and out of barges, up and down the ramp and up again. Even at Cape Kennedy they had seen nothing like it. As the flash bulbs clicked I felt I was floating on the little cushion of my bloated ego.

The press crowded around, I made a short speech, there was plenty to drink on the barge. Only one person spoiled the day when he said, 'I thought I noticed you had a little trouble going up the ramp.' (It was barely ten feet high.) 'How high do you think you will really get to in the Himalayas?' he continued. 'Ten thousand feet,' I said, unshaken. '*Ah oui*,' he said. This might be translated as, 'Oh yeah?'

Nor was the French Government impressed. After three months of negotiation with the 'Ministry of Sport and Youth', in which I had put some hope (what is the Ministry of Sport and Youth there for, except to finance a hovercraft expedition to the Himalayas?), I was told: 'Why don't you go to the Kayak Club?' The British Government showed more interest. Michael received a call from a director of the National Research and Development Council. The gentleman on the line, whom we hoped might be about to offer finance, declared that he was very worried lest we compromise the good name of the British Hovercraft Industry. We thanked him for his concern, but we had enough worries of our own. What did he expect us to do – call off the project for fear of failure?

For a Christmas present I received two letters from General Surendra Shaha. The first read:

My dear Michel,

Yesterday I sent a registered letter to you in reply to your official letter. So you can send your craft by air in the name of my office. When you arrive here, government officials will contact you for the necessary formalities and information. I am very hopeful about the success of your project.

Our best wishes to you both.

Yours sincerely,
Surendra

A week later the official document arrived. It read:

You are hereby requested to send your hovercraft by air in the name of His Majesty's Government, Remote Area Development Committee. I shall be grateful if you would indicate the approximate date of their arrival in Katmandu. The necessary formalities can be dealt with when you arrive.

Wishing you success in your project,

Etc. . . .

I was jubilant, but war still raged in Bengal, and no funds were in sight. A third letter soon came from Mr Brenninkmeyer, a friend of my family. It contained a cheque for £200 – a kind, spontaneous gift. In his letter Mr Brenninkmeyer quoted a proverb from his native Holland: 'Let one sheep cross the bridge and the others will follow. I hope this will mark a turning point in your quest for funds.'

I was most grateful but, alas, the rest of the flock seemed nowhere in sight, and we needed over £1500 just to fly our craft to New Delhi.

Then suddenly, faithful to the Dutch proverb, others did cross the bridge. Sir William Collins, backed by Robert Knittel, Senior Editorial Director of his publishing firm, boldly and imaginatively advanced a sizeable sum against the delivery of a possible book. Air France, too, now offered us free tickets to India. At last money was no problem; all that was needed was faith. After thirteen months our own faith, it seemed, had proved contagious. But could one cross the Himalayas on faith and air alone?

The giant sacred wagon of the gods, drawn through the streets by men to celebrate New Year, was the only mechanical means of transport known in Nepal before the introduction of cars and hovercraft. Below: raring to go. Our three craft at Tribeni.

Unloading our craft from the Royal DC3 at Katmandu's Gancher airport.
Below: Bob Cordukes assembles our craft in the hotel grounds, watched
by the servants.

This is what we now set out to prove. Panic set in, as we now had only a month before our scheduled date of departure. With frozen feet, we spent hours on the snow-covered grounds of the Heathrow Water-Ski Club (of all places), testing our new thrust units and propellers with the aid of a crew of volunteer engineers and mechanics. The new machine parts were only bolted down two days before the craft were to be shipped to India. The three hovercraft were then hurriedly compressed into eight crates, three of the crates so big that they could only fit into a Jumbo jet. The crates contained in all three hovercraft, three spare engines, and countless nuts, screws, bolts, belts, blades, pipes, cables, pins, rivets, filters, washers, plugs, gaskets, gears, levers, and handles in duplicate, triplicate, quintuplicate and hexi-whatever-it-is. There could be no turning back now. In the future there would be no more accessible nut and bolt shops, no more friendly hovermaniacs or local garages to solve our problems. There would only be us in a land of experts in growing rice, breeding yaks, cutting trees, and stalking tigers. One missing screw could bring our machines to a halt, our entire project could run aground on a single missing or damaged washer. Had we forgotten anything? I hardly had time to think as we prepared for the farewell press conference, to be held at the Collins's offices in London.

Michael and I felt like two Stanleys taking exotic leave as in the comfort of an elegant gilt room I addressed fifty-five members of the press, explaining our aims and goals. There was no pushing or shoving, no noise, only a respectful silence as the room echoed with my quavering voice throwing around statistics and names, reassuring words from which I hoped to gather the self-confidence I badly needed. Now, on the eve of our departure, it was as if a beam were focused on all the weak points of our project, picking out all the hazards and glaring down on the numerous unsolved problems that still lay before us.

The press was indulgent, even enthusiastic. The following day we read their comments with a mixture of pride and apprehension. The *Guardian* had us in headlines on the front page with a picture of one of our craft coasting down St James's Place; *The Times* devoted three columns to our plans, while every other newspaper in England and many abroad carried some story on our expedition.

Others might have found in all this publicity matter for self-congratulation; to me each article was a needle in my stomach – I was now committed publicly to succeed. Only by reading in print what we actually planned to do did I fully fathom its staggering foolhardiness. I feared that consciously or unconsciously I might have minimized in my mind the dangers involved, the crashing force of the rivers we planned to conquer, the thousands of tons of glacial waters that for millions of years had rushed towards the sea, cutting through mountains, bringing down cliffs, carrying boulders the size of houses, sometimes washing away villages in seconds while carving and scarring the Himalayas. Such were the rivers up which we planned to travel, seated upon minute fragile rubber dinghies which tipped the scales at barely 185 lbs. For the first time I wondered if we would return alive.

3 *Into a Forgotten World*

'Please fasten your seat-belts. In a few minutes we shall be landing at Palam Airport.' It was February 29th, 1972, a leap year, and the war in Bengal had just ended. Michael sat next to me as we drank champagne to celebrate our departure, all the panic of which was now too far behind us for us to worry. However, at the back of my mind I kept hearing the repeated whisper, 'Are we really ready?' Looking at Michael, I now saw him as the innocent victim of my optimistic enthusiasm, for he had never yet been to the Himalayas. Or was it that I in a way was a victim of his scepticism, which had made me struggle so hard to overcome every one of his perfectly reasonable objections? What if his pessimism was warranted? With a slight shudder the Air France jet touched down. It was 4 a.m. local time, and as the door opened the heat and fragrance of New Delhi filled the cabin.

No sooner had we set foot in India than unexpected problems arose. A hearty welcome by Mr Pande, the Nepalese Ambassador, assured us that so far in Katmandu all was well. It seemed we were eagerly expected; all we had to do was to reach Nepal. In ordinary circumstances this would have been easy but, as we knew only too well, there was nothing ordinary about our hovercraft. These now sat somewhere in the scorching sun at Delhi Airport while we discovered the true reason why no one in London or Paris had undertaken to guarantee their transfer to Katmandu.

Quite simply, our craft would not fit into any of the planes that fly between India and Nepal. In spite of the promises of our packers, our crates were just too large to go through the doors of any normal plane. This meant shipping them by road, and here a new problem arose. The war in Bengal having only just ended, and the Indian customs being what they are, there seemed little hope of obtaining clearance for our three machines to pass through what had been enemy-infested territory only a few weeks before. We thought of disguising the contents of our cases as ventilators and rubber dinghies, but the slightest examination would have revealed that together they formed a revolutionary machine bound to arouse the suspicions of the most amiable official. To transfer them by road in bond was also impossible, as there existed no right of way for Nepalese goods between Delhi and Katmandu. To cheer us up, the French Embassy advised us that pilfering of all road transport in India was estimated at 30 per cent, and that the overland journey would last at least three days and nights. I hated to think what damage other than pilfering our craft would suffer in bouncing over poor roads and dodging sacred cows, not to mention the trucks breaking down or crashing. Since we only needed to lose a few screws to jeopardize the whole project, we could not afford these risks. This seemed to leave no alternative. Then over the telephone to Katmandu, I learned that we might be able to charter the King of Nepal's private DC3, which happened to have double doors through which, with luck, our crates might be coaxed. The cost of chartering was by no means negligible, but we had no choice.

So on March 8th, to the uncertain roar of the ancient DC3 engines, Michael and I sat on a crate of whisky beside our eight huge crates that filled the fuselage of the King of Nepal's Royal Flight 2, as it headed slowly over the parched Indian countryside towards Katmandu.

Beneath us, veiled in the haze, sprawled the flat rice fields of the Ganges basin where the mighty rivers draining Tibet come to die, meandering in lazy loops as if lost, with no landmarks to indicate the distant sea. Monotonous India lay at our feet, the flat graveyard of men's ambitions which, like the rivers, lost their aggressiveness and their direction on reaching the plains. The course of India's history is similar to that of its rivers, as wave after wave of conquering tribes galloped down from the mountains, only to lose momentum and courage before becoming assimilated into the general torpor that had made the bravest into sheep, the ready victims of the next flood to surge down from the hills.

Little wonder that, throughout India, old men in the dusk of their lives leave their families and set off in search of the source of the great rivers that symbolize their birthplace, the fount of vitality and strength they have lost. All those born in the plains of India inevitably look north for comfort, up the trails for which we were heading. At last, looking through the windows of the plane, I noticed that a cloud was in fact a peak. We were now flying level with the great snow-covered ranges. Captain Rana, the King's pilot, asked us into the cockpit for a better view. The dry hazy plains of India had now given way to the rolling green of the jungles that border the Himalayas. In a matter of minutes the ground began to rise as the first tree-covered foothills sailed beneath us, scarred here and there by bone-white river beds. We peered at these with particular interest, searching for traces of the first large Himalayan rivers.

From the altitude at which we were flying it was hard to distinguish the features of the rivers, but our project seemed more than ever over-ambitious, for now we could see beneath us the chaos of the mountains rising in towering heights towards the snows. Was it possible that we might cross that formidable barrier, making our way between the hills and ridges, peaks and ranges, of the most disorderly cataclysm to have breached the surface of the globe?

A mountain slipped past our wing as we entered the Katmandu valley, a neat carpet of rice fields and little brick houses that marked the site of the greatest agglomeration of the Himalayan world, the seven small ancient capitals of the Newar Kings, the rulers of a race of artisans who for centuries had inhabited this narrow valley of Katmandu lost in the folds of the Himalayas. We had arrived.

Wedged between Chinese-occupied Tibet and India, Nepal is like a long thin rectangle, 100 miles wide and 540 miles in length. Its 54,000 square miles shelter close to 12 million

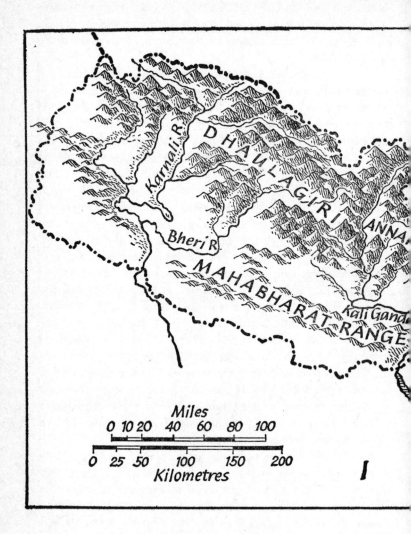

Map of major rivers of Nepal illustrating how they cut through the greater Himalayan chain before uniting to cross in three points the Mahabharat range that closes Nepal to the south.

people, giving the land a relatively high density of population, despite its ruggedness. Unlike most lands of Asia, Nepal was never a colony of a Western power, and until 1950 the country was practically closed to foreigners.

Having been isolated for so many centuries, Nepal is today trying to catch up with the rest of Asia, thanks to the combined aid of the United States, Russia, India and China, countries with which it maintains amicable relations, since Nepal is neutral in the East-West struggle.

Katmandu, Nepal's capital, is a city of contrasts. Here mingle members of every one of the country's numerous tribes, rubbing shoulders with Chinese Red Guards and young hippies, not to mention red-robed Tibetan refugees, a cosmopolitan colony of aid experts, and hordes of tourists. People of every description ambled in noisy crowds through the town's bazaar, in which only recently a few modern goods could be found among the fine handicrafts of the Newars, the original inhabitants of the Katmandu valley. On every street corner rise complicated temples dedicated to the saints and divinities of most of the major religions of Asia, which here combine their assets to the din of bells and the smell of incense. Through the city streets the varied crowd weaves its way on bicycles, tricycles, motor cycles, ponies, jeeps, horses, and other odd conveyances, among which, until our arrival, only the hovercraft was lacking.

With the help of General Surendra Shaha, our machines were cleared through customs, and then were hastily assembled on the lawns of our hotel near the royal palace, a vast conglomeration of buildings copying all the styles of Europe since 1870. We had expected that the Government or the army might give us a helping hand in organizing the complicated business of obtaining fuel and getting the hovercraft to the distant rivers. But we soon realized that no one in Nepal was even interested in looking over our unique machines.

In vain we expected to be asked to put on a demonstration for curious ministers, and perhaps even for the new young King, for shortly before our departure from London, King Mahendra

Transport in Nepal is by mule or pony in the north; by mule or on foot along rough, jungle-clogged trails in the south. Below right: a new and pleasant way of travelling through the jungle.

Mother and child on the banks of the Lower Kali Gandaki.

A ring in her nose does not impair this Mandi beauty's charm, and even the older woman below believes a ring enhances her smile.

The Marsyandi river cuts through the jungle south of the Mahabharat range. Below: Bob Cordukes drives out of the Marsyandi near Daveghat.

of Nepal had died suddenly and a twenty-day period of mourning had just ended as we arrived.

It soon became evident that we would be left to our own resources and could expect none of the government assistance we had originally solicited. It was now up to us to find means of getting our craft out to the rivers and setting up support bases with all that was needed to keep our creatures afloat on their cushions. This was to prove a difficult task; in Katmandu petrol is scarce, and outside the valley there was not a single petrol pump and hardly any roads, let alone a mechanic. We prepared alone for our first confrontation with a Himalayan river, according to a plan we had sketched out in London with the help of Colonel Wylie.

Seen from the air, the Himalayas look like a chaotic jumble of hills and peaks; on a map it is easier to see that the mountains follow a certain master plan. Eighty miles wide, the central section of the Himalayas, which in Nepal is nearly 600 miles long, is made up of three separate parallel chains. To the south, bordering a strip of dense jungle known as the Terai, rise the first foothills known as the Swalik Hills. These are a series of low ranges (1–2000 feet) that run across Nepal from east to west, forming the advance bastions of what is called the Mahabharat range. This second mountain chain is a little-known, compact ridge of mountains rising to 9 and 10,000 feet, forming a solid wall that seals off Nepal from the low Swalik Hills and the Indian plains. This range, running parallel to the Swalik Hills, has only three openings, three gaps through which all the rivers draining Nepal are obliged to pass. The third range is the famous Great Himalayan range which in Nepal is formed by a succession of such well-known peaks as Dhaulagiri, Annapurna, Gaurisankar, Chocyu, Everest, Lhotse, Makalu and Kanchenjunga. Although these peaks are the highest in the world, unlike the Mahabharat range they do not constitute an unbroken chain but are a succession of independent ranges separated by deep gorges and valleys, through which run the great rivers that drain southern Tibet. These rivers first flow south from Tibet between the famous peaks before striking the solid wall of the Mahabharat range; here they change course, going east or west in search of one of the three gaps through which they then proceed south through the Swalik Hills into the Indian plains.

We had decided that we would aim to try and cross successively all three ranges, beginning with the low Swalik Hills, then going on through the massive Mahabharat range before tackling the great Himalayan range itself. Our major problem was to decide which river we should follow, assuming it was possible to follow any of them for any great length.

Despite the many months I had spent trekking in Nepal, I had as yet no clear idea of any one river, for in the course of my travels I had seen only small stretches glimpsed from occasional primitive bridges. This view was often limited to the few hundred yards before the river sped out of sight round a bend down some mysterious canyon. As a rule, it is not possible for tracks in Nepal to follow the line of the rivers. One of the few exceptions was the trade route up the Kali Gandaki, where a mule path clings to the side of the gorge which the river cuts between Annapurna and Dhaulagiri. Walking along this trail to Mustang, I had been able to see for myself that with a little luck one might be able to shoot the upper course of this great river. All other rivers in Nepal were as much a mystery to me as to everybody else, for no one had ever been able to follow them for any great distance.

On the other hand, we had good reason to believe that we could travel up at least one of the other rivers, the Sun Khosi. This river has its source in Tibet and flows south between the Lamtang and the Gaurisankar ranges before striking the Mahabharat range and heading east a hundred miles until it joins two other rivers, the fearful Arun, that also runs down from Tibet near Mount Everest, and the Tamur, that runs down from Kanchenjunga. On meeting, all three rivers cut a deep gorge south through the Mahabharat range in eastern Nepal. The Sun Khosi had been surveyed, as this river had been the site of the daring experiment performed in 1965 by Sir Edmund Hillary and Mr J. O. F. Hamilton and several other New Zealanders, who pioneered Himalayan navigation when they brought two powerful jet boats to Nepal. These boats are without propellers but instead are powered by a jet of compressed water and are able to travel up many rivers where a conventional craft with a propeller would come to grief. This first experiment had shown the Sun Khosi to be navigable from near the Indian border up Dhaulaghat, some thirty miles from the Tibetan frontier and at an altitude of 2500 feet. Since then no other trials had been made with jet or other boats in Nepal, since in the course of this expedition one of the boats had capsized and been crushed to splinters in a rapid on the Arun river.

However powerful jet boats might be, they could never hope to go over rapids with visible rocks or up shallow or dry rivers. Indeed, the exploits of the jet boat expedition had been remarkable, considering the hazards that had to be overcome and the constant risk of hitting a submerged rock, which had eventually proved fatal for one of the boats.

From this experiment we presumed that the Sun Khosi could be considered navigable by hovercraft for a great part of its course, and that the best point from which to start our journey would be in south-east Nepal, from a camp we could establish at the place where the Sun Khosi, Arun and Tamur rivers meet. From there we could try our luck up these three rivers while tuning up our machines and learning our first lessons in handling Himalayan rapids. Then we could either try to go all the way up the Arun to within thirty miles of Everest, or leave eastern Nepal to go up the Kali Gandaki in western Nepal.

In accordance with this plan, Colonel Wylie in London had secured for us a promise of assistance from the British Gurkha military camp located at Dharan in south-east Nepal some thirty miles from where we thought of setting up our base camp. The British Ambassador in Katmandu had been advised and had kindly volunteered his assistance, although he warned us that, with the death of the King, everything was rather confused in the government and we should be careful to obtain in advance if possible all our permits to the regions where we wished to travel. As a rule, all foreigners need special permits to leave Katmandu, even for short treks. These are generally simple to obtain, but permits for expeditions to remote areas are always complicated. None the less, we hoped that these permits would be granted automatically on arrival, as our project had been planned under the auspices of the General and approved by the Prime Minister.

We never suspected that the sudden death of the King of Nepal would soon upset our well-laid plans. At first we did not notice that something seemed to have gone wrong already, although we were slightly surprised when General Surendra Shaha explained that we had better not mention our plans to the local press, as perhaps 'governments, people or someone might be suspicious . . .' Thinking this might be an allusion to the strategic undertones acquired by the hovercraft, we did not protest, but prepared to leave Katmandu for south-east Nepal silently and in haste.

When we arrived at Katmandu we had sent cables via the British Embassy to the Gurkha camp at Dharan; they replied that they were happy to welcome us and that, if we could fly our craft to a town called Birathnagaer, they could send a truck to collect them. Once we had assembled our craft at Dharan we planned to have them transported thirty miles over a dirt track to a place called Chatra, where they could be put on the Sapt Khosi, the river formed by the combined flow of the Arun, Tamur and the Sun Khosi. At Dharan the Gurkha officers assured us they could help us find petrol and porters, a cook and an aide whom we could send out on foot over the hills to set up our base camp at the confluence of the three rivers – a point beyond the reach of any motor vehicle.

'That's very kind of them,' commented Michael as we sat in our hotel room in Katmandu all ready to leave and waiting for Bob – that is, Robert Cordukes, the third member of our party.

The sudden appearance of a third member of the expedition needs a word of explanation. What with all the turmoil of getting our machines together, hunting for spare parts, taking

lessons on how to repair our engines, organizing press con-
ferences and raising funds, we did not have the time to find
what we badly needed – some sort of a mechanic to the expedition. This was because finding a companion for a venture such
as ours had proved a most difficult task. Unlike mountaineers
or other 'classical' sportsmen, we could not draw on a mass of
candidates belonging to clubs and associations. The few enthusiasts of the British Hovercraft Club we had met had shown
little real interest in our project, and none had volunteered to
cast in his lot with ours on the rapids of the Himalayas, since
they were having enough trouble navigating the Thames.

It was not that we lacked friends, even adventurous friends,
but none was free to come at short notice, since we only knew
that we could leave for certain a few weeks prior to our actual
departure.

A week before we were set to go we had still found no one.
Did we need a companion at all? Michael asked. I felt we did,
and preferably a mechanic, but mechanics, it seemed, had lost
their love of adventure and we could not afford union salaries,
hardship benefits, or the life insurance they demanded. Only
when Air France had kindly offered us three plane tickets in
exchange for a 3000-word article on our journey was I able to
secure the participation of the only person ready to come (as
long as the journey took no more than two months and I pay
his travel and field expenses). This was Bob Cordukes, the
Australian friend with whom I had tried out the hovercraft on
the flooded rivers in Spain. Thirty-two, well-built and bearded,
Bob had given his consent the day before we left. Then, that
same day, he had had a car accident while driving back to
collect his things. This was the reason why he had been unable
to travel with us. He eventually turned up five days after our
arrival in Nepal, and thus at last the three of us were set to go.

No sailor ever had such a strange craft as ours, and no craft
ever had a more unlikely crew. Michael was 52, habituated to
dining out, dilettantism and daily ablutions in a bathroom
furnished with a stuffed flamingo. There was no hiding Michael
was not 'normal'. To begin with, his English was a little too

correct and he himself a little too elegant and young-looking for his age – no great sin, but something to be frowned on when, with his habitual disregard for all things material, he would knock down every gatepost through which he tried to drive. At the least one had to admit (and Michael was a man to admit everything) he was not very good with his fingers, while his eyesight could have done with some improvement. The fact that he gloried later that our project had taught him what he had failed to grasp in fifty-two years – that screws screwed up clockwise – gives some idea of his practical bent.

When Robert Cordukes, who did consider himself normal, asked point blank why I had chosen Michael, I had to stop and wonder. Why, in fact, had I chosen Cordukes? Apart from availability, it was because I knew he was not as normal as he wished he were. Australian, and therefore already marked in my mind with something upside down, he had been successively a poet, an editor of the *Paris Review*, a novelist, a bar-owner, and now owned a boutique adjacent to the hotel he operated in Spain. All this good proof that he possessed a certain adaptability that could come in handy hovering through the Himalayas. He was a good sportsman, whose personality was interesting if undiplomatic, yet carried along by that irresistible gusto of a man with a liking for beer, girls and straight speech. He was also clever with his hands, if no true mechanic.

I, of course, was normal.

Yet, all told, it would have been difficult to find a more unlikely trio. We were well suited to our abnormal task.

In Katmandu we were able to get hold of an unscheduled cargo plane to fly to Birathnagaer. One by one the largest portions of the hulls of our three hovercraft were steered through its doors, along with twenty-two boxes, crates and bags, bundles and baskets, not counting twenty-one empty jerrycans and the anchors and paddles – these last items possibly the most important of our strange equipment. I had purchased them in London with much more of our incongruous kit, in which mingled the garments and tools of what are generally considered contradictory sports: duvet jackets and skindiver's boots, mountaineering clothes and life-belts, anchors and parachutist tents, flotation bags and an altimeter, fur hats and kayak helmets, not to mention waterproof trousers and – of course – the paddles. I had nearly forgotten one vital item. Michael had decreed that he would follow me to the ends of the earth, down any rapid or over any waterfall, but he had to have a comfortable chair specially fitted to his hovercraft. I thus brought along a sort of armchair, in the form of a moulded plastic seat, to make him happy.

We were perspiring heavily when the plane took off. The night before we had drunk what we thought would be our last beer, followed by dinner at the house of Hardy Furer, one of the most daring and gifted of the adventurous mountain pilots who are found in Nepal. It seemed he had landed a plane on everything from a runway down to a handkerchief, and had acquired something of a reputation. During his many years in Nepal he had flown over most of the country's rivers, and we could none of us forget this daredevil's comment on our project, pronounced with the sinister emphasis of a slight Swiss-German accent: 'Believe me, you are just plain crazy!'

Thus reassured, we flew towards Birathnagaer, a town claimed to be the ugliest in Nepal, and in fact the largest town in the country outside Katmandu. Bordering on India, and set on the edge of the plains three hundred miles from the capital, Birathnagaer has little to commend it. It was 110°F when we landed after a two-hour flight near this god-forsaken town, which although linked by road with India is accessible from Katmandu only by air.

At the airfield, a magnificent army truck and an equally new-looking khaki Land-Rover were waiting to drive us to Dharan, both chauffeured by two impeccably erect and smart Gurkha soldiers.

How many times had I heard the name of Dharan in the course of my past visits to Nepal! Lost somewhere in the foot-hills of eastern Nepal, the name conjured up in my mind visions of grim barracks rusting under a tropical sun in which were trapped a few homesick British officers busy recruiting Nepalese peasants to be shipped off to England or Singapore and trained to become world-famous Gurkha soldiers. Thus I had naturally expected to find at Dharan only a few barracks when, having journeyed over rice fields and through jungle, the Land-Rover pulled up at an impressive guard-house that marked the southern gate of the camp. And here, in the jungle belt of eastern Nepal, a land which remains one of the most primitive in Asia, was something even an atheist might have considered paradise. In a region with no electricity, no running water, where the local inhabitants still lived in thatched huts built on stilts, we found elegant air-conditioned bungalows set in a vast garden-like park of flowering shrubs and trees, bordered by a nine-hole golf course and boasting three swimming pools!

On our arrival, Captain Willsher led us to the Officers' Mess, where dark oak panelling set off leather armchairs, and the solitary skin of a leopard was the only reminder that the real jungle was not far off. A copy of the London *Times* (although two weeks old) seemed to proclaim that here at least there would always be an England.

At Dharan we had entered a small, closed, isolated colonial community, the kind which I had always believed had existed only in the novels of Somerset Maugham. England might have lost her Empire, but here at least in Dharan were preserved the traditions which had made its greatness. Dharan was also a triumph of organization and a brilliant demonstration of what can be achieved with a little discipline. We were caught off guard by such luxury, and were shamed when, on learning that it was compulsory to wear a tie in the Mess for dinner (served complete with the regimental silver), we discovered that we had not one tie among us. The entire establishment raised many fascinating questions regarding the two civilizations it confronted: occidental life as seen through the eyes of one of the West's most traditional armies, and that of the Nepali tribes surrounding the camp.

The Dharan camp was a recent creation, as until 1947 the British had recruited Nepalese mercenaries through agents who slipped into Nepal unnoticed, since the country was closed to foreigners. Although the Ghurkas were recruited from all the twenty-five tribes which constitute the population of Nepal, the British had soon formed a preference for four tribes of Tibetan origin – the Gurungs, the Magars, the Rais, and the Limbus – which they called the martial tribes, as opposed to the more pacific Hindu castes, the quiet Tharus who inhabited the jungles, or the artistic Newars of the Katmandu valley. Strangely enough, there are only a few real Gurkhas in the Gurkha regiments, Gurkha being the name of a town and region from which the royal family came. These Gurkha tribesmen of Rajput stock had conquered all the other hill people of what is now modern Nepal, overrunning the little Newar kingdoms of the Katmandu valley to form in 1773 a kingdom that for a short while had become a major military nation.

Led by kings from Gurkha, the Nepalese had caused the Tibetans, the British in India, and even the Chinese Emperor great concern. Eventually the Chinese in 1793 and the British in 1814 had set out to fight the Gurkha kings, who were severely defeated and their army disbanded. It was these soldiers who found re-employment in the Indian Army and became the elements of what grew into the British mercenaries. Meanwhile, the once arrogant Gurkha kings sealed off their kingdom from all foreigners and thus Nepal became a forbidden land, as it lost forever its short-lived military power. The Gurkha kings were soon to become hostages of their own Prime Ministers, who took over the Government in 1846. After ruling with a stern hand, in 1950 the Ranas were eventually overthrown by a bloodless revolution that reinstated the legitimate Gurkha kings, who now once again rule Nepal.

After the return of the Gurkha kings, and as a consequence of India's independence, the British were allowed to set up two recruiting stations within Nepal. Thus had been created the camp at Dharan, and eventually another at Bhairawa in the late 1950s.

On the evening of our arrival we read in the old copy of *The Times* how a hovercraft had overturned in England, killing four people. The story of the accident helped to divide the officers at Dharan into two groups: those who claimed the rivers we were heading for were quite unnavigable, and those who assured us we would have no trouble. I need not add which side was in the majority.

The truth was that, although everyone kindly volunteered advice, no one had ever been able to follow the rivers sufficiently closely to know how turbulent these waters really were. All the same, we were grateful for the assistance and advice we received, and carefully savoured the comforts of Dharan, as we knew they were the last we would enjoy for many days.

Three days after our arrival on March 20th, three trucks were loaded with our assembled craft, twenty porters, our cook and his helper, plus twenty-two loads consisting mainly of jerrycans, spare parts and engines, tents and cooking utensils – all broken down into loads weighing around sixty pounds. These loads were to be taken to Chatra and from there carried up by porters to the confluence of the Sun Khosi, Arun and Tamur rivers, while if all went well we hoped to travel up the river with our hovercraft and join the porters at what would be our first base camp.

Only at the last minute did our liaison officer turn up. A short little fellow, he was dressed in a brown suit, black patent leather shoes, and a tie! In spite of his odd dress, he declared he was ready and looking forward to becoming the first Nepalese to drive in a hovercraft. He was disappointed to discover that he would have to walk up with the porters as our craft would carry only one person, and that ties would not be necessary for dinner.

As if in retaliation for my remark and for having to walk, he handed me a letter from the provincial governor informing us that we would not be allowed to proceed up the river beyond a village called Tumlingtar, some thirty-five miles above base camp. This was bad news, for it meant that we could not go on up this river towards the Everest range, one of our alternate plans. I thought this was a mistake and immediately sent a wireless message to Katmandu to General Surendra Shaha, asking that we be allowed to proceed to Num, a village some thirty miles from Everest, set beside the Arun river in the Sherpa district. The reply was to be forwarded to our base camp from Dharan by runner; in the meantime, I set off with the liaison officer to join the others who had driven off earlier to Chatra.

Set on the banks of the Sapt Khosi, the village of Chatra was the only point where the river was accessible by motor vehicle. The road was a track winding in and out of the giant trees of the jungle that sprawled over the alluvial plain at the foot of the Swalik Hills. Grinding its gears, the truck bumped forward over rocks and stones. A fragrance of jasmine filled the air, coming from a little pink flowery bush growing in the shade of the trees. The heat was suffocating, and in this dryest period of the year the forest presented a carpet of fallen leaves. Nothing stirred as we drove by, occasionally passing small clearings where little huts stood on stilts beneath the shade of giant trees. Dark-skinned Tharus stared at us from these houses as we rumbled on. At one point the truck made its way for half a mile over bone-white boulders where a sudden flood had brought down tons of rock, cutting through the forest. This was a reminder that we would have to be on the lookout for the sudden rise of the rivers after a storm, as these floods could wash away our camp in a few minutes. In the Himalayas, rivers have been known to rise a hundred feet in a few hours.

The dirt road we were following had been built to give access to the site of a great irrigation project that was being undertaken at Chatra by the World Bank. If Dharan, with its swimming pools, golf course and air-conditioning, had been a white man's paradise, Chatra was the white man's hell. Under a leaden sun the indecent carcases of a mechanical graveyard were exposed, as hundreds of broken-down earth-removers and bulldozers lay rusting, evoking the fragility of all things mechanical. In the dead silence of the midday heat, vultures hovered overhead. As I arrived, a lone tern let its sad cry echo over the junk heap. All was still; it was the hour in which dogs cowered in the shade as the heat waves rose in shudders above a scene that exuded evil.

What a fitting place to start our journey! Had we covered thousands of miles to reach this dump – the new frontier of Western penetration, and also, it seemed, the physical limits of our modern technological world? What if we were the forerunners of further pollution? We were well aware that we were about to push the machines of man deeper into the sanctuary of nature, to disturb the silence of centuries. Was it worth it?

Michael and Bob waited for me, while the porters had struck out earlier, going up the river on foot, as here all roads ended. Beyond Chatra was a mystery. Perspiring heavily, Bob and Michael had attempted with little success to start their craft. After a while Michael's had begun to work, Bob's refused to operate. With a spanner and key we all toiled under the watchful gaze of a small crowd, but nothing could get the lift engine of 002 to start, and now our spare engines were somewhere along the trail that made its way north from Chatra towards the hills we could see in the distance.

Eventually I decided to set off with Michael to base camp and collect a spare engine. Two hundred yards from the shore, Michael's propellers broke. As it was getting late I decided to carry on alone, not realizing that Michael, on returning to where Bob was stranded, would be swept down by the current and would only manage to avoid being carried down into the plains of India by diving into the river and hauling the boat ashore.

Although we had originally planned to travel in pairs for reasons of safety, I now found myself facing the mighty Sapt Khosi river alone. Six hundred yards wide, its waters raced down to meet me, emerging from the hills through a wide gorge lined with tall cliffs some three miles upstream. Bouncing over the waves, I raced up towards the gorge where, as I rounded a bend, great rocks towered all around me. At that moment I caught sight of the first rapid, larger and wider than any I had ever negotiated before. A mass of foaming water barred my route. For a few frightening moments I feared I would never make it alive through the seething waves.

The craft shuddered, reared up and thudded down as the

water went swirling past. Tossing wildly, my machine began to slow down as spray rose over my bow, while a strong wind drove me off course towards the rocks by the shore. What if my engine stalled now? I thought I should never make this rapid, seeing in a flash my entire project end here. I had been warned it was folly to challenge these river giants. Yet somehow I pulled through. Ahead loomed another bend, then another rapid. I now knew for certain that I had misjudged the size of these rivers when I had tried to remember in Europe those I had seen from the safety of the land.

I had hardly crossed this second rapid when I saw a few yards ahead of me a low steel cable spanning the river. I was going too fast to stop, so at the last minute I ducked, passing a bare few inches under the obstruction.

The gorge grew deeper, the current swifter, yet my minute machine carried on. The river had now narrowed to some two hundred yards, and although it was not yet four o'clock, the waters were deep in shade. I reckoned I had covered about ten miles when, from behind another bend, loomed yet more whitecaps – an avalanche of water racing towards me.

Covered in sweat and spray, I carried on, the river growing steadily narrower. Chatra seemed miles away as, alone and dwarfed by the cliffs, I headed into more rough water, in the middle of which reared a large rock. I banged over this rapid, shaving past the obstructing boulder, bouncing dangerously on the crest of the waves. I was congratulating myself on having pulled through when I caught sight of another rapid, bigger and rougher than all the rest. I was so fascinated by it that I did not notice that to my left another river had joined the main stream. This was the Tamur; without realizing it, in less than thirty minutes I had reached the proposed site for our base camp.

Just before striking the new rapid I saw some figures on the beach. I managed to pull in, and came to a stop hovering up the sandy shore in a shower of grit and dust. Shyly, a few figures came towards me, staring in awe as if I was from outer space. Apprehensively, they looked alternately at my craft and at me, naked save for bathing trunks and a bright yellow life-jacket.

'Tribeni?' I asked, giving the name of the confluence. 'It is here,' remarked a man in Nepali. Only then did I notice the confluence behind me. Taking off my life-jacket, I sat down to rest, thinking of the others on the scorching flat sandbanks back at Chatra.

While waiting for the porters, I began looking for a site for our camp. Starting up my craft again, I went downstream to below the junction of the Tamur, where a little sloping beach formed a perfect harbour. Landing here, I got out and looked around. Upstream, my view was barred by a lake of foam where the Tamur clattered down a steep stone-strewn incline and rushed into the combined flow of the Arun and the Sun Khosi. These met just five hundred yards upstream, their waters forming the huge rapid below which I had stopped. Looking south, I saw the turbulent waters of the rapid with the great boulder stuck in the middle up which I had come. I was hemmed in on all sides by rushing waters, whose angry roar echoed against the steep hills rising in tiers above my head.

It was only 4.30, and all I could do was sit and wait for the porters to arrive. I felt lonely and exhausted and strangely out of place, lying beside my incongruous machine. Soon I was surrounded by another small crowd of strange-looking half-naked men and several dark bronzed-face women with rings in their noses.

I was a bit shaken, for in the last hour I had seen far rougher water than I had anticipated, and this upon the river we believed to be the easiest in all Nepal to negotiate. We should probably never get beyond this point, even assuming the others managed to make it to base camp, for I now recalled that neither Bob nor Michael had much experience in handling the craft. I was deep in these depressing thoughts when the first of our porters came staggering into sight up a ledge above the river carrying a large empty petrol drum. The rest followed close at his heels.

I had hurriedly to decide where we should set up camp and deposit our fuel and equipment. There was no flat land except right at the water's edge where I was lying. This was dangerously close to the river in the event of a sudden storm, but I had no choice and selected a large rock by which I made the men place our jerrycans and the large drum, which was then filled so that four porters could set off back to Dharan to collect yet more fuel.

I then had the crate of spare engines opened, selected a new one and had it sent down by one of the porters to Michael and Bob at Chatra, as it was too late for me to risk going back alone.

Our large mess tent was soon erected, and a smaller one set up for the liaison officer, while the cook built a fire. We hurriedly got ready for the night, as I knew well that in the Himalayas all activity ceased at sundown, and in a few hours it would be dark.

I went to sit on a rock above our camp. As night fell I saw the mountains begin to blaze, as forest fires raged all round, drawing mysterious glowing designs in the sky. Occasionally a tree would explode, illuminating our camp for an instant in weird shades of orange. All around us peasants were setting fire to the forest, where they would later plant corn on the ground they had thus reclaimed. The trees burned with vicious rapidity in the dry evening breeze, and the roar of the fire mingled with that of the rivers. Dharan and Chatra seemed very far away, and I felt once again all the mystery of the Himalayas, with their countless inaccessible valleys, home of a captive population.

That night I could not sleep, so I got up and sat on the warm sand, torn between joy and anguish. I had at last broken the bonds of that other world below the rapids, the world of the plains with its pollution, miseries and luxury. In the mountains the only reality is that of the elements, which are sometimes cruel, but always beautiful. That night for the first time I fully measured the dimensions of the challenge I had accepted.

4 *Accident on the Arun*

It was 5 a.m. when I awoke. The cold dawn light shone on the mountains. The water rushed past, more menacing than the day before. Swirl after swirl, the river clawed at its banks, drawing rocks and gravel out of sight, down the great gorge through which I should have to descend to help my companions. It was cold. I did not want to go; I was afraid.

Getting up, I put on my life-jacket, tucked tools and spare parts under the canopy of the hovercraft, and then pulled the starter ropes. Pushing the lift lever, I sailed down the beach in a flurry of sand and on to the water, only to be immediately sideswept by the rapid. Carried over the turbulent waves, the craft bounced on the crests of foam that rose on either side of me, hiding lethal rocks. The engines roared on, and soon I felt exhilarated as, over 'hump', I now skidded down the gorge at considerable speed. I sailed round a bend, then clattered over a rapid, shooting rocks, sandbanks and curves. Another big rapid approached, a sea of unruly white caps; in its centre I feared the larger waves might swamp the engines. The river now widened, the banks receded, the hills flattened, and soon I was shooting down smooth water, the plains lying below me at the end of a crystal carpet of water. I could at last relax, and noticed a naked man on the shore watching aghast as I sped by.

The jungle lay bare in the morning sun when Chatra came into sight. I hugged the shore before coming up in a cloud of spray to where Michael and Bob stood waiting. They had spent a rough night in the cold, as they had slept out beside their craft. Yet now, at only 8 a.m., the sun was already a blazing ball in the dusty sky as they struggled with the spare engine which the porter had just brought down.

For two hours we wrestled to get it into place, suffering for the first time the torture of burning light on white sand and the bitter agony of exertion in the tropics, caught between the sun and its glaring reflection on the water.

My worries about the other two's inexperience returned. Would they be able to manage the rapids up to camp, and would the six temperamental engines keep working in this heat? Two of our craft were new and not yet broken in, and could be expected to give us trouble. We would have to see!

Having at last got all engines running and everything in order, we set off. Fifty yards from the shore, in midstream, a sinister noise announced that Michael's fan blades had exploded again. His craft fell to the water and started going downstream. Michael jumped off and waded ashore, pulling it. We joined him on a sandbank, and began on an operation which would soon become only too familiar: changing fan blades. A loose bolt had shattered the plastic blades, which had exploded into sharp slivers and caused damage to the plastic base plate, as well as cutting the wire control cables. A light grille was our only protection against these dangerously sharp needles of plastic. Before each future run we would check every bolt, as the vibrations of the two engines would loosen the most resistant nut.

When all was ready and we were about to set off again, Michael's starter cord broke. We repaired it, but the engine now refused to start. An electric contact had been cut. For fully four hours we toiled on the same sandbank in the sizzling heat. Every five minutes we had to slip into the water to cool off. Our throats were parched, our hands bleeding. None of us had eaten that day, and our water jugs were empty. All was deadstill in the midday heat, and the glare of the river was unbearable. We began getting on each other's nerves as we fought with the engines. Not until one-thirty was everything repaired. By that time we were exhausted, yet, as we set out again, we needed all our energy for the run up the river.

To begin with, Michael shot on ahead and I followed, but Bob fell back with engine trouble. I went back to see what the matter was, but Bob rapidly adjusted his carburettors, and we carried on up together. Michael in the meantime had disappeared. The river was four hundred yards wide before it began to narrow gradually as the cliffs rose on either side. The current got faster as we crossed the first rapid. All was well so far, although Michael was still nowhere to be seen.

We did not suspect that he was living through a moment of terror. Advancing at full speed, he had not seen the cable strung across the river. I had warned him, but had reckoned on showing him where it lay and how, by hugging the bank, one could pass underneath it.

Two yards away Michael suddenly saw the rusty line barring his route twenty inches above the water. A second later he would have been decapitated. As it was, he flung himself to the floor, and the cable missed his ear by a few inches before smashing into the fibreglass duct of the thrust unit. The duct was ripped open, the cable swung up, and the craft, after being spun round, kept going.

Quite ignorant of this mishap, we eventually caught up with Michael.

Together we negotiated the next rapid, and I admired the way Bob and Michael were managing their machines. We soon reached the last fast rapid before camp. At his first attempt Bob bounded madly, was thrown against the bank, hit a rock and was swept back downstream. Fortunately his engines were still running, and he tried again as I pulled up beside our tents. This time he made it, but overshot the camp, going on up to the next furious rapid. Realizing his mistake, he soon came back to join me on the beach.

We then noticed that Michael had engine trouble and had pulled his craft into a small cove below the rapid, so Bob and I went back for him. It took us half an hour to adjust his carburettor. Finally we all made it back to camp, exhausted, sunburned, but happy. This seemed to us a great achievement, yet we had only travelled fifteen miles. We now understood that nothing was going to be easy on this journey. Gone were our dreams of travelling fifty miles a day with ease.

That night we had our only meal of the day and then lay down in the tent. Neither Michael nor Bob had air mattresses, and so they slept on the sand with their lifebelts as pillows.

The following morning we were up at sunrise. Our problems of the day before had made us decide to give our engines a complete overhaul before tackling the rough water of the three rivers that met beside our camp.

Michael had brought along a fishing rod and various lethal-looking lures with steel traces. He was hoping to catch a mahseer, the great Indian sporting fish that can weigh anything up to ninety pounds. Michael explained that the strongest trace was necessary to stand up to the powerful teeth that lie encased in rolls of muscle at the back of the fish's throat. The mahseer likes rough water, he said, and should then be running up this river in pursuit of the small whitebait-sized *chilwa* we could see leaping out of the water in their thousands, to the delight of the local fishermen who were squatting at various places along the bank scooping them in with nets. Michael was waist-deep in the foaming water casting out hopefully when Bob and I decided to go for a short ride. We called to him to join us, but he was so busy tugging away at his line that he did not hear us, and moments later we slithered down the beach, hit the water, drifted down a few yards, then headed upstream under full power.

Just north of the camp we struck the large rapids, where torrents of water rushed together to form great white waves rolling over hidden boulders. Here the Arun's grey mass emerged from a deep vertical-sided canyon to meet the green flows of the Sun Khosi.

Although in theory our craft had no real contact with the surface, the drag of the fast waves on our skirts slowed us down, and we barely progressed as we passed this rapid before heading up the deep gorge of the Arun. Here the water ran smooth and swift, perhaps fifty feet deep, between the vertical walls of the narrow, mysterious canyon.

The Arun is one of the most famous rivers of Nepal, a mighty waterway that runs for 175 miles through Tibet before breaking through the entire Himalayan chain. I could not help recalling that we were only a few miles from where one of Hillary's jet boats came to grief.

As we advanced I noticed that my thrust engine was rapidly losing power. Then suddenly I started sliding backwards. Using my paddle, I made for a little sandbank nestling against a cliff. Bob joined me and together we worked on the engine in the sun. At first I could not find out what was the matter; it was only an hour later that we discovered that the main axle pin had broken; the craft was beyond repair. Bob consequently decided to proceed a little way upstream alone.

Half an hour later I saw Bob's craft creeping towards me . . . empty! I had visions of disaster when suddenly Bob's head appeared from behind the hull. When I had pulled him ashore, he explained that he had decided to turn back after proceeding some miles upstream. On coming down a rough rapid, a wave had broken through to the lift propeller, shattering it. He had no alternative but to float down, and eventually had to swim behind the craft to push it towards the beach where I remained stranded.

On inspecting his machine, I noted that the accelerator cable had been dented by the shattering fan blades. We had no spare cable with us, so both craft were now out of order. We debated what to do. Only with difficulty could we hope to climb the cliffs enclosing our beach, and anyway walking back to camp might take anything up to six hours. I recalled what Michael had told us on the basis of his experience during the war in the 'Special Boat Section' of the Commandos: 'With our inflatable hulls we can always float down any river.' I had disagreed with him, yet Michael had sounded positive: 'A rubber boat can float down anything,' he claimed. I had always loathed the idea of floating down rapids without means of controlling our craft, but Bob reassured me: 'It's only a few miles back to camp.' To camp, where we could at last have something to drink. We decided to push off.

A few yards from the shore the current took us in tow. Slowly, then more quickly, we floated over the water. Occasionally we were caught in a backwash and had to paddle out to midstream, but all seemed well.

Bob was in front of me. As the current grew faster, he moved farther and farther ahead. My ears soon echoed with the roar of the big rapid where the waters of the Arun and Sun Khosi combined above our camp.

I lost sight of Bob. My craft gathered momentum. I was utterly helpless, heading inevitably for the thick of the rapids. From my low level I could see only the whitecaps immediately in front of me. Then I caught sight of the first big waves, far bigger than I had expected, because on coming up we had clung to the river's edge; now in midstream the true size of the waves was revealed.

Thousands of tons of water from the two rivers met with a growl. They rushed together over hidden rocks, scalloping out the river bed before rising in a backward swirl to break and crash into whirlpools. In a flash I saw clearly what lay ahead. Waves four, five, even six feet high broke in my direction, as inevitably I was borne towards the biggest. I knew disaster was inevitable, and desperately looked ashore. Far away I could see a man waving, as if urging me to hold on. I was now swept directly into a huge wave that towered above my head, breaking in a voluminous crash of white water. The bow of my craft rose vertically then, as the crest caught it, the whole craft turned over and slapped down with tremendous force on top of me.

Everything was in slow motion. I was in the water, trapped under the craft, I could see orange light, sunlight through the canopy. I flailed out, trying to free myself while hurtling down the river like a leaf caught in a flood. I was rolled about, head over heels, banged against rocks, and carried over more rapids. I could not breathe. In a flash I knew I was lost. This was the end. I choked . . . saw bubbles and the distant light through water. Thrashing desperately, I came up, but no sooner had I broken the surface than I was caught by another roller and forced under again.

What must have taken at the most a few minutes seemed like

an hour. I had a horrible conviction that this was the end, I was about to drown. And how logical it all was! I had willed it all, I had been warned, the forces against us were just too great.

My head ached, my stomach contracted. As I surfaced again I saw light and caught sight of a rock in midstream. Desperately I lunged for it, only to see my hand as if belonging to someone else miss the rock by a few inches as I was borne on. Just then my fingers hit a submerged portion of the rock. I grabbed it, hauled myself up somehow, and collapsed vomiting. Never before had I seen death so clearly. My back was cut, my hands bleeding, but I had been spared a fatal blow on the head. I was alive. The sun, the river, everything appeared beautiful. I dared not believe it.

It took me some time to realize all this, as I felt sick. Only later did I notice my strange predicament – I was alone, stranded on a rock in the middle of a great rapid, unable even to shout, since the river's roar would drown my voice. It was a ridiculous situation, yet I was happy to be there.

Where was Bob, I wondered? I prayed that he was alive. In fact, at that very moment he was wrestling to keep his head above water. His craft had met the same fate as mine, but he had had the good fortune and wits to hold on to the upturned hull which sped downstream as he clambered on to it. As the craft neared our camp, Bob, who had done duty as lifeguard on the Sydney beaches, dived into the swirling water and grabbed a line in a courageous attempt to swim ashore. But the current was too swift and he was dragged by the rope as the boat approached the second large rapid just below our camp.

Bob managed to pull himself back on to the upturned hull just as it battered through the largest waves, barely missing the great rock in the centre of the rapid. For four hundred yards he was carried on down until the water eventually slowed enough for him to jump off and drag the wrecked craft on to a beach.

I was naturally unaware of all this, and was measuring my chances of making it to the bank if I jumped back into the river.

These seemed small. I was dizzy and still trembling. Five, ten, perhaps fifteen or twenty minutes later a man appeared on the bank close to me – an old man, with very pronounced Mongolian features and little slit eyes. He waved me to stay on the rock while he went off, returning soon with a long bamboo pole. It was too short to reach me. A few minutes later I saw four men downstream clambering along the steep rocky bank and dragging something – my craft – upside down.

Desperately I tried to signal that there was a rope in the craft. In a few minutes it was all over. They found and threw me the rope, which I tied around my chest. I remember tying the knot and reflecting what would happen if it came undone. I then took a deep breath and lowered myself into the foaming water. Hand over hand, they reeled me in. At first I was too relieved to find myself still alive to worry much about what had happened. Now, safe at last, I slowly came back to normal and began to realize that it was all over, that – as in a nightmare – nothing had really happened, not at least to my life. All was as before: the sun still shining, glinting on the water, catching the spray; the hills rising serene around me; the little men jabbering, commenting on the incident.

I now began to worry again about Bob. Then, slowly, I grasped the full extent of the disaster. All those months spent on getting the expedition together, and now this. The machines were total wrecks, and Bob was possibly dead. Even if he was alive, this stupid incident had destroyed all my plans. Yet I refused to accept the evidence of failure.

I went over to the upturned craft and noted with surprise that it was not punctured. I felt certain that the fibreglass rim and steel frame of the thrust unit which protruded above the craft must be warped and smashed, along with the rear engine. Yet when the machine was swung over I discovered that only a small portion of the fibreglass duct had been broken off. It was surprising indeed how little apparent damage the machine had suffered. I had of course lost all the tools in the cockpit and one of the wooden boards that held up the canopy, while the canopy itself was ripped and its frame shattered. That seemed all; except that the engines were full of water and the steel frames were most probably beyond repair.

I was looking at this pitiful sight when from across the river came shouts. Looking up I saw the black hull of the large canoe that every day is hauled up the rapids from Chatra to Tribeni. This boat also served as a ferry across the river below the rapids near our camp. The boatmen now proceeded to come to my rescue. They pushed out into the fast water, pulling at the oars, when suddenly one of the men slipped and fell in. He was hauled out in the nick of time. At a second attempt, pulling with all their might, they made it. Five minutes later the boat came slowly up on my side, dragged along the bank against the current. This was my first encounter with the captain of the boat, the headman of the Chu-ba Rais, the tribe which ruled the area in which we had set up our camp.

Knowing a good bargain when he saw one, he began discussing how much I would pay if he took me and my craft back across to our camp. The headman was no exception to the worldwide tradition of ruthless ferrymen, and asked a fee beyond all reason. Being in no state to haggle, I had to agree. Slowly the hovercraft was slung across the boat. Still shaky, I clambered on board. The men pushed off, and in twenty seconds we were hurtling downstream, a man with a great bamboo pole manœuvring the tiller that steered us diagonally to the other bank. In a few minutes I was on the beach of our camp. There stood Michael – and, to my relief, Bob.

From the beach where Bob had managed to drag his craft and right it, he had taken the risk of swimming across the river and had reached the bank some three hundred yards below where he had started. From there he had made his way to camp on foot.

To my surprise Michael seemed indifferent to all this commotion. He was angry that we had set off without him. He had not heard us shout that we were leaving while he was playing with his rod and line; he had caught nothing and in the end his rod had broken. It was a bad day all round – and as we were to discover, the day was not yet over.

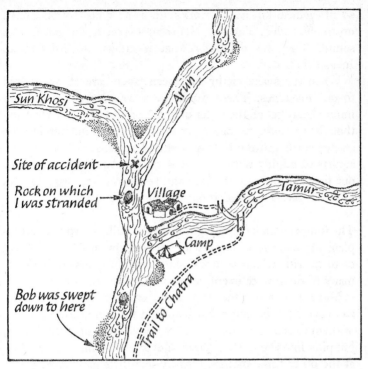

The base camp at Tribeni

Further negotiations with the ferryman persuaded him to retrieve the other hovercraft and bring it back. Having to use his canoe represented the triumph of man over machine, and we felt very foolish as the crew of fifteen half-naked men rowed off to collect our second craft.

I gave a generous present to those people who had hauled me off the rock. I should have liked to lie down, but when the canoe returned with Bob's badly damaged craft we had another problem on our hands. When 002 was picked up a white snake had sprung from under the hovercraft and bitten one of the crew members. The lad was now in great pain, and the less optimistic said he would die. Bob, who was in charge of our small medical kit, got to work with a razor blade and opened up the boy's leg. The boy, clenching his teeth, did not utter a sound. This was definitely what is known in India as an Inauspicious day.

When the snake victim had been taken care of, we looked to our machines. These would be a write-off if we did not immediately get all the water out of the four engines. Exhausted though we were, we began dismantling them and pulling the starter cord, spitting out through the spark-plug hole endless squirts of muddy water. It was dark when we stopped to have our first and only meal – rice and tasteless curry, with one tin of pineapple. Thus ended our second day in camp.

The following morning we got up in the chilly dawn to contemplate the damage to our machines. We now had only one set of tools with which to work. This was a serious problem, as many of these were irreplaceable in Katmandu.

More serious was the state of our engines. Would they ever run again? Three hours' hard work in the sun and we got one of them to start. We were wild with joy. Working even harder, jumping into the water to cool off every few minutes, we toiled at the other three motors. One by one their parts were dried, replaced, and then came the moment of truth. Would they start? They did – all of them. We could hardly believe it. Our luck also decreed that, in spite of bashing over rocks upside down, not one of the steel frames had been bent.

With the planks of an old wooden crate brought from Dharan, we worked on making new supports for the canopies and re-paired the other broken wooden spars with tape. By nightfall we were exhausted, but the three machines were operative.

This incident made us appreciate how completely our lives depended on our machines. So far these had proved far too unreliable, in need of constant adjustment and repairs. Could we ever overcome these problems? And ought we to continue to risk our lives at the slightest mechanical failure? Such was our dilemma.

To cheer us up, our liaison officer produced a bottle of

Rakshi, rice alcohol, whose poor taste was offset by its fortifying effects, so that we were soon in the best of moods again.

That same evening, naked save for a piece of cloth attached to a string, a fisherman paid us a call. He spoke only the Rai language, so our cook had to act as interpreter. We offered him a cigarette and began to inspect his tackle with the same curiosity with which he inspected our craft. He carried with him two long poles tied together to form, as it were, two great antlers, to the ends of which was attached a rectangular net. All day long he and other primitive-looking men spent their time waist-deep in the river, scooping up the water in these strange nets and blindly trying to grab the small fish that were seasonally moving upstream, out of the opaque and muddy water.

These same men had also set up fishing rods supported by forked stakes in the sand near our camp. These they left out overnight, placing beside them eggshells and flowers – an offering to the river gods. Our contact with these fishermen marked the beginning of a whole series of encounters with members of the little-known fishing tribes of Nepal, people who thrive in a marginal world of water, leading lives far different from those of the rest of the Himalayan peoples in a world unsuspected by those who scale mountains.

While a peak is by definition the highest point of a given area, the rivers mark the lowest point. Thus at Tribeni we were only 1000 feet above sea-level, while above us rose hills reaching to 8000 feet. It was on the crests of those hills that most of the local population had settled, living in another world where the temperature was some ten degrees cooler than in the deep gorges.

Altitude is one of the main factors affecting population distribution in Nepal. If one were to draw up a map of the regions inhabited by the country's twenty-six different tribes and races, this map would follow the altitude contours of the hills, each altitude having its own particular population. Thus a hill might harbour three entirely different races speaking three quite distinct languages, although all living within sight of each other. Similarly, from hill to hill similar races speak different dialects, thus turning Nepal into a giant tower of Babel.

In eastern Nepal we were in the home of what are known as the Kiranti people, a race divided into two groups, the Rais and the Limbus. At Tribeni we were in Rai territory, although not far from the territory inhabited by the Limbus. The origin of the Kirantis goes back nearly two thousand years, when they apparently ruled much of Nepal, including Katmandu. Yet the Kirantis were not an aboriginal tribe of Nepal, for according to legend they came originally from Tibet. This is further confirmed by their language, very similar to that of the land of the snows, although their physical appearance is very different from that of the Tibetans. Very short, Rai men scarcely exceed five feet four inches tall. Their faces look far more Mongolian than those of the Tibetans, or even true Mongolians. One could believe one had found in them the prototype of all Mongolians as Asiatic people. The Rai are almost a caricature of a Mongolian, with their very high cheekbones, blunt features, and flat faces that frame very narrow eyes. It was impossible to think of them as handsome, yet their women, with gold rings in their noses, were somehow attractive. However small they might be, the rugged Rais are a people to be reckoned with, and they, together with the Limbus, have a great reputation as soldiers. Their marked features have no doubt become accentuated by their long isolation in the hills of Nepal. Cut off from all contact with the outside world, in a few thousand years they have developed into an easily recognizable type in which are concentrated the physical traits of their land of origin. Yet even among the Rais there are different physical types. Thus the fishermen, for instance, were darker skinned than the farmers, and may originally have come from another race altogether.

Professor Tucci, the noted Italian Tibetologist, wrote of Nepal that its ethnology is 'one of the most complex in the world.' This is certainly true today, but is only a relatively recent phenomenon according to Dr C. S. Coon and other scholars, who claim that ten thousand years ago there were only very slight physical differences between the peoples of the world. Yet in this short time have sprung up such varied races as the seven-foot tall black Dinkas of Sudan and the tiny yellow slant-eyed Rais. As Professor Tucci has remarked, if ever there was a good breeding ground for producing different physical types, it is the Himalayas.

It would be interesting to know exactly what produced these changes – not so much why blacks are black or whites are white, but why are the Rais so different both from their Tibetan ancestors and from their closest neighbours, the tall dark-skinned Tharus, who live just thirty minutes downstream by hovercraft. A logical answer would be climate and general ecology, but even if Nepal had as many micro-climates as it has different races in many similar climatic regions, similar types of people have not evolved. This is true even when they have been from the same stock. The answer seems to lie in the intricacies of genetics as the result of constant inbreeding rather than in ecology. But inbreeding results from interference on a human level – through political, social and religious taboos – rather than from isolation or other geographical imperatives. Most tribes of Nepal are endogamous, which means that they forbid their members to marry outside their tribe.

Yet a tribe may also at the same time forbid its members to marry within a family group. The Rais, for instance, have a ban on marrying close relations down to the seventh generation, although they tolerate and even recommend inbreeding between certain cousins, boys being allowed and even encouraged to marry their mother's brother's daughters. In theory this should lead to everyone looking alike, and that is very nearly what happens. It takes surprisingly little time for a tribe to achieve physical identity. In terms of evolution a new type, or 'cline', is created overnight.

What is true of physical appearance is true in part of certain traits of character linked to genetic factors. In the case of the Nepalese tribes of Tibetan origin, these traits seem to be their courage and aggressiveness, which also appear to have little connection with geography. Ecology, we began to appreciate, is perhaps less important in shaping a race than is generally believed.

5 Not too Welcome

Once our machines were repaired we set about testing them, learning a little more about how to handle them on the three large rapids just around our camp prior to fighting our way up the dangerous Arun once again.

On the opposite bank of the Tamur to where we had pitched our tents was a small Rai village where the ferryman and several of his crew lived. As we tried out our machines a crowd gathered on the beach, and though they stared in amazement at our machines they were there for another purpose. A big celebration was under way. Women were busy preparing a feast that would soon gather together all the local villagers. We were asked to join them by the boatman who had rescued our craft. As headman, he was paying for the celebration, no doubt sharing the large sum of money he had made rescuing us two days before. Eager to know our neighbours better, we warmly accepted their invitation.

To begin with we were served 'jar', millet beer, a delicious white drink which looks like watery porridge with a few red millet seeds floating in it. It tasted better than it looked, and was a welcome change from the wretched river water we had been drinking, which contained a lot of clay and allum, which parched our mouths and left us even thirstier than before.

Unlike the Hindus, who will not share their plates or touch the cup of another man, everyone drank from the same drinking cups, which were constantly refilled by the happy crowd. A woman then served us on large leaves helpings of rice with curried pork, bristles and all. We swallowed it rather reluctantly.

I now learned that our neighbours belonged to a clan called

the *Chu-ba*, which in Tibetan means 'those of the river', a reminder of the Rais's ancient northern origins. This clan was in fact master of the great rivers of the confluence, being all ferrymen by vocation. Until three years before, when they had collectively acquired the large boat with which they travelled down to Chatra, they had owned several small dug-out canoes.

A recently built footbridge suspended over the Tamur and one farther upstream over the Arun have taken away some of their ferry trade. On the other hand, their new large boat – which could carry at a pinch forty persons – allowed them to travel up- and downstream to Chatra in the dry season, and was thus a new source of wealth to them.

The ferrymen's lives were dangerous, as we well knew. The very fact that they could take their boat up the river at all was remarkable and, as for going down, it was not without considerable risks. The true head of the clan, we now learned, was an old woman who was the guardian of all the mariners' secrets, of knowledge accumulated over the years on how to make use of the backwash and counter-currents to fight one's way upstream. It was hardly comforting for us to learn that they never ventured upstream beyond the rapid where we had come to grief, let alone beyond the larger ones we proposed to challenge the following day on the Arun. It was late in the afternoon when we left our new friends (a little tipsy from drinking) to start our craft and cross the swift waters back to our camp. Our farewell was a gay one, but it became painful to recall when we learned that, two weeks later, their precious boat capsized going downstream, drowning sixteen. How many among the victims were our friends we were never able to find out.

After the feast we attempted a practice run up the rapid that marked the few hundred yards where the Tamur dropped down to meet the main river. This drop of some 30 feet in a short distance was over rocks and boulders, and looked terrifying, although there were no huge breaking waves such as had caused us to capsize on the rapid higher up.

Since leaving Chatra we had learned a few useful lessons

about our hovercraft. For one, we knew that when floating on air our tiny machines could successfully bounce over waves up to four feet high, the only risk being that rushing spray and fast water could progressively slow us down, making us lose momentum and often causing us to slide down backwards. On the other hand, to drive too quickly up turbulent waters made our craft dig suddenly into a big wave which would then violently throw us back. The art, it seemed, lay in approaching the rapids at the right speed, not too fast and not too slowly, and then relying on our quick reflexes to avoid very big rocks or turbulent waves. This was no easy task. Seated barely ten inches above the water, it was impossible to see over the bigger waves to what lay ahead. It was a matter for last-minute thinking as one entered a rapid or came out round a blind bend in the river. Only after several unsuccessful attempts were Bob and I able to ascend the steep step-like rapid of the Tamur at the trijunction.

Finally, we now knew that the art of negotiating rapids was a matter of steering one's course around or between the large crescent-shaped breakers, avoiding where possible the mainstream of the river.

It was such a spectacular sight to watch our craft battle against the rushing, foaming waters that I decided to film Bob in action. Looking through my lens, I saw him take off, gather speed, and turn in a great arc in the mainstream before heading for the rocky steps and, steering a course between boulders, bouncing over foamy crests and smaller rocks, being slowed down almost to a standstill. Then, as if by magic, he slowly gathered forward speed against the spray. All the time Bob was simultaneously correcting the side drift caused by the wind, by centrifugal force, and by the drag of the current against the skirts.

All this needed quick co-ordination and a good sense of direction. On pulling up above the rapid, Bob lost control for a moment, and his craft went hurtling into a rock. Back at camp, we noticed our first puncture. This was repaired under the watchful eye of a pretty young lady who had joined us, together with another girl of about fifteen. This girl, we soon discovered, was mentally retarded. Later that night the unfortunate child refused to leave our camp and eventually spent the next six days sleeping beside our tents. She was a pathetic yet charming companion who smiled at all we did, even when we tried unsuccessfully to chase her away. We soon came to adopt her, and the day she vanished we were all quite upset.

Just before sundown, when all was ready for the next day's run up the Arun, we took a walk along the Tamur river. A steep goat's track led us above a deep vertical gorge through which the river ran for about half a mile. A great variety of trees grew on the steep hillside above the track. Looking across the gorge, we could see the dark patches left by the forest fires of the preceding nights. Clambering down, we came out on one of the many beautiful beaches we had already encountered. These bordered unpolluted water caught between great rocks, and to walk on their fine sand was a delight. We had a swim, while Michael laid out nine different kinds of fern he had collected on the way.

From reading, Michael had acquired a surprising knowledge of the local flora, yet neither he nor anyone else could ever hope to identify all the plants we might meet. There are believed to be over a hundred varieties of orchids alone in Nepal, not to mention the different strains of grass, moss and trees, among which must be counted the hundreds of rhododendrons, varying from the little pink to the huge red varieties, and often reaching more than 30 feet in the forests that cover most of the hillcrests of central Nepal.

The forest fires we had seen burning all around us were reminders of the population explosion which had struck Nepal in recent years. In two decades the land's population had leaped from 9 to 13 million, requiring the forest to be burned so that squatters could find new slopes for their small terraced fields of corn and rice.

Back in camp, we discussed our plans once more. Tomorrow we would survey the Arun as far up as we could go. This might be only a few miles; in any case, 30 miles was our maximum range, for we could only carry fuel for five hours.

On this journey I hoped to find a site to which we could send porters to establish a new petrol dump. This was provided we received permission to proceed up to Num, for we were still restricted to going no farther than Tumlingtar, 35 miles upstream. Every day we expected a runner to come with a reply to the cable I had sent to Dharan, but none came.

The following morning I had butterflies in my stomach as I recalled the hazards we were up against. Michael had declared jokingly that going up these rapids was 'dicing with death'. The formula had made us all laugh, but now it did not sound amusing at all.

The truth was that we were constantly taking calculated risks – risks fully justified so far by the positive aspect of our journey. All told, our craft had proven surprisingly efficient. Even Sir Christopher Cockerell would have been impressed by the way they battered up the river over waves as large as themselves, surmounting the flow of thousands of tons of rushing water.

The main danger lay in the engines breaking down, which would turn our hovercraft into mere floating boats. Had our craft been bigger, the risks might have been less great, but bigger craft would have been impossible to fly over to Nepal. As it was, our small, light machines were ideal for prospecting uncharted waters, for two of us could lift them with ease. We could always manage to carry them round a waterfall, for example, while with bigger boats this would have been impossible.

We had decided to travel together up the Arun, but when the time came to leave Michael's craft broke down once more. He was certainly unlucky. From the first we had each operated a specific craft because, although they were all theoretically the same, every one handled differently from the next as a result of the delicate balance of pressure inside the bag of the skirt. The exact cause of these differences lay in the mysterious laws of that new science, low-pressure aerodynamics, a field of research only just beginning to reveal its secrets to hovercraft engineers.

When his machine refused to start, Michael sportingly let us go on ahead without him. The journey soon proved eventful. Just above the rapid where we had capsized, Bob's thrust engine stalled. His craft was swept backwards towards the huge waves in which I had nearly drowned. Aware of the danger, Bob got up and pulled his starter. The engine roared again, just in time. Together we carried on through the dark narrow gorge of the Arun, each bend revealing a new perspective of turbulent water.

Emerging from the deep gorge, we struck a wide, fast rapid curving around a bend – the rapid where Bob had broken his lift blades three days before while I had been stranded with a broken axle-pin. Bouncing and slowing down, we hugged the rocky bank and painfully made our way up. For a few hundred yards the water smoothed out, although it still ran very fast. Then came another rapid. The flow here was as fast as any we had so far encountered, and I picked a course between the largest whirlpools. Looking round, I noticed that Bob's craft had dug in and was being swept back. He eventually pulled it round and started upstream again, this time following on behind me on a relatively easy stretch of water to yet another rapid, which we could avoid by hugging the shore even more closely.

The last rapid was where we presumed the jet boat had sunk. This was hardly surprising, for everywhere rocks broke the surface. These were no obstacle to us, but they would inevitably be lethal to a craft that floated in water. We had little time to enjoy the scenery, for it took all our wits and reflexes to steer our craft, spot the obstacles, estimate the current, and decide on a course, as bend after bend revealed more rapids, leaving us only seconds in which to decide how to tackle them.

A few miles up, we struck another rapid whose bounding waves barred our way. I made one attempt at it, but the spray and current were so strong that they brought my craft to a standstill. For a few seconds, I sat poised above the rushing water, then slowly I drifted back until a wave hit me broadside and spun me round, hurtling me downstream. I fell back fifty yards, steered towards smoother water, turned up, and tried again. This time I made it, but I was advancing only at a snail's pace when I reached the even swells that marked the top of the rapid. Bob was having the same trouble, and I soon lost sight of him as my machine gathered momentum, shooting swiftly forwards between the steep banks. More bends, more rapids – I lost count, for there was a rapid every few hundred yards.

By rapids I mean a stretch of white water breaking over rocks and boulders as opposed to fast water with an even surface. Although each rapid differed from the next, we soon recognized three distinct kinds. The first type is found when a river goes down over an even, steep incline; these we came to call 'straight rapids'. The second and most dangerous are 'curved rapids', where on a bend the water comes up against one bank, swirls round, and then shoots across to crash into the other bank. Shaped like an 'S', they are the most difficult to ascend, because one is obliged to travel in midstream through the biggest waves, while on a straight rapid one can usually hug one side of the river. The third kind is an 'obstructed rapid', one with many large boulders in it. These create many cross-currents, with consequent steering hazards. Frequently all three types are combined. In addition, each can be graded as to speed of water and, more important, volume, for it is volume rather than speed which creates the hazards of great vertical whirl-pools. These are formed when a depression is created in the river bed into which water sweeps down before curling up to break like a surf wave. These waves and the hollow behind them can only be properly seen when going downstream; going up-stream, one cannot appreciate how deep the depression is. Needless to say, even between rapids there was always a fast current, with sinister upheavals breaking the surface or forming backflows that lead to whirlpools.

After crossing some ten rapids I lost sight of Bob. We had made it a strict rule to stick together, partly in case of accident and partly because now we had only one set of tools. I therefore drove on to a low sandbank to wait for him. I could not help but marvel each time I sailed ashore at the versatility of the hovercraft, the only true amphibian machine in the world. From dangerous water, one could float to the safety of land in an instant, so long as the banks were not more than two feet high. This low clearance height did not prevent us from being able at a pinch to bounce over much higher rocks when encountered in midstream.

Soon I heard Bob's engine, and saw him coming up the water steps to where I stood waiting. When loaded with petrol, his craft had a greater tendency than mine to dig in, so he had had to make several attempts up some of the rapids. Very soon, with a little more experience, Bob was to prove the best pilot of the three of us, while his machine also turned out to be the most robust and trouble-free.

As we stretched our legs on the sandbank and refilled our tanks from the jerrycans we had brought, we noticed above us a crowd peering over the edge of the steep embankment. We were near some village whose inhabitants had been startled by the noise of our engines. From all sides they had come running to see what was the matter. They were too high and far away for us to speak to them.

It struck me that although we had been less than thirty minutes under way, we were possibly a day's walking from the confluence, perhaps two, as the tracks could not follow the river and had to scramble over several very high hills. We were now in sparsely inhabited country, the local people (still Rais) preferring the height of the ridges to the hot valley. It was strange to realize that the people we could see on either side of the river (which we could now cross with ease) were probably total strangers to one another, there being no canoes to ferry them over and the nearest ferry and bridge standing more than a day's walk away. Two full days' march thus separated these neighbours, who could look at each other yet never shake hands! We were soon to discover that in many places each bank of a river was inhabited by entirely different races, speaking a different language yet living only a hundred yards apart.

After a quick drink of water from our flasks (the river here was too murky) we set off north once more up a long, relatively smooth stretch. There were only a few minor rapids here, which allowed us to proceed at nearly 30 m.p.h. until we hit another large rapid where once again Bob's craft was swept back. I carried on alone again around more bends, up more steps, in and out of obstacles, playing with the thrust and lift engines in quick succession to keep control.

I had now come out on the other side of the Mahabharat range, that east-west barrier that cuts across southern Nepal, and was about to enter the deep, wide valley of the Arun, whose hilly sides were the lower ends of the buttresses that slowly rose to merge into the formidable Everest range to the west and the less known Lumbasumba range to the east, both about seventy miles away.

After a while the river began to run through a straight, sheer-sided gorge rising vertically some thirty feet from the water. I wanted to stop and wait for Bob, but this proved impossible as there was not a beach in sight. Carrying on for a few miles, I came to a very large rapid that rushed down between the rocky walls bordering the river. There my machine seemed to have met its match. I slowed down and inspected the foaming water that was just short of being a true waterfall.

I estimated that we had covered about 25–30 miles since leaving our camp. This left us with so little petrol in reserve that I decided to turn back. A few miles downstream I ran into Bob and waved to him to follow me to a sandbank. We emptied our remaining petrol into the tanks and set off back to camp.

Going down was not easier than going up, as one might expect, because of the strange phenomenon of 'going over hump'. To get out of the depression created by the lift fan while going downstream required considerable forward speed, as the depression was carried along with us by the rushing water. We were thus obliged either to crawl at the speed of the current and lose much of our independence of movement, or to speed along so fast that steering accurately became quite a problem. Fortunately all went well until, just before entering the narrow gorge of the Arun, the fan-belt of my thrust engine suddenly began to slip. I had to stop and repair it before carrying on down to camp.

Our run up the Arun marked our first penetration of a river never travelled before. We had succeeded in going where jet boats and all other craft had so far failed. Adding our journey from Chatra to that up the Arun, we had at least proved that hovercraft could in a couple of hours reach places only accessible by foot in the course of a three days' march. I now began to feel more optimistic, and regained some of the confidence I had lost when we had capsized.

On the other hand, we now appreciated that overloading considerably reduced the craft's manœuvrability over rough waters. This meant that we could load less petrol than we had originally planned. All the more so in that safety required us to carry a considerable load of spare parts – fan blades, rubber skirt and hull repair kits, cables, and so on. All this weight, plus the paddles, the anchors, the rope and a little food or drinking water, left little room for more than three jerrycans. Consequently we could not travel more than 70 miles without refuelling, which meant only 35 miles if we had to return each time to base camp. Seventy miles might sound like a very short distance, yet by Himalayan standards this would allow us to penetrate nearly to the Tibetan border, this being as far up the Arun as we could ever hope to travel short of penetrating into Tibet. It had originally been planned to send some porters ahead of us to establish a petrol depot some thirty miles up the Arun. This would allow us to go up, refill, shoot on to the head of the river, and return.

Our problem was to secure the permit from the Nepalese Government to proceed beyond the town of Tumlingtar, 35 miles upstream. With this permit, our only obstacle would be to negotiate the large rapid I had seen and other possible big ones. These we could negotiate by carrying our light machines along the shore, if need be. Going up the Arun, we felt, would prove a worthy task, taking us to within 30 miles of the summit of Everest – a good objective for a boat or for any mechanical vehicle short of a plane. It would also allow us to investigate

No boat can travel upstream on fast-flowing, rock-strewn water like this on the Arun. Above right and below: when our craft capsized, these Chuba-rai ferrymen rescued it. Three weeks later their own craft capsized and many of them were drowned.

Our craft is dwarfed by the cliffs of an untravelled gorge on the Tamur.

the Tibetan-speaking inhabitants of the upper Arun region – a region rarely visited and unknown to me. Since no message arrived from General Surendra Shaha, we decided in the meantime to continue investigating the area around our camp, going up the Tamur and the Sun Khosi.

By five o'clock that evening the sky had become overcast, and grey clouds hung angrily about the hills to the north. As we got ready to have dinner, a sharp wind began moving the fine white sand surrounding our camp. As it grew stronger, we were soon caught in the midst of a small sandstorm. Our tents were slowly invaded with dust. There was sand everywhere, blowing past us as we tried to patch the leaks where the wind forced entry.

With great trouble, the cook and his helper stoked a small fire in the open – brewing tea whose murky river water was further thickened by sand. It was dark when we ate. The gale howled and a few streaks of lightning outlined the black hills. It was not raining over our camp, but it was undoubtedly pouring on the high mountains, so that any minute I felt the river might begin to rise. I now recalled the warnings we had been given of flash floods, and began to fear that our craft might be swept away in the night. We hauled them a little higher up on the beach, but the move was mainly symbolic, as high water could well sweep right over our tents.

That night I tried to sleep listening to the wind and the rush of the water, imagining the roar to be ever-increasing. Next morning when we awoke we were coughing and covered in dust. The wind had abated a little, but the clouds still hung black and menacing to the north over the Arun. One by one we refuelled our craft, toyed with the engines, and prepared to set out up the Tamur.

Michael's engine as usual gave us trouble before finally breaking down once more. Reluctantly we had to leave him behind. From our short walk up the Tamur, we had gathered that this river would prove difficult to negotiate. Apart from the rapid where it plunged down to join the main river by our camp, it showed signs of being littered with boulders, as in this season its flow barely covered the large rocks and stones of its bed.

As I set off with Bob the thrill of the unknown gripped us once more. Our craft was neither plane, boat, nor car, but seemed to have inherited the disadvantages as well as some of the advantages of all three. Like a boat, we could capsize; like a car, we could crash; while like a plane, once we were off, we had to stay airborne, for we could not afford to have engine trouble going over rough water.

Even by combining all three modes of locomotion, it would be difficult to convey the exact sensation of hovering up a fast river whose course is utterly unknown. It was like flying at ground level in a forest of rocks, skidding round obstacles without any firm contact with land. Every bend required to be planned ahead, for we could not make a sharp turn or come to a sudden halt. All we could do in an emergency was to land the craft on the water, but this was like leaving the frying pan for the fire, as we would then be swept downstream – possibly into another, even more dangerous obstacle. Speed was our principal enemy, since it meant we could lose control, yet it was equally dangerous to go slowly.

The thrills I had felt in Spain and France when cruising up untravelled reaches of well-known rivers were now sharpened by the knowledge that no one had ever seen the landscape we admired from behind our canopies. Within a mile there would be a hundred inaccessible little coves at the foot of the cliffs, a hundred beaches never trodden by man, a thousand forbidden vistas of water – some turbulent, others reflecting mountain views – a whole new world such as I had never dreamed of when in the Himalayas before. There I had been but a pedestrian, but once on the water one was entirely alone against the forces of nature. And what forces! Many have described the horror and power of a flood, but what is a flood compared to the mainstream of fast mountain torrents, especially when these torrents are wider than most of the rivers in Europe?

Having battered our way up the first rapid of the Tamur, we eased our craft around a bend and entered a narrow gorge whose cliffs rose vertically like those of a Chinese print. The noise of our engines echoed as we bumped over rounded waves where the water compressed by the canyon rushed down against us. Spray and wind in our faces, made us squint as we scanned each bend, picking out a large rock ahead or the tell-tale white water indicating a rapid.

A few miles from camp, we emerged from the canyon to encounter a wide bend where the river fanned out and divided in two as it rushed over boulders in a fury of foam. I bore left up the smaller of the two channels, Bob hard on my heels. The channel now narrowed to become only six feet wide and strewn with rocks, on one of which my craft grounded. Bob managed to pass me and carried on ahead. I jumped out, leaving my engines running, and, slipping on the rocks, managed to free my craft and hop back in to proceed slowly up. The incline was steep, and although the engines were going full blast my craft barely made headway up the fast shallow water.

I could see Bob just ahead of me, slowed nearly to a standstill. Across our path was a tree-trunk, thrown there no doubt to allow fishermen to walk across to the main channel of the river. We were able to hover over it without the slightest trouble, only to find more boulders and swirling water which eventually brought us to a halt. It was a strange halt, for although we were making no headway, water rushed past under us at over 15 m.p.h., so that in effect we were standing still above a rushing river, defying all laws of gravity and motion, since we were moving at 15 m.p.h. in regard to the water yet stationary in regard to the bank. This could never get us anywhere, so I slowly drifted backwards until a wave caught my bow, spinning me around.

In the meantime Bob had managed to jump ashore, pull his craft up a step and carry on up the rapid out of sight. I made another attempt up the rapid, creeping over the rocks and up water steps till I was again brought to a standstill and then swept back. This time I jumped on to a rock, holding the rope attached to my craft whose engines I had left at full throttle. Hovercraft left on their own, I now found out, have a tendency to misbehave. Relieved of their passenger's weight, they bounce about and pull backwards, throwing water in your face. Soon I was engaged in a wrestling match, a sort of aquatic tug-of-war with my craft, losing ground rapidly as my feet slipped on the mossy boulders. For a moment I was in some difficulty through falling flat over a rock, my craft pulling like mad and threatening, if I let go, to go shooting off alone. In the end I clambered aboard and turned down the engines in order to drift back over the log to the bottom of the rapid. From there I gathered momentum and swept up again, only to come to a standstill below the same obstacle – a step of water between two boulders. I just could not work out how to jump out as Bob had done and give my machine that extra pull it needed. In the midst of this scramble my craft gave a deafening howl, lending more urgency than necessary to a ridiculous situation.

The banks of the river were too steep to run the craft ashore, so I finally decided to drive back to a more hospitable place and catch my breath. A few hundred yards farther down, I was approaching a medium-sized rapid when suddenly my lift engine stopped. Immediately my skirt deflated and I fell into the water. Once again I was an ordinary boat being dragged downstream at the whim of the current, heading for waves large enough to make my heart sink. I bumped clumsily through the first, while the second broke over the bow of my craft, filling it with water. For a moment I felt the seeds of panic, for several large rapids lay ahead. With my paddle and the aid of my thrust engine, I made it ashore on to a sandy beach just above the entrance of the canyon. While I was struggling to empty the water out of my craft and get the lift engine started, I saw Bob bouncing towards me. He hovered about while I got my engines going, and we carried on together back to the camp.

For a trial this had hardly been successful, although Bob was able to carry on up for four to five miles, encountering more boulder-strewn rapids and eventually a village populated by very Mongolian-looking people, probably Limbu tribesmen, the second of the Kiranti people, who generally live north of the Tamur between it and the frontiers of Sikkim.

Michael, who had missed all the 'fun', was understandably furious with his machine. Since we arrived, he had spent most of his time fussing with tools. I now let him have my craft, and together with Bob he practised shooting up the rapids of the Tamur river near our camp. Meanwhile, I struggled to change his engine for a new one. Things were beginning to seem depressing when we suddenly recalled that it was Easter Sunday – a fact that seemed confirmed by the visit of two young American Peace Corps men who, hiking up the trail, had been attracted by the noise of our machines. We welcomed their visit and invited them to share what we promised would be a great Easter dinner, for as usual we had not eaten all day. Somehow we had become indifferent to food, so absorbed were we by our devilish machines, tending to their breakdowns while neglecting our own bodies. The weather now conspired to stop our planned Easter feast, for the storm that had been brewing suddenly broke. A howling wind rushed up the gorge, blinding us with sand and ripping open our tent so that we had great trouble preventing it from flying away. Singing 'Happy Easter' to myself did not seem to help, as I found out that it is harder to pitch a tent on a beach than to build a house on sand.

Soon we were in total chaos: Michael clinging to the guide ropes, I latching on to a flailing flap, Bob buried under more canvas, and the Peace Corps boys goggling at us, our equipment and our craft, and trying to make up their minds if we were mad or not. The reason for their alarm was that it was not Easter: we had simply lost count of the days. All that mattered was that we thought it was, but when it began to rain and the rain blew into the tent and turned the dust to mud, we had to confess that there would be no Easter dinner as our cook had fled to a nearby hut. The liaison officer lay hidden in his small windproof tent – my best – and we sat huddled around a tin of cheese full of sand, followed by spam which we munched in humiliation, accompanied by roasted rice our new friends kindly handed out to us from a plastic bag.

The following day was Easter Monday by our reckoning. At dawn our house guests stalked off, no doubt for the more comfortable shelter of a sturdy Nepalese home. Our festive mood vanished when we discovered that our little friend the mad girl had weathered the storm out in the open, sleeping nearly buried in sand. For some reason she had fallen in love with us – sure proof that she was mad. We were somewhat concerned for her, as we gathered she had been abandoned by her parents. We really did not know what to do. To make matters worse, I was feeling ill, the prelude to the same stomach trouble which had attacked Bob the day before.

Overnight the rivers had risen, especially the Tamur, whose blue waters were now *café au lait*, and the contours of the nearby banks had changed. The Tamur had hollowed out a large sand cliff opposite our camp, while our swimming hole was filled with boulders. The rapids below the camp had partially disappeared under the rising water. All told, the rise of the rivers had made things slightly easier. Still feeling unwell, I sent Bob and Michael out alone to go up the Arun and investigate the rapid where I had turned back.

It was 8 a.m. when they disappeared, leaving me to speculate on what would break down next. There is nothing like a real stomach ache on a fake Easter Monday to bring one down to earth, and I had ample time to meditate on the past few days and worry about the future. Our machines, despite their frequent need of adjustment, had performed remarkably well on rough water; but the rivers were much rougher than I had expected. This was worrying, for we believed these eastern rivers to be the easiest in Nepal, and it was still our intention to cross the entire Himalayan range. So far we had only reached an altitude of 2000 feet. What would happen at higher altitudes, where we would have to battle against the combined effects of height and isolation? My worries increased when the Assistant District Commissioner of eastern Nepal arrived, having come up the river on foot, escorted by two armed soldiers. He had been dispatched to our camp because of rumours that we had drowned, the story of our minor disaster having been magnified into a major calamity. I politely informed the District Commissioner (somewhat to his disappointment) that we were all alive and well, after which I asked him to tea, worrying that it was now 3 p.m. and there was no sign of either Michael or Bob. Fortunately they arrived in time, though Michael's craft was suffering from belt slip and crept along, Michael helping it with his paddle and affording a sight hardly calculated to impress the local official. To make matters worse, Michael ran out of petrol and had to pull ashore on the opposite bank from our camp and call for help. Our guest soon left, after handing a letter to our liaison officer.

That night the liaison officer, who seemed slightly bloated with importance, explained to us in difficult English that there was to be no 'anthropology'. 'No anthropology!' I echoed. 'What do you mean?' 'I don't know,' answered our liaison officer. 'What do you mean – "I don't know"?' 'Well,' he explained, 'I know you are not to anthropologize, but I don't know what anthropology means.' He then produced a letter written in Nepalese and re-read the word anthropology. 'Is there a mention about our permit to go up the Arun to Num?' we asked eagerly. 'No,' answered our liaison officer. 'You cannot go beyond Tumlingtar.' This was a severe blow. No anthropology, no Num, and now the liaison officer informed us that we were not to go up the Sun Khosi either!

This was ridiculous. We had mentioned to the General in Katmandu that we would be making an ecological and anthropological study of the river people, and he had approved. So why this formal ban on 'anthropology'? We did not then suspect the sinister implications of this decision, nor the size of the storm brewing in Katmandu which was soon to represent a hazard far more disastrous than the worst rapids.

Faced with a ban on going up the Arun or the Sun Khosi, there was little we could do but revert to our original plan, and consider our stay in eastern Nepal as a trial period in which we familiarized ourselves with our craft, their capabilities, and with the character of the Himalayan rivers, before returning to Katmandu to tackle our major objective – the run up the spectacular Kali Gandaki river right through the Annapurna and Dhaulaghiri ranges. Ten days had elapsed since we had set up camp. We now planned to return in two days' time after a last short run up the Sun Khosi which our liaison officer said would be all right.

Our last night in camp was a pleasant one. Since we had arrived the sun had turned us all into dark-skinned ruffians, and in the short time we had been at Tribeni each of us had lost over ten pounds, the combined result of strenuous days of struggling with our craft in the heat and our spartan diet. Up at five, we had often spent ten hours by the water, many of them exposed to a midday sun which should have driven the maddest of dogs to shelter, to say nothing of Englishmen, Frenchmen or Australians.

Since our arrival at Tribeni, we had come to know each other better, and now formed a close-knit team. Michael, for instance, had emerged as the gentleman he truly was, with a heart as big as his heavy frame. A poet in a strange sort of way, he viewed life with a remote detachment which placed him far above – perhaps too far above – all personal and material concerns. He never ate, would fall asleep anywhere at the drop of a hat, and showed a general disregard for everything concerned with his body, which seemed indifferent to heat or cold, rain or flies. In fact his only material concern was finding his glasses – by now they only had one lens – which he was constantly losing. I had accepted that he would never make a mechanic, yet at the controls of his craft he showed unexpected skill, as witness his successful run up the Arun. Michael's conversation was always enlightening, and his life was more characteristic of those of nineteenth-century travellers in which mingled beautiful women and rugged natives. We had little trouble imagining Michael pacing the world impeccably dressed for every occasion, fussing over the harsh treatment meted out to mules or temporarily adopting children, for children everywhere, as we were soon to witness, had a passion for him – a passion not only due to the sweets and small coins he was constantly distributing, but to the patience with which he tolerated their antics while dispensing advice on hygiene and good manners in an impeccable Oxford accent.

As for Bob, the rivers had given him ample occasion to show his skill and daring, while he had become the best of us as regards keeping his craft in good working order. His life and education could hardly have been more different from Michael's, yet, like Michael's, it had its contrasts, since he had tried his hand at a thousand contradictory occupations. He was constantly torn between his need for an occupation that was both physically and intellectually demanding, and his wish to bring a little democracy into a world which he persisted in regarding as the monopoly of a caste represented by Michael, the public school boy.

Occasionally I was caught in the inevitable conflicts between these two, but most of the time we spent speculating about the rivers, our craft, and what lay in store for us when we set off on the trail that, we hoped, would take us to 10,000 feet and closer to solving some of the mysteries of Nepal.

Since our arrival, the three of us had totalled approximately 400 miles, of which, alas, only 45 miles from Chatra to our highest point on the Arun could represent anything like penetrating a mountainous region otherwise inaccessible. Yet the total number of miles proved so far that what we had done was well within the scope of our machines. Hovercraft as a means of communication up rapid rivers was beginning to become a reality.

All our equipment was loaded on to the ferry boat and sent downstream with the liaison officer – a trip far more dangerous than hovering, as we realized when the same boat capsized a week later.

We remained behind to shoot a film of our craft bouncing over the rapids, then we set off, all three in a row like angry water-flies chasing each other, minute orange and grey dots dwarfed by the steep, ever-widening canyon as we headed for the plains. On the way, we stopped at Barachatra, a Hindu shrine which marked the northern limit of the Hindu religion. Slowly we climbed the two hundred steps that rose from a sandy beach to a series of temples, where the statue of Shiva recalled that all the world's rivers flow from his sacred head. All rivers are therefore considered sacred by Hindus, particularly their sources and confluences, the most holy river of all being the Ganges, on whose banks at Benares it is fitting to die.

Having visited the shrine in the company of a small crowd of children, we pushed off, to emerge a few minutes later into the suffocating plains. Chatra, with its scrap-iron graveyard, was there to meet us.

Bob and Michael were soon busy dismantling our craft, while I settled accounts with the District Commissioner and the officers of the camp, and got ready to fly back in advance to Katmandu. But first of all I celebrated Easter, for the second time, at Dharan – this time on the right day.

6 *Up in the Air*

I reached Katmandu on April 3rd and called General Surendra, expecting a word of explanation regarding our being forbidden to proceed up the Arun. With his habitual charm and oriental evasiveness, the General appeared quite surprised. 'Why,' he said, 'I spoke to the Prime Minister on receiving your cable from Dharan, and he said you could go anywhere in Nepal except in the restricted northern areas.' To my knowledge Num was well within such limits. The General gave no further explanation, but asked that I send him a report of how things had gone. Before I hung up, he explained kindly how relieved he was that we were all alive, as in Katmandu he had received news of our deaths by drowning.

That evening I paid a visit to Boris. Boris must be one of the most colourful foreigners to have lived in the East and was my best friend in the valley. A big game hunter, he was once a dancer with Diaghilev. The road that had led him to Nepal ran from Odessa, to Monte Carlo, then, via Buenos Aires, to Shanghai and finally Calcutta, where he had founded and operated the famous 300 Club. Boris's eccentricities were well known in Nepal, and ran from catching elephants to organizing a Hollywood safari with a brace of maharajas. Artist, sportsman, and bon vivant, he for ever surprises his friends and acquaintances. These include Queen Elizabeth and Prince Philip, for whom he once organized a banquet in the jungles of Nepal, in which 240 different types of game were served!

In 1950 Boris became one of the first foreigners to settle in Katmandu, and it is thanks to his endeavours that Nepal's doors were thrown open to tourists. In 1956 he persuaded the late King of Nepal that foreigners would be fascinated by

Katmandu's ancient charm, and later he opened the famous Royal Hotel in Katmandu, a hotel whose bathrooms sported stuffed tigers and in whose corridors one might well have met in quick succession Mr Nehru, a panda, and several Russian astronauts – not to mention countless other personalities that mingled there with the world's most famous mountaineers. In 1963 I had written a book, *Tiger for Breakfast*, that attempted to record Boris's never-ending fantasies and our friendship dated from that time. His hotel had recently closed down and Boris was now reduced to running a restaurant, the *Yak and Yeti*.

When we arrived there, Boris was so pleased that we were all still alive that he nearly drowned us in vodka, before insisting that my companions and I come round the following Saturday night for his great Easter banquet. Surprised, I was going to make some comment to straighten out this Easter problem when he added, 'The Russian Easter, of course.'

With the knowledge we had acquired in eastern Nepal of the capabilities of our craft, I could now consider it worth while making an aerial survey of the new rivers we planned to ascend – in particular, of the Kali Gandaki, whose source lies on the border of Mustang and Tibet.

Millions of years ago this river, like the Arun, had drained the high Tibetan plateau, flowing gently down into India. Then suddenly, in one of the world's greatest cataclysms, the Himalayan range had arisen, raising its massive peaks along the edge of the highlands of Tibet, forming a jagged lip to the vast Tibetan plains. Overnight the Arun and the Kali Gandaki with other rivers, had found their southward routes obstructed. The result was that most of these rivers were forced to make a huge detour to the east. They combined to form the upper Brahmaputra, which today circles the entire Himalayan range before being able to cut south through Assam. But not so the stubborn Arun and the Kali Gandaki, which both decided, as it were, to flow uphill. For it is a fact that along the first seventy miles of the Kali Gandaki's course this river flows against the general slope of the north face of the Himalayas. How this came about had only recently been explained. When the rising Himalayas cut the Kali Gandaki's route to the south it formed a gigantic dam. Eventually, having built up to a deep lake, the river broke the dam in a weak spot and was able to overflow it and carve out a channel through the mountains. It ultimately dug so deep that not only did the lake disappear, but the river resumed its old course south unobstructed against the general slope of the land. This unusual performance is well illustrated by the fact that all the tributaries of the Kali Gandaki north of the Himalayas flow downhill in the opposite direction, only changing course when they join the Kali Gandaki.

The Kali Gandaki is not only a freak of nature; by cutting through the Himalayas, it has dug the deepest gorge in the world – a gorge far deeper and more impressive than that of the one-mile-deep Grand Canyon, for in parts it is fully three miles deep. It was through this gorge that I hoped to be able to travel to the very edge of the Tibetan plains.

I now set about hiring a plane to survey the river from the air, but I soon found that it was no simple matter to fly over and behind the Himalayas, on to the Tibetan plateau and then through the great Himalayan breach. The main problem was to find a small plane that could fly high enough to go over and through the Himalayas and stand up to the turbulence caused by the high-altitude jet streams running into the 25,000-foot peaks.

Himalayan aviation is no easy affair; in fact, those few pilots who fly in Nepal are all exceptionally gifted. One of the best of them, Hardy Furer, we had met before going out to eastern Nepal. We remembered him only too well because of his having declared us 'plain crazy'. I now learned that in Nepal only he or a pilot by the name of Emile Wick, also Swiss, were capable of taking us safely where we planned to go.

As for the plane, the *Pilotus Porter* was the obvious choice for such a tricky job. This plane takes its strange name from a mountain near Lucerne where it is built. To the uninitiated, the *Pilotus Porter* looks like any other small single-engined private plane. This is deceptive. Its nose conceals a 700 h.p.

turbo-prop engine, making it possibly one of the highest powered light planes in the world. Its extra wide wings and reversible propeller allow it to stop, when not too heavily loaded, in ninety-five feet, the width of a six-lane highway!

It so happened that the Royal Nepal Airlines possessed such a plane for hire, and a French friend, M. de Millville, who worked for the airline, was able to obtain clearance for us to fly over areas close to Chinese-held Tibet.

Of course, however powerful our plane, it could not fly right over the Himalayas, so what we would have to navigate was the Himalayan breach between Annapurna and Dhaulaghiri just above the river. This was more easily said than done, since at 10 a.m. every morning a gale-force wind was known to rush up through this breach, making flying practically impossible after that hour. More dangerous still, the breach could fill with clouds or mist and, with no weather station in this remote gorge, there was no way of knowing if the passage was open except by going to see.

Eventually Emile Wick was designated to pilot us. A short, stout, smiling character, at 46 years of age Emile was a veteran of Himalayan flying. He had spent nearly six years pioneering flights in Nepal, interrupted by short leaves of absence to fly into the jungles of New Guinea and Africa.

In 1960 he had landed on a glacier at 18,750 feet on Dhaulaghiri, while accompanying a Swiss expedition to this peak. This made him probably one of the highest 'landers' in the world. I say 'lander' because, when it came to take-off, the plane crashed. Emile had to walk all the way down the mountain back to Katmandu.

Emile thought this very funny, but Michael and I frowned a little. We might be at ease with hovercraft, but planes had never inspired much confidence in either of us. Also, why did Emile seem so excited about our flight? Could it be that it was dangerous?

At 7.30 a.m. we turned up at the 'cow field', the name of Katmandu's airport. It was a clear day, although here and there a few clouds floated. Of course there was no plane in sight. We hung around in the company of four middle-aged ladies whom I had talked into coming with us for the ride the night before to ease a little the cost of chartering the plane. Neither they nor we realized that our flight was to prove something more than a routine operation.

It was 9.30 a.m. when the plane arrived, having been delayed on an earlier flight to Lukla, an airfield close to Everest. When I saw the time my heart sank. We would never make it through the breach before the gale winds closed it to air travel. Emile did not seem unduly concerned. 'I think it will be all right,' he said. '*I think!*' We eyed him suspiciously.

Then, since flying low would consume extra petrol and we planned to fly close to the river all the way down to the Indian border, one of our passengers had to be left behind so we could take on extra fuel. At last everything was set and we took off at 10 a.m.

Once in the air, Emile looked at the clouds and decided that we should never make it unless he took a short-cut and flew round Annapurna. This meant flying over the 17,500-foot Manang Pass. Would our ladies stand such an altitude? Emile asked. There was only one oxygen mask on board. Did they have weak hearts? I did not know. 'Let's try,' I shouted in his ear. We changed course, heading towards the massive wall of ice, rock and snow that barred our horizon to the north. Slowly the wall grew larger and larger, higher and higher, as we laboriously approached, gaining altitude, heading apparently right for the heart of the icy range. Beneath us the hills were veiled in haze, but not for long. They too now rose up towards us, each summit higher than the next, until we were only a few hundred feet above them, while the great peaks soared right above our heads. We were nearing 17,000 feet, the pilot now steered wingtip against the flanks of Annapurna while asking Michael and me to keep an eye on our fellow passengers. We passed the solitary oxygen mask from hand to hand as we entered what seemed like the entrails of a crystal world, dwarfed by the craggy north face of Annapurna as we skimmed the snowfields of the barren Manang Pass.

Sweeping between the peaks, we emerged on the northern side of the Himalayas. It was as if a curtain had been raised. To our left sprawled the barren immensity of Tibet. Brown rolling desert stretched for a hundred miles, capped here and there by ancient summits sprinkled with ice. Seen from the air, Tibet appeared a great waste – a desolation that matched my own thoughts as I recalled how this great land suffered under foreign occupation. At second glance I perceived better its particular beauty, which spoke more to the soul than to the heart. This was truly the land of the gods.

My heart beat faster when I caught sight of the great peaks of Mustang. I could easily recognize the passes and ridges along which I had toiled for days behind my slow caravan of yaks. More than ever I appreciated the marvel of flying, feeling the exhilaration born of possessing for an instant the all-encompassing vision of a demi-god. How small our world is, seen from the air. And how great.

As we began to descend I recalled the object of our mission. In a few minutes we would be over the headwaters of the Kali Gandaki, above that part of its course which cuts through the edge of the Tibetan plateau.

I had followed this stretch on foot to go to Mustang, but now as we flew over it I took in every detail. North of Annapurna the river ran through the barren wastes of Mustang, a region beyond the reach of the great monsoon that drenches the southern flanks of the Himalayas. This entire area is within what is known as the 'rain-shadow' of the Himalayas, a sheltered spot where clouds never break.

This 'rain-shadow' explains why the upper valley of the river has such a parched desert-like aspect, without so much as a single tree and little if any grass. The absence of vegetation accounted for the river cutting such a sheer-sided canyon through the soft alluvial deposit of the edge of the Tibetan plateau, which trillions of years ago had been a great sea bed that was somehow, aeons before the Himalayas existed, raised 15,000 feet towards the sky.

On reaching the river, Emile headed north for a short

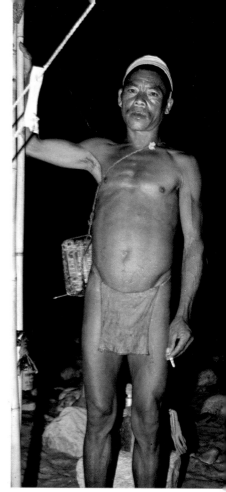

Above left: one of the dozen ingenious fishing devices of the little-known Himalayan river people. Above right: primitive fisherman comes to our tent at Tribeni. Below right: at work. The origin of this near-pigmy subtribe of the Rai people has yet to be established.

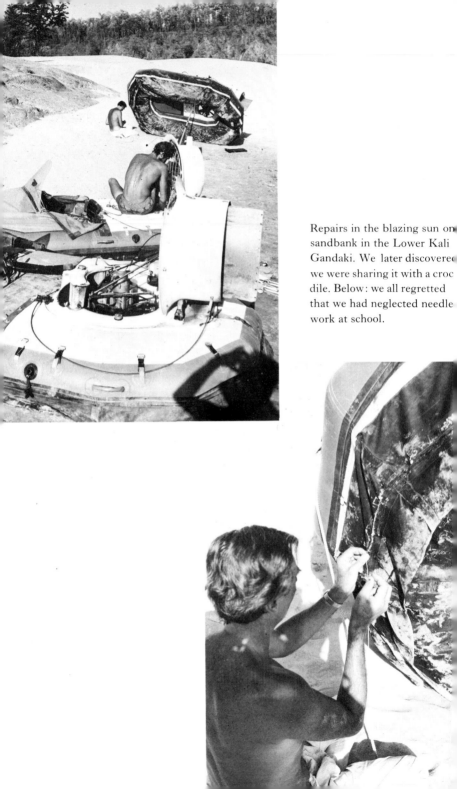

Repairs in the blazing sun on a sandbank in the Lower Kali Gandaki. We later discovered we were sharing it with a crocodile. Below: we all regretted that we had neglected needlework at school.

distance before turning round. We were now dangerously close to Chinese Tibet. From the air we could see the banks of the river and the oasis-like wheat and barley fields of little villages. These were inhabited by Tibetan-speaking people descended from lords, who in the fifteenth century erected great fortresses all along the upper course of this river. From these they controlled the caravans that plodded through the Himalayan breach, carrying salt and wool to India and bringing back rice and spices to Tibet.

I had hardly time to admire the fortified villages before we were diving in between Annapurna and Dhaulaghiri, heading for the great breach through which the silver line of the river slithered. I just had time to recognize Jomsom and Marpha, the former marking the northern limit to which travellers are allowed to penetrate, since Mustang and the rest of the Nepalese border zones in this part of the country are restricted areas.

Although the pilot clung to the flanks of Annapurna and flew only some three hundred feet above the river, it was difficult to estimate accurately the speed of its currents or the size of the foaming breakers that marked its rapids. Were they two, three or six feet high? I could not tell. What was certain was that north of Annapurna the floor of the gorge was relatively wide and flat. At this season the water, far from filling the river bed, meandered between the cliffs of the canyon at what seemed a reasonable pace. We should not have too much difficulty on this stretch, I thought.

As we descended I noted a smile of satisfaction on the face of Emile Wick. Only later did I discover the reason. In deciding to take a short-cut by flying behind Annapurna, he had taken a slight risk that the Himalayan breach might be closed by clouds. If it had been, we should have been trapped and obliged to fly back the way we had come – providing that in the meantime the Manang Pass had not itself been blocked by fast-moving mountain mist. As it was, all was clear and – exceptionally – there was no wind rushing up the gorge.

Words can hardly describe what it was like to fly through the breach. On either side of the plane rose the flanks of the

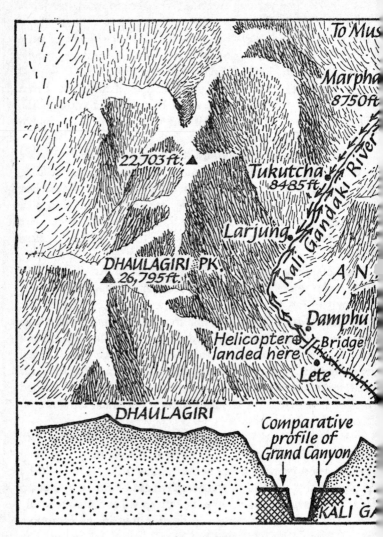

The great Himalayan breach

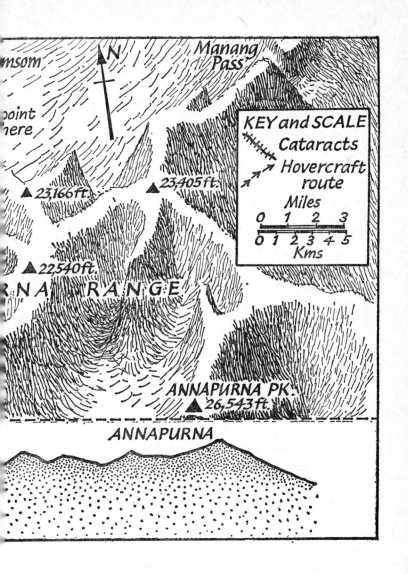

Manang
Pass

N

msom

point
here

▲ 23,166 ft.   ▲ 23,405 ft.

KEY and SCALE

Cataracts

Hovercraft
route

Miles

0   1   2   3

0 1 2 3 4 5
Kms

▲ 22,540 ft.

NA   RANGE

ANNAPURNA PK.
▲ 26,543 ft.

ANNAPURNA

two great Himalayan giants towering 15,000 feet above us, so high indeed that we could not see their summits. It was as if we were flying through some gigantic tunnel, for nowhere could we see the sky. At one point the gorge was so narrow that we could not have turned in it, nor in the little *Pilotus Porter* could we have risen clear of its sides – all above 23,000 feet high.

Looking down at the river, I wondered if we would ever be able to make our way up it with our hovercraft, especially as more and more frequently we saw beneath us the white shimmer of rapids. Then, just as we were emerging on the other side of the great Himalayan breach, we saw the river turn pure white, take a dive and disappear down what seemed like a hole. From then on for twenty miles the Kali Gandaki was nothing but a series of cataracts plunging ever deeper. It was out of the question to hover up these falls; we should have to portage along this section as the river dropped 4000 feet in less than 20 miles. At the foot of the cataracts the river became more docile, although every three hundred yards there was a foaming rapid. Michael looked at me and winced; it would not be easy, even if it were possible. We could not tell for sure, being too high to appreciate those minute differences in wave height that could spell disaster on the water.

In all, our flight lasted three hours, as we slowly followed every bend of the sacred river from its head-waters behind Annapurna down to where it entered the jungles that topped the steep eroded flanks of the Mahabharat range. Along this west-east section the river lost much of its momentum, and meandered slowly in great loops. Again here was a stretch that should cause us little or no trouble. There remained the gorges through the Mahabharat range, but we were unable to estimate the extent of the rapids, as we were running out of fuel and were obliged to gain altitude and head back for Katmandu.

Only when we had landed did we fully appreciate how daring had been our flight. Emile admitted that it was only the second time in his six years flying in Nepal that he had been behind Annapurna, and the first time by this route. Weeks later he was still jubilant over this trip, making us realize how unwittingly privileged we had been to have had such a pilot and such luck in successfully completing this circling of Annapurna.

Our lady fellow-travellers may still not have realized how unique was their flight along the only trans-Himalayan route still open, for elsewhere China controls all the northern face of the great chain. One day this flight could become a famous tourist attraction, for what with its view of Tibet and the hair-raising trip down the world's greatest gorge it is far more spectacular than the classic air trip to Everest.

In a few hours we had lived through the condensed story of the Kali Gandaki as it passes from Tibet to India down a ladder of varying climates and vegetation. But although our flight had brought out the advantages of air transport it had also underlined its limitations. It was now up to us to pioneer a way of travelling up the river in contact with the land, so to speak, up to us to investigate yard by yard the terrain we had overflown and get to know those who lived there, to get the feel of what we had seen only from a distance.

Back at the hotel, I found a letter waiting for me from Roy E. Disney, whom I had met six years previously when his father and his Uncle Walt were still alive. Roy Disney, now a Director of Disney Productions, was enthusiastic at the idea of filming our expedition and ready to send a camera crew to Nepal. Unfortunately his letter had been delayed in India and there was now little time left to plan his participation, as we hoped to leave very shortly. As we sent him a cable by teletype, I could not help but marvel at how fast things had changed in Katmandu, linked today with the rest of the world by this modern device, whereas when I first arrived fifteen years ago there were no telephones in the valley, practically no cars, not one truck, and Nepal did not even belong to the International Postal Union! Now from its capital I could speak in a matter of minutes to the entire world, although there were as yet no telephones linking such centres as Katmandu and Birathnagaer, Nepal's two largest towns.

We were excited by Roy Disney's enthusiasm, although we did not fully see how his camera crew could follow us up the river's banks. Immediately after dispatching our cable I called the General to ask when we would get our permits to leave the valley, telling him also of the film prospect. He seemed glum and evasive. 'You must wait a little,' he said without giving an explanation. Why wait? We were burning to go, and a week previously had filed our official request to travel up the Kali Gandaki, also asking permission to proceed beyond the restricted areas to study the mysterious cliff dwellings along the river's upper reaches.

Our craft too were now all ready to go, as Bob had repaired them with the help of Mr Everatt, the army engineer at Dharan, who had also made us a device that would stop our fan-belts slipping when wet.

Days dragged by, and we were still stuck in Katmandu, while the General became more and more evasive about when we would be allowed to leave. At first we put this delay down to the fact that just after our Russian Easter party with Boris the Nepalese had held their New Year's celebrations. We were now entering the year 2028, a year we hoped would be auspicious.

On New Year's Day, April 12th, ceremonies were staged in all the towns and villages of the valley, where great crowds gathered to witness the holy Jackneys (magician-priests) plead for rain and foretell the future. Dressed in white, holding a large drum, they pranced about behind gigantic carts carrying the bronze effigies of deities, which were drawn by hand through the brick-paved streets. Prior to the introduction of cars, these sacred carts were the only wheeled vehicles in the valley, for in most of Nepal even bullock carts are unknown, the terrain being too rugged for any kind of wheeled transport.

We watched these festivities, but our hearts were not in it. We yearned to get on with our plans. The reason for the delay, we now thought, was that with the New Year the young King was taking over the reins of government after the death of his father, and there was talk of a great political shuffle in which

Ministers might be changed. We therefore concluded that no one wanted to take a decision regarding our expedition at this critical moment.

Forever awaiting a phone call from the General, Michael and I sat in our room speculating on what was the matter. We remembered all we had been told by the British Ambassador about the necessity to secure all permits before leaving England. Yet we could not believe that the General would let us down; after all, our project had been approved by the Prime Minister in person, who had reconfirmed that we could go anywhere in Nepal except the restricted areas. We hoped everything would turn out all right, yet there was that strange message about 'No anthropology' and the fact that we had never been allowed to continue up the Arun. What did it all mean? I recalled how in the past many climbing expeditions had been delayed for months or had their permits cancelled at the last minute . . . Then my project was no ordinary enterprise; why, even in Europe officials had been suspicious of our machines. Possibly in Nepal someone had suddenly become alarmed by our venture. I spent several sleepless nights before a call came from the General, asking me to go immediately to his house.

A taxi dropped me at the door of a modern home, built in the gardens of what had been a family palace. Two servants in white jodphurs and black fez-like hats (the Nepalese national dress) bowed me in.

The General was visibly upset. 'I cannot explain,' he said. 'I do not understand, but I think it would be better if you were to go to India or Bhutan.' I suddenly felt faint. What did all this mean? The General could not clarify beyond insinuating that someone in the Government had taken objection to our project. There was nothing to be done; someone had decreed that we were not to go into the high mountains of Nepal.

This was ridiculous, I argued; we had officially been asked to come to Nepal, had already spent a small fortune to do so, and had risked our lives already on some of the lands and rivers. Although we were undertaking a private scientific venture, I argued, Nepal would still be the principal beneficiary of our experiment. We hoped that our project might lead to a minor revolution in communications that could have many benefits for the country. In answer to these arguments, the General repeated his suggestion that we leave Nepal and try out our machines in other mountains, those of India or Bhutan. This was of course impossible at such a short notice. When I suggested appealing to the Prime Minister himself for our permit, the General informed me that he had just left for a fifteen-day visit to India. What about the King? I queried, certain that the young monarch could not fail to be interested in our project. The General seemed doubtful. To reach the King would take a long time. I knew well that when someone in the Orient admits that a thing will take time, this could mean months. By then the monsoon would have broken, the rivers would be a fury of mad water, and the roads quagmires of mud. What could we do, and why this sudden ban on going to the mountains?

The General would give no explanation. I began to think that perhaps the reason was linked to my past journeys in Nepal. Some member of the Government might have eyed suspiciously my scholarly interest in the Tibetan people. Or perhaps my book on Mustang had overstressed the ancient historical autonomy of the rajahs of Mustang, a statement of fact that certain officials had disapproved of in a land composed of many different races all presently struggling to minimize their differences and achieve national unity.

Could it be that overnight I had become *persona non grata*, or that my hovercraft were unwelcome? In the past I had always been on good terms with the Nepalese Government. Yet someone had had cause enough to contradict the Prime Minister. Who could it be? The King himself? Or just some petty official who in the intricate bureaucracy of Nepal had the power to block our entire project?

The General could only suggest that in the absence of the Prime Minister we continue our expedition in the southern regions of Nepal and await his return. Having no choice, we decided to go down immediately into the central jungles near the Indian border and start working our way up the Kali Gandaki from there. The uncertainty about our future unfortunately cancelled any possibility of Disney's participation, but, even worse, it meant we might never be able to take our craft into the high mountains, thus ruining our project of crossing the Himalayas.

Michael tried to comfort me as we continued to speculate wildly on the reason for this ban. Bob in the meantime was busy combing Katmandu for clothes for his boutique and seemed to us more concerned with bringing his girl friend to Nepal than with worrying about the outcome of the project. Bob, of course, was primarily anxious for action, action of any kind, and we could not blame him for his impatience. He had come to do a job and was doing his part well, but he had little concern for the intricacies of Nepalese politics.

Once again Michael and I pored over the map of Nepal. We saw that there were only two approaches to the Kali Gandaki which would enable us to get our machines on to the water. The first was via the road that linked Katmandu with India and then turning west along the yet unfinished east-west road that was being cut through the southern jungles of Nepal. This road crossed the Kali Gandaki just below its confluence with the Marsyandi, a river which runs down from the Manang Pass, each river draining a different side of the Annapurna range.

The second road, which cut the Kali Gandaki farther upstream, was a new one that the Chinese were completing and ran from Katmandu to Pokhara before turning south towards India. The southern section of the road cut the Kali Gandaki just where it turned east parallel to the Mahabharat range, after running down through the great Himalayan range. It seemed clear that we would not be allowed to go to this point so close to the forbidden mountains, so we decided to set out for the first area in the heart of Nepal's famous jungles, the last refuge of the land's great tigers and the rare great Asiatic unicorn rhino.

Starting in the south, we could traverse the jungle, then the

Swalik hills and the Mahabharat range, and proceed west to the foot of the great Himalayan range. Then, if all went well, we might be allowed to proceed through the great Himalayan breach, which would mean we would have crossed the entire Himalayas along the Kali Gandaki river as originally planned. That is, if we could raise the ban on our going north, and if we did not drown!

Colonel Jim Roberts, another old friend and possibly the man with the most intimate knowledge of Nepal and its hills, helped us prepare for our new departure. A former Gurkha officer, he also, like Charles Wylie, had been military attaché to Nepal. On retiring, Jim had set up the first trekking organization in Nepal to help expeditions and casual trekkers on their way to the mountains. He had led many large expeditions himself, including a successful expedition up Annapurna and one up Machupuchari, the fish-tail peak, not to mention many others to mountains all over the country. Having no brigade of Gurkhas to help us out as at Dharan, we appreciated his assistance. Not only did he lend us all the equipment we needed, but he found us two young sherpas to act as cook and general helpers.

Three days before we left, Nyma and Lhakpa, the two young men in question, aged 18 and 19, reported for duty. Neither spoke much English, which did not matter as I spoke their language, a dialect very similar to Tibetan. Lhakpa, the elder of the two, was in charge; Nyma, slightly fatter with a baby face and curly dark hair, acted as his second. I had never seen two more enthusiastic young men. When not breaking their backs in an effort to be useful, they spent their time laughing.

Our party now consisted of five people and was further augmented the day before our departure by the arrival of Marie-Ange, a shapely French brunette with a solid character and a passion for Bob. I had my reservations about a girl in the camp, possibly inherited from my nanny's stern upbringing, but I could see no good reason why she should not come along provided she was prepared to remain at base camp and cause no trouble. She and Bob pledged that she would, and on the whole we were glad of the company. I did not believe that Marie-Ange quite appreciated what she was letting herself in for, but then we didn't either. Thus it was that at dawn on April 24th the six of us boarded a large truck packed high with our hovercraft, spare parts and countless jerrycans. Our destination was Bharatpur, a village on the edge of the Narayani river somewhere in the heart of Nepal's densest jungles. On our maps we figured we had three hundred miles to travel, yet due to the condition of the roads the driver announced that it would take us fifteen hours to reach our destination.

The sun was just striking the valley when our truck swung round the first of a thousand bends that would slowly lead us over the many jagged hills that separate Katmandu from the plains. As we climbed above Katmandu, we could see below us Kiritpur: one of the smallest capitals of the Newar kings who ruled for so long over the heart of Nepal. Perched upon a table-like hill, Kiritpur's houses presented a pink bastion dominating green fields. When the Gurkha king had conquered the valley, in the late eighteenth century, Kiritpur had given him considerable trouble and for months his soldiers had besieged the town. The king's patience was at an end when at last he forced an entry into its narrow streets, and his men set about punishing the town's stubborn inhabitants. All prisoners had their lips and noses cut off, and it was by the weight of these gory trophies that the king measured the extent of his victory. Ever since then the inhabitants have been known as 'the noseless ones', a sad reminder of their ancestors' courage. Today Kiritpur stands in peace and beauty, its stone- and brick-paved streets opening on to sunny squares, in whose fountains the townsfolk bathe when not engaged in weaving or spinning cotton in the city streets.

The snail's pace at which our truck progressed reminded us that wheeled transport was not the best means of travelling over mountainous terrain. A twisting road meant that it took us eight hours to cover a distance as the crow flies of less than 35 miles.

The only alternative developed, short of flying, had been the use of cable-cars. The first cable-car system in Nepal was built by the Rana maharajas in 1928, prior to the building of a road. The wires had looped from pole to pole in what was nearly a straight line from one crest to the next right down to India. In 1959 a new cable system had been installed whose cars we occasionally saw from the road as they swayed dangerously above gorges or clattered against the pillars that clung to the sheer sides of steep cliffs. These cars were restricted to cargo, and despite their slow pace could reach Katmandu in less time than a truck.

Both road and cable-way had cost a considerable sum of money, not to mention the thousands of lives lost through accident when the road had been blasted through the hills. Would it not be possible, we wondered, to reach Katmandu by travelling up the rivers by hovercraft? On our maps the rivers ran far straighter than the road.

Lying on the roof of the cabin of the truck, we had a grand and often frightening view of the mountains and gorges. As the vehicle nosed round hairpin bends, wheels inches from disaster, there were, it occurred to me, some deaths more fearful than drowning. I recalled the answer given me when, on a similar road in Bhutan, I had asked if there were many accidents. 'Oh,' answered the driver, 'there are no wounded, only dead.' Indeed, to go off the road or to crash on such ledges nearly always meant plunging into a gorge, but the risk did not seem to deter our driver nor the other drivers we encountered, and there was an inevitable screech of brakes as they emerged at full speed around bends.

Towards 2 p.m. we stopped at a little thatched shack that served as a wayside restaurant. We were now close to 8500 feet in altitude and surrounded by great forests of rhododendron trees whose pink trunks were veiled in moss and whose branches supported dozens of white and dark blue orchids. These were the mist forests that cover the high ridges and are veiled in fog for most of the year.

In the shack we shared the usual Nepalese meal of rice and

dhal, dhal being a pale lentil. To these two staple foods were added in minute helpings a little meat and vegetable curry. This constitutes the exclusive diet of most Nepalese of the middle hill areas.

After lunch the truck made its way to an 8600-foot pass, the highest point of the road. Looking north, we could see the entire Himalayan range from Mt Everest in the east to Mt Dhaulaghiri in the west, a spectacular panorama. The road we had been following was built in 1956 by Indian engineers and is Katmandu's only link with the outside world, apart from the new Chinese road built in 1963 which links Katmandu with Lhasa in Tibet, and is closed to all foreigners and most Nepalese. Before its completion, the very few cars to be found in the Katmandu valley had had to be carried over this pass by coolies. They were carried over not, as one might think, dismantled into parts, but in one piece on great bamboo trays, under which toiled a hundred men. More remarkable still, a steam roller had been carried over this pass, though that had been broken down into parts. It would be amusing to record all the strange objects that have 'walked' over this range: thousands of fragile Venetian mirrors for the great palaces of the Ranas, as well as bath-tubs and crystal chandeliers; everything, in fact, which had reached the isolated capital of Nepal, including visitors, who were often carried on sling chairs.

The first Englishman to have come this way had been W. J. Kirkpatrick in 1793, but prior to him Italian and Portuguese monks, starting in 1675, had crossed Nepal on their way to and from Tibet, before opening a mission near Katmandu, where they resided for nearly twenty years. Even before these missionaries came to Nepal, it is believed that an unknown mysterious European traveller may have penetrated the forbidden valley of Katmandu, as is testified to by a multilingual inscription set at the foot of the old palace in Katmandu's main square, with a caption, in Roman letters, reading 'Autumn, Winter, Hiver'.

Protected in part by mountains, Nepal had been able to keep to itself its delightful temperate climate that contrasted with the

icy highlands of Tibet and the steaming plains of India. Yet it
was not so much the mountains that explained Nepal's isolation
as the jungles – the extensions of the jungles of Assam and
Bengal that border Nepal along the edge of the Indian plains.
The reason why the jungles were such an effective barrier is
not the tigers, snakes and other dangerous animals, but man's
most deadly enemy, the mosquito, the carrier of those fevers
that killed most travellers and annihilated entire invading
armies from India. Only the aboriginal tribes who by some
process not yet fully understood had built up a certain degree
of immunity, were able to live and travel freely in the jungles.
Until a few years ago these fevers, among them fatal cerebral
malaria, were still rampant in southern Nepal; now they have
practically disappeared, thanks to a very active malaria eradi-
cation campaign. One unexpected outcome of this campaign
has been the destruction of tigers and rhino. Once the fevers
were gone, the hill people of Nepal and Indian squatters poured
into the jungles, cutting trees, grazing cattle, killing wild life
and eventually turning into rice fields many of the vast areas
where for centuries the aboriginal tribes and some of nature's
most beautiful beasts had lived in harmony, protected by the
mosquito. There are few places in the world (with the exception
of Assam) where Western medical knowledge has brought
about such a radical ecological change. When the English first
arrived in Assam, and until the middle of the nineteenth century, this province had a population of under 100,000; today,
with the elimination of malaria, the population is 60 million.
The proportional increase in Nepal's Terai district is much
less, although the population of the Terai has increased by
some three million in ten years.

From the summit of the pass, the truck began a vertical
descent towards the hot plains. Through a series of hairpin
bends we fell from pines to rhododendron forests, then round a
curve to a mixed forest soon bespattered with palm fronds
followed by banana plants, before entering the outlying parts of
the southern jungles that overlap the foothills. We had crossed
the Mahabharat range, but taking much longer by truck, we

noted, than when we had crossed the range for a similar distance in eastern Nepal in our hovercraft.

On reaching the foot of the hills, we followed briefly the dry rocky bed of the Rapti, a river born in the Mahabharat range, which flows west between this range and the Swalik hills. The road now straightened out as we sped towards the town of Hetaura, once set in the middle of the jungle but now surrounded by clumps of trees.

At Hetaura Michael and Bob busied themselves filling our jerrycans with petrol, while I left them to travel on alone to Birganj, the site of the residence of the Governor of the Narayani district in which we would be setting up our camp. They would travel on alone to Bharatpur, where I hoped to join them the next day.

An old bus drove me to Birganj, which I reached at dusk. Situated on the Indian border, Birganj is possibly one of the most depressing towns in the world. It is not really a Nepalese city, being Indian in its architecture, climate and general aspect.

The Kipling-like enchantment of the towns of the Ganges basin has been praised for too long. It is time to write an elegy, or rather an epitaph, on the modern Indian bazaar, of which Birganj is typical. Its approaches are masked by great brick walls surrounding several derelict-looking factories, walls that seem never to have been completed and which bear an odd assortment of slogans ranging from posters advertising Coca-Cola to political symbols scrawled in a shaky hand. Yet these walls, however dilapidated, are the straightest thing to be seen for miles. They support shacks whose rusted tin sides are interwoven with bamboo matting, the homes of hundreds of families. Everyone wore rags the colour of earth, real earth being only occasionally visible between cement, abandoned railway lines, telegraph poles, and an inordinate number of city cattle. These sacred cows litter the pot-holed streets and rusty buses, trucks and countless spider-like bicycles pedalled by thin-legged, loin-clothed ruffians, forever puffing at cheroots. The cheroots themselves are sold from behind small packing crates under dirty rag awnings. As I went deeper into the centre of town, the factory walls were replaced by façades, still decorated with graffiti and overlapping posters. A din of clanging bells, horns and whistles drowned the shuffle of a thousand barefooted, perspiring pedestrians menaced by vehicles, goats, sacred cows or packs of dogs. Men, women and children rushed about on endless errands, coughing, chatting and spitting blood-red saliva from chewing betel nut.

I knew I was near the heart of the town when overhead the spider's web of wires appeared like a net poised to capture the swarming mass beneath. From the various vehicles came the stench of all grades of grease and oil which mingled chaotically with the strong smells of leather, urine, copper, steel, plastic, and tar. The place could not have been farther from those scents traditionally associated with the Orient. There is no city planning here, nothing but greed, slovenliness and squalor.

The following morning I met the Governor, a man as handsome as his capital was ugly. He gave me a warm welcome and did not require me to take a liaison officer – asking only that I contact the local district administrator in Bharatpur, to whom I was to report all developments. It was with relief that I hired a car and left Birganj to join the others.

Returning to Hetaura, I left the metalled road to take the new East-West Highway which will one day stretch right across Nepal's jungles along the Indian border. The Russians, the Indians and the Americans are each building one section, while the stretch along which I drove was being undertaken by the British. On the side of the gravel road squatters had cleared the jungle down to the wide stony bed of the Rapti river, whose course we now followed west. We were heading for the Chitawan district – a vast 'protected' section of the Terrai jungle, the heart of which encompasses 250,000 acres set aside as a game reserve.

After two hours, my face grey with dust, I reached a clearing in the jungle – scattered with new buildings set up to house the police and local administration. There I met a young, sturdy Nepalese, the deputy district commissioner of Bharatpur.

It had been suggested in Katmandu that we establish our base near the confluence of the Kali Gandaki and the Marsyandi rivers at a place called Daveghat – ten miles north of Bharatpur, and accessible by a rough dirt track through the jungle. My driver left the new road and reluctantly steered his car between the tall trunks of the majestic sal trees. Looking through the vegetation, I felt the fascination of this area we were about to explore, so different from eastern Nepal. We were now in a land of shade, an Eden ruled by animals in which man is but a guest, one of many living creatures in the underbush. Whereas mountains tend to elevate man's soul, giving him a vertical view of the world, jungles are a lesson in humility, a prison that limits man's horizons and which underlines his own frailty.

Driving on, I caught sight of the Narayani river just below the confluence. Seen from the shade, it was a fleeting vision of light. I suddenly appreciated how water and sun were the sources of all the life teeming in the shadows. Yet the river and its banks were another world, one to be approached only with caution and in darkness, when beasts could master their ancestral fear of coming out in the open.

I was relieved when at last we emerged unexpectedly on to the blazing whiteness of a wide rocky beach where the trail came to an end. I had reached Daveghat. It was still early in the afternoon, and the silence of noon, when even the crickets are too tired to chirp, hung in the hot air. It emphasized the hushed whisper of the river rushing by, its waters endlessly churning in their struggle to reach the plains.

I found the others lying under the thin shade of our tents, pitched on the edge of the vast stony field that extended down to the water's edge. Our equipment lay beside them, where it had been dumped from the truck that morning. Michael explained how they had spent the night at Narayanghat, a dingy bazaar that stretched along the vulture-clustered banks of the river, a few miles from Bharatpur. Nyma and Lhakpa, the sherpas, had slept in the truck. Michael had shared a dirty room with 'two smelly ruffians' and the thousand creepy creatures that flourish in such hospitable places. Marie-Ange was still expressing her surprise at the local standards of hygiene, while Bob rested from the exertion of a morning spent unloading and assembling our craft. I paid off my driver, who immediately headed back to the beauties of Birganj.

Whether it was the heat or the memory of Birganj I do not know, but I felt depressed as I brooded on the risks we should again have to take and recalled how disappointing the general indifference to our venture had been all along. No one in Europe and now no one in Nepal seemed to care for our enterprise. Was it just a stupid idea? I began again to have my doubts, as I felt the full weight of the responsibility for our being here. For a moment I wished I had been dispatched under orders or was on some official mission so that I need not constantly question the validity of our attempt to develop a new means of transport and scientific investigation. I also recognized that we could expect no sympathy if we failed.

Were there not enough hazards in daily life, I wondered, that I had to solicit more? I stood to gain nothing from this expedition beyond the personal satisfaction of realizing a mere figment of my imagination. I began to appreciate that what had brought me here was that same morbid curiosity I have always had for the unexpected, the unknown and the new – a curiosity that has driven me since childhood to place myself in odd situations. Was it a disease? I wondered.

Only on looking again at the great rivers were my doubts dispelled. Daveghat represented the end of the road, the end of man's possibilities of penetrating to the east and the north, for here the two rushing rivers emerged from deep jungle-crested cliffs, cutting their way through steep ranges along a route that till now had been the exclusive monopoly of fishes. Soon this trail might be ours. Along these turbulent waters our new quest would begin.

7 *Shores of the Gods*

Daveghat was no ordinary place. A few miles away, the ruins of a 3000-year-old shrine hidden in the depth of the forest recalled that here for thousands of years man had perceived holiness. We were on sacred land. Daveghat – or, in Hindi and Nepalese, 'Deoghat' – comes from 'Deo', god; 'Deo' also means two. So the merging of two waters is a holy place. All over the world, it seems, whenever primitive man beheld two rivers meeting, he saw there the residence of a god. Daveghat was no exception. High upon the peninsula above the two rivers, and behind us under the dark fronds of the bordering jungles, nestled dozens of shrines set in holy villages. 'Ghat' means 'shore'; so 'Daveghat' means 'shore of the gods', and the village was inhabited by the 'divine' cast of Brahmins. These Brahmins were not the haughty rich breed that one encounters in India, but were agricultural – poor peasants.

These villagers were our first indication of the variety and type of people inhabiting this area. Vestals of the rivers, guardians of the temples, servants of Shiva and sons of Ganga, they tilled the earth, and paid homage twice a day to the water gods, coming down silently to bend and dip their brow at sunrise and at dusk. Draped in light veils of cotton that clung to their thin bodies, they revealed to all their frailty, their dignity, and their piety. Daveghat was certainly no ordinary place.

Our camp site, too far from the water, too hot because of the radiating bed of white boulders, had to be changed. After assembling our craft in the late afternoon, I set out in search of a better place. Four hundred yards up the south bank of the Marsyandi, the boulder bed came to an end where a small hill rose from the water. Here were three grass-covered ledges shaded by tall trees. The site was ideal, as it dominated a smooth sandy beach sheltered by a rocky cliff – a perfect harbour and landing-stage for our machines.

Early next morning we moved camp. Directly beneath us was the Marsyandi, emerging down a gorge, swirling along an incredible mass of grey water, hurling it against the foot of a steep cliff on the far bank and into the blue-green waters of the Kali Gandaki. This river leaped out from steep green hills – the last of a seemingly endless series that barred our horizon, the great Mahabharat range.

The time had come to make plans – no easy matter, as we could not tell what obstacle might lie hidden round the first bends of the rivers. Our objective was twofold. First, to travel the Kali Gandaki river as far north as possible within the limits of the ban forbidding us to penetrate the greater Himalayas; and, second, to make a comparative study of the flora, fauna and people who lived along the banks. By going all the way down the Kali Gandaki to the Indian border some sixty miles to the south, and then back up through the Mahabharat range, we should have crossed half Nepal. If we could obtain permission later to go right up to the Tibetan border, then we should have crossed the entire Himalayas. This would give us a continuous picture of the evolution of man, animals and plants according to altitude and climatic levels. Tribeni had marked a stage in our experimenting with our machines; now we were ready to tackle our main objectives.

We all felt fit and hardened for our task, our dark skins now quite accustomed to the sun, and our calloused fingers skilled in repairing our machines. Towards five in the evening we were keen to set out and pit ourselves against the rivers. Leaving Marie-Ange and the two sherpas to prepare dinner, we walked down to the beach. As we fastened our life-jackets, our minds momentarily lingered on the possibility of being at any moment hurled into the rushing water. Yet I felt confident, and even Michael, whose sceptical mind would find a flaw in the perfect diamond, said little to counteract my renewed enthusiasm. The previous day he had confided in me that he was beginning to believe in our craft. Such a compliment had filled me with bliss.

Soon the engines were purring. One by one, like ice-cubes on a slanted table, we slithered down the sandbank, hovered a while over the current, and then headed east up the Marsyandi. White egrets rose from the banks as we advanced up the widest river we had yet encountered.

We kept a lookout ahead for the first large rapid. It soon appeared, wide and booming, four monstrous waves hugging one bank while the other was lined with steps of rock forming a cascade, obstructed by the occasional tripods of wooden stakes – native fish traps. Swinging in an arc, one behind the other, we chose to batter up the watery steps over the rocks rather than risk the proximity of the large waves. A shudder, followed by a slight loss of speed, and we were up and over and on to a flat stretch of water. On both sides rose rocky banks, and an occasional large boulder lay in midstream. High above us birds of every description rose dark against the evening sky. Power was my first sensation – a dizzy feeling of superiority, as we sped on at a good twenty knots, spray spattering our faces. We soon hit another rapid, and had to decide on which side we should pass. I hugged the left, then, as more boulders appeared, I moved to the right. I went up some steps, but was slowed down as first Bob, then Michael, passed me. Suddenly I noticed I was slipping backwards. I pulled my steering lever and turned to the left, gripped by fear as I was drawn back towards the thick of the rapids. My machine swung round, faced the large waves a few yards away, then hit a rock on the shore and stopped. I jumped out and held on – safe on firm ground. I waved the others to carry on, but by then they were already disappearing round another bend. As I cut my engines a strange silence fell. The sun was sinking on the horizon, and a slight chill rose from the river. I felt cold. Where was I?

Leaves rustled above me and a form appeared. A man, nearly naked, stalked down the bank and stopped a few feet away. Without saying a word, he stared at my machine in astonishment. I felt foolish, standing there draped in my bright orange life-jacket. What could the man be thinking? He must think me a demon or witch, yet I was wet, and he could see that my muscles were no stronger than his – he must know that I was only human. I looked at his dark skin and slightly Mongoloid features; he was taller than a Rai, and had a darker complexion. Soon a second man, then a third crashed down the bank as if they had been hiding. Each was attired in the same fashion, wearing nothing but a loin-cloth. Where was their village, and what was their tribe? I realized that in twenty minutes we had covered perhaps a day's walk.

I tried to communicate with them, but they did not seem to understand my poor Nepalese. Were they Gurungs, I asked, or Magars? I went through a short list of the tribes to which they might belong. Finally I got down to work before my audience, feeling like a circus act as their eyes followed my every gesture.

I soon had the fan-belt, the cause of the trouble, fastened again, and asked the men to give me a hand in holding the craft while I started the engines. They approached shyly, but did not understand. I got in and promptly grounded on a rock. One man pushed me off. I could not even wave goodbye, as I was grabbed by the current and swept back before I could go over the hump wave and pull up to the head of the rapid. I now gathered momentum and passed my strange companions as I headed on after the others. After several miles and many minor rapids, I hit a long stretch of very fast water. Still hugging the boulders of the near bank, I slowly reduced my speed.

Now the sun was getting low – gold glistened on the crests of the waves, tree-trunks on the banks shone warm while the rocks glowed yellow. Ahead was a large bend and suddenly a dot in the distance. Two hundred yards away, bouncing towards me and growing steadily bigger, were Bob and Michael on their way down. They pulled up as I turned, and indicated that we should all go back to camp.

The return was like flying, the sun setting in our faces as we headed west. The river was a flash of gold, our craft hardly causing a ripple. The banks loomed dark, and the rocks seemed to rise above pools of blood as the jungle cut a black line before the bright red of the sky. A bird darted across the river. I had rarely seen such beauty and was filled with an inner silence. We were floating in the sky, riding a reflection of the sun, sailing on a highway of light. In neat formation, one after the other, we pulled ashore. The sun set as the air echoed with the cry of a tern and the shriek of a flock of egrets homing for the night. All was still near the crackling fire, as we crowded round a steaming pan of rice.

Michael and I were up at daybreak, having slept in the open. The family of mynah birds in the tree above our heads were already practising their acrobatics. A flock of noisy parakeets, flashing green, darted across the river. Below us, a silent procession of figures made their way back and forth to our beach: Brahmins from the village coming to collect water and perform their ablutions and prayers by the river. It was a scene of grace and peace, and Michael was rightly worried lest our camp disturb the village worship. Brahmins are the highest caste in the Hindu hierarchy. They range from the Thakuri Brahmins (warriors), through the Chetri, all the way down to the occupational castes – tailors, cobblers, blacksmiths and goldsmiths. Only the Brahmins can officiate as priests at the numerous and often very complex religious ceremonies that mark every Hindu event from birth to death. Most important of a Brahmin's duties is that of preserving his caste – not to lose his rank through impure acts or contacts, through alliances with people of lower caste – or, worse, with 'untouchables', those who are not Hindus.

The purity of the race is maintained by these taboos, by which intermarriage of Brahmin children with the other castes is automatically forbidden. To enforce this strict endogamy, the act of marrying one's son or marrying one's daughter to the 'right' man is the most important religious duty of a father, and the primary means by which he can gain *punya* (merit). In consequence, to quote a Hindu friend and anthropologist, Mr B. Bista, 'a young daughter is considered a sacred object – more so even than a sacred cow.' A son is naturally considered even more sacred, since he alone can aid his father after death to cross the limbo of the spirits into paradise. Because of this, the eldest son in all Brahmin families is invariably spoilt by his parents.

To ensure the rapid accumulation of merit, marriages are arranged before the children are thirteen, frequently when girls are only six or seven. The weddings are long and elaborate affairs, and last two or three days. Discounting the money to be given to the Brahmin priest, it is a costly operation for both families, who will often go in debt for years to satisfy the requisites of a perfect Hindu wedding, not so much to please their children, but to gain merit for themselves. Indeed, a Brahmin with no children will often adopt a little girl, just for the merit derived from marrying her off.

It is the parents who decide the match, yet astrologers check for incompatibility and decide the day, which must be in a time when Venus is visible.

A gay procession preceded by musicians (a low caste) is formed to carry the groom in a litter to the bride's house. The future wife's family and friends then entertain the groom and his party with a feast. The actual wedding takes place the following day at the exact time appointed by the astrologer. To begin, the bride and groom exchange garlands, symbolizing that they have chosen each other to be husband and wife – although often it will be the first time the two have met. At the appointed time, the groom is given the girl in marriage, and receives the dowry. The bride is then dressed up in the fine clothes presented to her by her husband. Later, they make a series of ritual offerings to various Hindu deities – among them the elephant-faced god Ganesh, the keeper of households.

After a second feast, the bride and groom are carried off to the groom's house in a noisy procession. Here ends all bliss for the bride, who now becomes servant, not to say slave, to her mother-in-law, while she overcomes the traditional resentment of her in-laws and all her husband's family. She may often spend several years, if not the whole of her life, under the command of her mother-in-law.

The lot of women in Hindu society has never been enviable. A man may take several wives if he chooses, and these are

Elephant meets hovercraft at Tiger Tops, where we encountered civilization after travelling 50 miles over shallow, rapid rivers from our camp at Daveghat.

A wise old Brahmin looks in awe at our devilish machines. Below: girls
in their best clothes on the banks of the Kali Gandaki.

Sunset over the Indrawati with a hovercraft in the foreground.

Preparing corn beer by beating fermented corn mash with river water. We lived on this nutritious beer for twenty-four hours when our craft broke down. Below: curious onlookers contemplate the stranded craft on the Indrawati.

treated by many Hindus with little respect. Women must know their place. They are rarely educated, although today this is beginning to change in Nepal, as in India.

Watching the Brahmins bathe in the river recalled to me how the complexity of Hindu ceremonies is nothing in comparison with the number and intricate hierarchy of the divinities of the Hindu pantheon. The most famous gods of India are Shiva, Vishnu and Krishna, and the monkey gods Hanuman and his attendants who rule alongside the countless spirits and lesser divinities that populate the ancient Vedic tales, which were imported three thousand years ago from Persia.

Unlike Buddhism or Christianity, Hinduism is not governed by a strict creed or an established body of men constituting a Church; further, it lacks a true dogma, so that it is hardly a 'religion' in the generally understood sense. For most Hindus, their beliefs are primarily the basis of an ethical and social code, one in which all humans by birthright are divided into well-defined classes – the famous castes. The real evil of the already much criticized caste system is that it breeds among Hindus a great self-righteousness and considerable scorn for inferior castes. Scorn is the hereditary trait produced by Hinduism, somewhat like the scorn for the lower classes that was a common trait in the rigid society of nineteenth-century Europe. But if castes are the weakness of Hinduism they are also its principal asset, and explain why it is one of the most dynamic religions of the East, if not of the world, in terms of growth.

The reason for this is that in the Indian subcontinent most people, unable to fight the caste system, try to join it. This is particularly true in Nepal, where whole tribes have switched to becoming Hindus for the social and economic advantages it brings. Admittance into the caste system is achieved by a little historical falsification or simply by mass conversion – when this suits a political purpose. Most orthodox Hindus naturally disapprove of these newcomers, but this is less true in Nepal, where nearly all the avowed Hindus of the hills are converts. Thus most Nepalese Hindus have a somewhat unorthodox legal right to the caste to which they claim to belong. The social attraction of the caste system is so great that today there are practically no Buddhists left in India, and Hinduism is spreading all over the subcontinent, although the followers never preach conversion as believers of other religions do.

Many years ago a young prince born only a few miles from Daveghat reacted against what the scholar L. Austin Waddell has called the 'caste debasement of man'. He decided to fight what Hinduism had become and still is – 'an agnostic idealism', based on a social code. This man was none other than Sakyamuni – Lord Buddha, who was born at Lumbini in Nepal. Now, 2500 years later, his birthplace is practically devoid of his followers, as throughout Nepal Buddhism gives way to Hinduism. Buddhism flourishes now only in countries other than those of its origin.

At Daveghat, as in certain parts of western Nepal, there are still some 'ethnically pure' Brahmins who originally came from eastern and western India, entering Nepal when fleeing the Moslem persecutions of the twelfth century. Among these were the Hindus of Rajput descent, who settled fifty miles north of Daveghat upon a mountain-top, and founded there the little town of Gurkha where, at the end of the eighteenth century, a Rajput exile rose to power and fame as he eventually conquered the twenty and twenty-four kingdoms of western Nepal, before seizing those seven kingdoms of the Katmandu valley and conquering the Rai and Limbu peoples. This was Prithvi Nayaran Shah, the first Gurkha King.

At Daveghat, the Brahmins were not of Rajput descent. Their pale features suggested a different origin, yet one we were unable to ascertain. All we could do was speculate as we watched them pace proudly towards the river to render homage to its flow – bend down to dip their brows, and sprinkle water to the four horizons. For them, as for us, a new day had begun.

8 'Beyond the Wildest Dreams of Kew'

After trying out the Marsyandi, we planned to tackle the lower Kali Gandaki. We had not surveyed its course on our flight with Emile Wick, as we had had to turn back towards Katmandu for fear of running out of fuel. We now prepared to come to grips for the first time with the river up which we eventually hoped to travel all the way to the Tibetan border, the same river whose source I had found in Mustang, the river that 'ran uphill' across the great Himalayan range before carving out the world's deepest canyon.

The goddess Kali from which the river gets its name is the wife of Shiva, so that more than the goddess Ganga, Kali is in a sense the mother of all rivers. The Tibetan-speaking people of Mustang call this river the 'Tsangpo', 'the clear one'.

Daveghat marks the beginning of the second of the three gateways that open into inner Nepal through the Mahabharat range, the only outlet through which the waters of the Himalayas can run south. This gateway was not only a geographical gap; it also marked a limit of vegetation and of populations. At Daveghat, with the homes of the Brahmins, the world of the Indian lowlands ended; north of Daveghat we would be entering the fringes of the Mongol world, the home not of the short, slant-eyed Rais or Limbus but of a host of less defined tribes – Magars, Gurungs and Bots. The last of these, the Bots, were the most intriguing for, if their name sounded the same as that generally given to the Bhotias – that is, to all the Tibetan-speaking people of the Himalayas – it was pure coincidence; they in fact formed a completely different group, composed of three ancient tribes believed to be indigenous to Nepal – the

Dunwars, the Maji, and the Darai. These three groups speak a common language which, to my knowledge, has never been studied. Indeed, little is known regarding their origins and customs. The Darai are believed to number only 1500, a minute figure when compared to that of tigers – (there are some 2000 left in India) – a species considered menaced by extinction. I wondered if we would meet some of these tribesmen.

Leaving Daveghat, I set off ahead up the Kali Gandaki, clattering down the rapid below our camp before turning in a great arc into the mouth of the river. Three hundred yards later, the Kali Gandaki began to show its true character. Although cutting through the same hills as the Marsyandi, it looked entirely different.

The Marsyandi had been majestic, wide and forceful; the Kali Gandaki was less bold, but dark and mysterious, its banks steeped in shade and its beaches slightly muddy between moss-covered cliffs. It was faintly reptilian as it quickly slid between steep mountains covered with hostile jungle, and its meandering course and shallow rapids exhaled a sense of evil, recalling that Kali is also the goddess of death. I pulled ashore to wait for Michael and Bob. The river water was dark green, not opaque, yet not altogether clear, and surprisingly warmer than that of the Marsyandi – no doubt because the Kali Gandaki had to run from west to east along the northern flanks of the Mahabharat range, while the Marsyandi came down direct from behind Annapurna. Taking care not to be swept away by the current, I lay blissfully on my hands in the water, my body floating while I cooled off. It was a case of ignorance being bliss, for these waters were, in fact, alive with crocodiles – and not small alligators, but giant, long-nosed gharials and monstrous muggers!

Sitting in the river, I recalled that in Mustang the Kali Gandaki river was so small I could jump across it. I also remembered fording it howling with pain as the blistering cold numbed my legs and clawed at my very bones.

When neither Bob nor Michael turned up, I began to worry,

and getting up I saw three men in loin-cloths picking their way towards me across the stones of the beach. I did not feel at ease alone here, but their smile reassured me. Imagining that the others had run into engine trouble, I decided to go up a little farther and see how the river made its way on through the mountains.

I zoomed off – to the surprise of the three men, who probably had never seen so much as a bicycle – and after crossing three rapids in succession and going round a great bend, I seemed to be getting ever deeper into the mountains, yet still could not imagine how the river managed to break through the chain. Eventually the river narrowed, and I saw ahead rough waves among boulders. Preferring to leave this stretch to be tackled in company, I decided to turn round. It was hard to estimate how far I had gone – perhaps ten or fifteen miles.

Going back, I stopped on a large boulder bed. It was a relief not to have the roar of the engines. The silence seemed all the greater as I peered into the jungle around me. I was about to go for another swim when, with great agility and speed, a naked figure on the opposite bank quickly worked his way down, Tarzan-fashion, clinging to branches, and finally flung himself into the river. With a powerful crawl-like stroke he slowly propelled himself across the current and scrambled ashore on the other side only three hundred feet below where he had begun.

The fellow had an unpleasant face but looked a little shy. I then saw four other men coming out of the forest, on my side of the river – two, I noticed, were armed. The men were poachers, for one had a large dead black bird hanging from his belt and bleeding down his thighs. Their rifles were antique muzzle-loaders. They looked odd – half-naked, yet armed, but in my bathing suit, and puffed up by my life-jacket, I hardly looked better.

The five men poked around my craft, marvelling at the bouncy texture of the inflatable hull, and one of them passed his hand over my life-jacket. He must have thought me as weird as my machine.

I asked the men in Nepali from what tribe they came. They admitted to being Magars, adding that farther up there was a Gurung village. They did not reply when I asked if there were any Bots living in the area. My Nepali was not very good, and perhaps theirs was no better, as the Magars speak a Tibeto-Burmese dialect. I then inquired about *bhag* (tigers). The men explained that there were plenty, and pointed to one particular spot where I presumed they had encountered one, or at least seen pug marks. The hills were very steep, but I knew well that tigers are in fact good climbers and have been encountered up to heights of 10,000 feet – although, contrary to general belief, a tiger cannot climb trees.

Leaving my admirers to their shooting, I turned my machine round and started back downstream to where the rivers burst out to meet the Marsyandi. In a matter of seconds I then glided up to our beach and found Michael and Bob both in a bad mood because of mechanical trouble. Marie-Ange also seemed moody and bored, although Bob had taken her for a ride in the hovercraft – a perilous experience, as the overloaded craft had fallen backwards down part of the rapid near our camp. Nevertheless, it had managed to come up slowly, proving we could load our craft a good deal more heavily than previous trials had led us to believe.

There was little for Marie-Ange to do in camp, what with two energetic sherpa housekeepers already. Nyma was always running around, even when he had two cups of tea and two plates in his hands. I used to speak to them in Tibetan, which made me a favourite. We joked a lot and I coaxed them to learn how to swim. Water, I knew, had never been a sherpa's best friend – they tend to prefer salty tea or barley beer to drink, and, as for washing, the word they have for it is never actually understood to relate to one's own body. Our sherpas, though, were an exception, thanks to lessons from Colonel Roberts. Nyma instantly fell in the river and thought it a great joke. I had to warn him of the dangers of going beyond his depth – especially since there was a strong current a few yards from the beach.

In spite of having a French girl and two sherpa cooks at our disposal we had little appetite, so that none of our meals was worth mentioning, and tinned pineapple remained our favourite food, with rice and curry our daily diet. Grey river water was our ever-present salvation from thirst. In camp, Michael spent his time spotting birds and insects, regaling us with the stories of their habits, or thrusting larvae into our faces in the middle of meals. His knowledge and enthusiasm about everything that creeps and crawls, grows and growls, were contagious. I marvelled at how he, who could not see a screw or nut a foot away, could spot a praying mantis under a rock in the dark. This feat afforded us the sinister spectacle of the mantis catching and devouring the insects attracted by the light of one of our candles. Somehow the praying mantis was immune to the exciting effect of light, which sent all the other insects spinning in small circles as light stimulated the wing nerves on the opposite side from those of the eye that perceived it. This is proof that insects, like humans, have a crossed nervous system, the right side of the brain directing the left side of the body. Why was this, I wondered? Like Michael, I had always been fascinated by those natural phenomena that are affected by left and right, north and south, the seasons and time. Why do certain animals change their sexual cycle on changing hemisphere, while others do not? What are the effects of climate and altitude on the cells of animals and plants? What is the mechanism that makes these cells perceive time or the shortening and lengthening of the days, not as a visual or a sensitive phenomenon but biologically? What tells a larva that it should proceed with its metamorphosis, or informs a cactus that seven years have passed and it is time to bloom? These are perhaps small questions; but what of all those insects that look like birds or flowers or rotten leaves because they know that their predator does not like those birds or flowers that they imitate? How can genes transmit techniques as in the case of those French beavers who for two hundred years had never built a dam, yet suddenly, on being released from cages, knew how to start building intricate irrigation works?

Michael and I were firmly convinced that it is not only evolution nor only natural selection of haphazard mutations that is responsible for animals looking as they do. Surely the mind can somehow imprint something on the genes so that some lesson learned can be transmitted – just as certain gifts are transmitted from father to son.

We decided in the next few days to try and cross the entire Mahabharat range, which is higher and wider here than it was at Tribeni.

All three of us planned on going up the Kali Gandaki together, Bob carrying additional petrol which he would deposit at a site where Michael and I would spend the night before carrying on the following day.

We were now to attempt to travel farther from base camp than we had ever done before. It was an exciting moment. Having loaded our craft with food and a small tent, Michael and I set off ahead.

At first, all went well, and after about twenty minutes we stopped and waited for Bob. We then noticed that Michael's skirt had become torn, his craft being the one in which we had carried out all the trials in Europe. We busied ourselves with needle and thread, our not-so-nimble fingers having trouble with this feminine art. I should like to compare stitching a hovercraft skirt with the manly art of sewing sails, but the skirt material is so thin that it needs a woman's fingers and we regretted Marie-Ange's absence. When we had finished, Bob had still not turned up. We decided to push on a little farther and wait again.

We soon passed the point where I had turned back the day before. Travelling over a large rapid that cut through boulders, the river was constantly encased in the hills that rose vertically above the water. We climbed bend after bend as if up the steps of a giant stairway, each rapid leading to a higher one, on which we emerged covered in spray, only to see yet another step ahead. We had long ago lost count of the rapids when we saw ahead of us a rough stretch of a kind we had never previously encountered. The entire river was funnelled between large rocks so that it formed a narrow bounding strip of white water rising menacingly in great swirls over successive steps of rock. I leaned forward as the spray hit my bow, slowing me down. Looking over the side at the fantastic rush of water I corrected the drift, but my craft's power was failing. At any moment I expected to be swung round and hurled back down as I nudged into the shore, grazing the sharp boulders but making no headway. I could reach out and touch the rocks as for a minute I hung in the balance upon those watery steps. Then, at last, very slowly, I began to pick up speed and pulled in at the head of the rapid, where I made for a little beach. Jumping out, I saw Michael approach and rise halfway up before a wave broke on his bow, spinning his craft round and knocking it twenty yards down. Michael regained control and turned upstream to rush the rapid for a second time. Again the breakers slowed him down. I kept my fingers crossed, but in the end his overloaded craft was swept back, slithering sideways dangerously close to the large stone steps on the far side of the river. Eventually Michael turned downstream and steered his craft to shore.

'The stupid thing keeps digging in,' he remarked angrily. 'Let's haul it over on the edge.' This was more easily said than done. We emptied the craft and solicited the help of one of the inhabitants of a small leaf-covered shack set upon the beach upstream. The three of us were stumbling over boulders, tugging at the hovercraft, when suddenly Bob's craft roared into sight.

At full speed he rushed the rapid, keeping his bow heading well into the onrushing water. He was about to make it up when a wave spun him round and swept him back. If ever there was a struggle against the elements, this was it. We were really fighting the river foot by foot. As Michael had observed, we were experiencing an entirely new sport. At his second attempt, Bob made it and coasted up alongside my craft.

Bob, we discovered, had had great trouble starting his

engines just as we disappeared out of sight. After a lot of sweat, we eventually carried Michael's craft up to join the others. We were ready to set off again.

Base camp felt far away as we sped yet farther up the river, knowing that now there was no going back except by machine, since we were locked between vertical moss-covered cliffs. The massive shoulders of the mountain ran down to the river, whose rare calm waters reflected the craggy peaks. The noise of our three craft echoed loudly in the gorges as we bored deeper into the heart of the Mahabharat range – a succession of deep valleys and towering jungle-covered peaks. Rounding one bend, we saw thatched huts and, on the shore, a crowd of some fifty people staring in awe as we skidded by, taking short-cuts over sandbanks, or rushing low boulders before plunging out of sight. We were drunk with speed and spray, with that feeling of power and airy aloofness that characterizes the short spells between rapids, when once again we were reminded of the frailty of our craft. Only the perspiration on our brow beneath the spray betrayed the tension of steering our machines, the alertness needed for the split second decision on which side to pass a rock or tackle a sandbank. We passed another village, another amazed crowd, taking it in turns to lead the procession and overtaking each other in festive mood when the river allowed us a little rest.

We lost count of time and direction, and it was only on looking at my watch that I realized we had been on the water for over four hours. Michael was in the lead when I decided to stop, the other two soon joining me.

Emerging from the jungle, a small crowd soon gathered round us. We felt like Martians parachuted on to a new planet – and looked like them, to judge from the amazed stares of the villagers. Quite probably the youngsters had never seen a European before. To them we must have seemed frightening giants, especially Bob, with his beard. Three pretty girls with bright blue turbans and gold nose rings stared at us with shy smiles – no cultural gap needed to be bridged for us to appreciate their charms! A loud chatter rose from the crowd, as

spectators excitedly explained with their hands to latecomers
what they had seen of our manœuvres.

Although it was early in the afternoon, I felt it wise to stop
here and spend the night. Bob had to return before dusk so as
not to leave Marie-Ange alone, and, to the amazement of all,
he slid down into the river, in a cloud of sand, bounced over a
rapid, and skidded out of sight. A strange silence set in; the
crowd broke up and we followed the last stragglers back to
their village, leaving a few children to look after our machines.

On entering the village, I had the same impression as one gets
on sailing into New York Harbour or on entering a Venetian
palace by its canal entrance – the feeling of sneaking into a new
world unannounced by a back door. It was as if we had been
parachuted into these primitive surroundings, for there was no
logical link with the rest of the world, no footpath or trail with
landmarks to help us retrace our route.

Looking up at the ridge of mountains that enclosed the
clearing, we wondered how one could reach such an isolated
place as this by means more conventional than ours. 'How far
is Daveghat?' we inquired. 'Two days' walking with a load, one
long day for a fast walker,' a man explained, pointing to the
distant summit of the ridge, where a footpath no doubt led out
of the gorge.

The village was a small settlement inhabited by Magar
tribesmen. Its few fields of brown clay cleared from the jungle
did not boast one blade of grass. We gathered that a famine had
set in here, for we were in the peak of the dry season and the
previous year's crops had been poor due to an early monsoon
season. Most villagers, having run out of other grain, were
surviving on a handful of lentils a day. They had their cattle
killed and eaten before they died from lack of fodder.

The houses were squat, well-built rectangular constructions
of thick, vertically planted posts supporting palm-thatched
roofs and surrounded by low verandas. The largest served as a
wayside inn for those passing through the village on a trail
that runs from Bharatpur to Pokhara, some fifty miles
away.

We were now in the very heart of the Mahabharat range, and the climate here was a good deal cooler than at our camp. Overhead we could see Chir pines, the lowest growing conifers of the Himalayas; they yield a resin used to make turpentine. The forest below the pines was mixed, ranging from shiny leaved magnolias to acacias, walnut, rosewood, ebony and eucalyptus trees. I could not help marvelling at the variety of plants we encountered. I had believed this to be due to the climate and altitude, but I now learned from Michael that the reason lay in the fact that central Nepal marks a crucial meeting-point of flora, so that one finds plants of Mediterranean origin alongside plants of south-east Asian and Chinese origin, as well as certain plants from Tibet and India, and the numerous varieties indigenous to Nepal itself.

Central Nepal is thus a botanical crossroads, and time and time again Michael recognized the originals of shrubs and flowers that had been imported to England and become familiar there – so confirming Kipling's verse that 'The wildest dreams of Kew are commonplace in Katmandu.' Indeed, there is no more spectacular botanical garden than the Nepalese Himalayas, in particular the central section in the Mahabharat range. Yet in spite of this, in this village we found famine; not the noisy, clamorous famine of the Indian cities, but an anonymous, gnawing hunger – and this in one of nature's most generous gardens.

Once in the village, we made for an isolated house set in a parched field where lived the father of the child we had left on the beach to keep an eye on our things. This man had seven small children, yet his patience and kindness betrayed nothing of the tragedy of famine, and he generously bade us drink tea and offered us a share of their meagre meal of lentils from a copper plate. We accepted the tea but refused the food. We would have liked to give the man a present, but discovered that in all our plans we had forgotten to bring any money. We found out later that we had only three rupees among us, hidden in the folds of the small pockets of our bathing suits.

After our tea we set out for a walk along the banks of the

river. Coming to a beach surrounded by huge blocks of granite, we found bright red sand bearing traces of ferrous oxides scraped away from some distant mineral cliff. The sand, I knew, also contained gold torn from the hills of Mustang. Looking into murky pools we could see thousands of minute frogs breeding in the tepid water and were reminded again of the peculiar richness of the region, and the many forms of life it nourished. I thought, looking at Michael and myself, how far away London seemed, the sophistications of our culture, whose intricate traditions and obligations, laws and taboos now seemed strange, far removed from the bare essentials of creation – sun, and water, and organic food. It seemed *we* were the real primitives, with our peculiar customs and rites, our awkward clothes, our strict social code – all the paraphernalia of our daily routines. To shave, to dress in shirt and tie; to clothe the feet in nylon and shiny leather shoes; to change one's dress according to the hour of the day; to sleep between sheets, blankets, eiderdowns and pillows – only custom has made us accept these things so easily, so much so that it came as a surprise to me that naked on a beach we looked so human, so much like everyone else. How man delights in complicating his daily existence! Some believe this to be a sign of sophistication. Yet a genius can walk naked: the sages of the East have only a loincloth and a begging bowl. And in truth our rituals are less sophisticated in comparison to those of the wildest tribe of New Guinea.

We left the beach and returned downstream to our craft to have some very Western food: a loaf of bread home-baked in a saucepan at Daveghat, a can of meat, a tin of pineapple – the lot spiced with sand. As it was getting dark, we set about finding a place to erect our small tent. We first thought of the edge of the jungle under the trees, but eventually chose the open beach a few feet from the water. We were still blissfully ignorant of crocodiles, and no one had yet had the kindness to warn us that to lie at the water's edge was like sleeping in the dragon's mouth, for it is at night in the hot season that the lazy reptiles emerge from the cool water on to the warm sand. In the event, the tent was too small and stuffy, so in our innocence we decided to sleep outside, with just our heads under shelter.

It was too early to retire right away, so we picked our way through the trees back to the village, and came upon the wayside inn. Here we found several villagers crouched on the floor around a fat old lady. We joined the group. The dancing light of the flame of our linseed-oil lamp lit eager faces that stared at us in silence. The ring of light bound us together, and after a while, at a remark from the old lady, all began talking again, trying to draw us into conversation. I examined the faces around us, the faces of Magars – dark and full with slightly Mongoloid features, but without noticeably slanted eyes.

I had always been fascinated by the Magars. This is not because they presented a remarkable culture, or any very distinctive characteristics, but because they were in a way a cultureless race – or, rather, a race with many cultures. The Magars inhabit mainly western Nepal, yet unlike other tribes they are found both near the snow line and down in the jungle, their settlements covering the whole climatic range of Nepal. Likewise their customs and culture reflects the variety of cultures to be found in the land, for the Magars readily adopt the culture of the people near whom they live. In the north I had encountered many Tibetan-Buddhist Magar communities, while these tropical Magars claimed to be Hindu. What intrigued me was that Magars, the cultural chameleons of Nepal, consider themselves primarily as Magars, yet have little or no peg on which to hang their identity.

By definition, a race or tribe will usually have its own definite culture. Not so with the Magars; for them the tribe is only a matter of language and blood lines. Magar speech is of Tibetan origin, as I now learned as I began asking the name of this and that object around the camp. The villagers' replies were practically pure Tibetan. Among others, the words for road, fire, eye, nose, earth and wood are identical with their Tibetan counterparts. The only variations I found in a short list of key names were for the word water, *di* instead of *chu*, and *yum* for house instead of *khang* or *khim*.

The old woman was amazed that I knew, as she said, 'how to speak Magar', so she generously poured Michael and me a glass of rum, soon followed by two more for which she accepted payment. By the time we left we could not have told a crocodile from a frog, and we were persuaded that the Magars were the best people in the world. Nevertheless, I had been sober enough to take notes and to recall that the Magars, together with the Limbu, the Rai and the Gurung, were one of Nepal's warrior tribes. Prior to the unification of Nepal, Magars had ruled over twelve small principalities in western Nepal. Today they are divided into dozens of clans who all claim to have come from some ancient forgotten Magar kingdom.

Considering the similarity between the Magar and Tibetan languages, one might postulate that the Magars stemmed from the great days of Tibetan supremacy in the seventh and eighth centuries when the Tibetan kings conquered Nepal. *Magar* in Tibetan means army camp or military camp, and it could well be that the Magars are descended from the soldiers left in Nepal to guard Tibet's old frontiers.

Language, far more than religion or customs, is the least changing heritage of a people, the clearest pointer to a race's origin. A people might be projected from the Stone Age to the atomic era in terms of cultural development, yet their language tends to remain the same. In fact, a people's physical features will change more quickly than their speech. Language is the root of all culture. The ability to communicate through language is the main difference between men and animals, and it is language that is directly responsible for tradition and culture, which are little more than combinations of concepts derived from language and formed into laws and taboos only comprehensible to a people who have agreed to the same definitions.

Lying on the beach under the stars, I thought how little we really know of the nature of man. Who is he? What is life? Why do we live? Such questions every man has asked, and every tribe has answered in its own fashion, inventing and improving fanciful theories to reassure its members. Having experienced so many faiths, and so many different lives in different worlds,

I realized that the only thing certain and universal is man's anxiety. Truth cannot be multiple, yet faced with a choice, who can rest assured of having taken the right decision? Perhaps God himself is anxiety? Or so I felt that night, lost in the deep inner folds of the dark Mahabharat range.

9 *On How to be Eaten by a Crocodile*

It was cold at sunrise, for the sun only grazed the tips of the steep ridges around us. The river roared past, a reminder of what we had yet to accomplish. I remembered the early dawns I had seen when sailing across the Atlantic. The only difference now was that the weather gave no hint of possible storms, and I could not chase away the anxiety and fear I felt at each new departure. Anxiety had a power of its own, which made self-deception about the future impossible. 'I wouldn't mind walking,' Michael confessed to me, and I agreed. But our machines beckoned and there was the watery route we had laid out for ourselves to conquer.

Hastily we packed our tent, chewed some left-over bread, and prepared to leave. Our main incentive was to see how the river managed to force its way through the steep mountains. So far, every loop through and around the mountains had come as a surprise, so massive did the barrier seem as it rose above us; yet we had not yet encountered a really steep waterfall.

It was 6 a.m. when we pushed off. The moment we hit the water we were entirely absorbed by the river, struggling to keep our craft heading upstream, calculating the speed of the current, the size of the oncoming waves, the direction of the wind. Forgotten was our interlude in the Magar village; our only preoccupation was the uncharted river. I wondered whether the early navigators and explorers had had the same feeling that constantly assailed us: the realization that every yard we achieved spelt as many new hazards for the return journey. Every rapid we climbed meant another rapid to descend, and going down, we knew, was no easier task than going up.

All during our journey, the fact that we had no reassuring precedent from which to seek courage weighed heavily on us. On previous journeys, when in fear or doubt, I had been able to recall ancient travellers and find comfort in their experiences. Here we were completely alone. At every rapid we had to decide for ourselves whether we could make it or should even try, knowing full well that the penalty for a mistake was to be dashed into the turbulent flow.

All this left little time to admire the beauty of the river, whose virgin bed revealed ever more beautiful waterscapes. At one point we found ourselves navigating between huge grey icebergs, blocks of granite lapped upon by an angry sea. Easing our way around them we came dangerously close to the bank. Our speed and manner of turning reminded me of skiing, only our giant slalom course allowed for no mistakes.

It was bitterly cold. We sat soaked by a fine spray blown up by our lift fans and further chased by a slight wind that soon began to freshen. We were now on the northern face of the Mahabharat range, and hoped any minute to emerge into the wide valley along which the Kali Gandaki meandered in its search for the gap through which we were riding. From our aerial survey with Emile Wick we knew that once we reached this stretch our troubles would end, for the river from there on was a wide rapid-free throughway until it turned north to head up towards the inevitable Himalayan cataracts.

We had with us fuel for approximately five hours, yet of this we needed to keep at least three hours' worth to return. We therefore planned to go no farther than the northern limit of the Mahabharat range where the river flattened out. Our only alternative, had we wished to proceed farther, would have been to send on porters with more fuel, an operation that was hardly worthwhile, since it would take a week, and would only lead to a quite unexotic territory, anyway beyond the limits of our temporary permit. Our goal now was simply to get across the Mahabharat range, which here in central Nepal was at its widest.

Michael was in the lead when, about an hour after leaving

our village, we were hit by a strong wind that drove spray into our eyes and chilled us to the marrow, while seriously impairing the steering of our craft. We lost considerable forward speed, and wherever possible we were obliged to hug the steep rocky riverbanks to find shelter from the howling wind that whistled down the gorge like a giant draught. At one point I fell under hump, and decided to pull up on a sandy slip to adjust my carburettors to obtain maximum power.

Pine trees now clothed the steep sides of the river, rising to a mountain beyond which appeared a patch of blue sky. Here at last was the gap, the northern exit to the Mahabharat range, and we now headed for it up several turbulent rapids. We had made it at last, through the only breach in the whole central section of the range. We now emerged into inner Nepal, where the river ran its lazy course westward along the northern face of the range.

We had wanted to shoot up a dozen miles along this easy stretch, but by now the wind was so strong that we were making practically no headway, even though our engines were at maximum throttle. By this time I had caught up with Michael, who was attempting for the third time to go up a rapid between two large boulders. Unfortunately the wind did not allow him to gather enough speed, and each time he was slowly shoved backwards by the combined effect of wind and current drag on the skirts of his craft. I, in turn, tried unsuccessfully to negotiate this rapid, and eventually also surrendered to the power of the wind.

We were now faced with a choice either to pull ashore and wait for the wind to drop, or to call it a day and turn back. As there was no telling when the wind might drop, and since we had succeeded in crossing the range, I thought it wisest to end our prospecting of the lower reaches of the Kali Gandaki at this point. My decision was also influenced by the knowledge that we now had practically forty miles of rapids to negotiate before reaching our base camp. Any time lost here meant spending another day on the river, which did not seem warranted: we could only proceed a dozen miles farther because of lack of petrol, and then only when and if the wind stopped. Having made it across the Mahabharat range, there was no real point in doing more until we had the permit which would allow us to carry on up north from our present position. We could then join the river again at the point where the road running south from Pokhara crossed it fifty miles upstream. We therefore decided to return, happy at having successfully found our way across the Mahabharat range, and so opening a new door into central Nepal.

As we came down, Michael and I stopped on the first sunny beach to dry our clothes, refuel and warm ourselves a little. So far everything had gone well, and as a result we had become somewhat over-confident of our little machines and of our capacity to control them. The spill that had nearly cost me my life seemed far away, and I chose to believe that all my anxiety was no longer justified. Whether due to over-confidence or just plain bad luck, our return trip was soon to remind us of the true hazards of our enterprise.

After a short rest we set off. The strong wind (now at our backs) impaired our steering a little, and we were constantly blown off course and made to go faster than we wanted. I was busy coping with these problems as I headed for a rapid that swept round in a great arc of foam between rocky banks when Michael shot past me at what seemed – and indeed was – a reckless speed. Since hovercraft float on air above water, there is in theory little or nothing to slow down a hovercraft when going downhill. Michael entered the rapid at full speed, bouncing madly on top of the waves, and was swept straight into a massive boulder. In a volley of spray, I saw his craft hit the rock and rear to a near-vertical position from the impact. The craft then bounced back, falling flat on the water. Although Michael was wearing a life-jacket, I realized he had no crash helmet. The instant the craft flopped down it was immediately swept away by the rapid. To my dismay I saw that the pilot seat was empty.

I rushed forward just in time to see Michael in the water, but with one leg over the side of his craft. Having been thrown overboard on to the rocks, he had somehow managed to hold on to his craft as it cavorted out of control down the rapid. Eventually he managed to scramble back on board, and carried on down for a few hundred yards before pulling on to a sandy beach. I found him still dazed, only just able to realize how close he had come to disaster. By rights he should have been knocked out on hitting the rock, and it was fortunate that he was still alive. That the craft was not punctured was amazing. The wind had made him gather too much speed, and then he had completely lost control. As soon as Michael had recovered and we had repaired the craft's damaged canopy, we carried on down, bend after bend, rapid after rapid, forging our way slowly back across the range. Looking around us, we could see why the Mahabharat range is one of the wildest and least inhabited areas of central Nepal. Its tropical forest and sheer vertical hills have combined to discourage most settlers, even those rugged Nepalese peasants who have managed elsewhere to survive upon the steepest of ridges and up to altitudes of over 14,000 feet.

About halfway down the river we stopped on a wide beach, where there were three slim dug-out canoes which were used as ferries across a relatively calm stretch of water nearby. Made of hollowed tree-trunks, these dug-outs were particularly thin, yet with a very heavy fan-like stern. The men who operated them, we learned, were Bots. Above the steep far bank was a large Gurung village, or so we were told by a smiling man whose three daughters stood on the beach where the ferry had dropped them.

The Gurungs of west Nepal are a race generally found living in higher altitudes. Like the Rai, the Limbu and the Magars, they are Tibetan in origin and are also famous as soldiers, but unlike the Magars, who tend to adopt the customs of neighbouring tribes, the Gurungs are very faithful to their own culture – or rather to the culture they have developed on their own as an offshoot of Tibetan culture. Their religion is related to Lamaism, yet involves many magical practices of ancient origin.

Gurungs are easily recognizable, for their round, full faces, although Mongoloid in aspect, do not have slanted eyes, nor are their features as flat as those of the Rai. Gurung women are even easier to identify as, covered in gold and semi-precious stones, they look like walking jewellers' shops. A Gurung apparently places all his wealth upon his wife, and most of these ladies have as many rings as they can afford on their fingers, huge discs attached to the lobe of their ears, little discs sewn into the top of the ear, and one or sometimes two large rings in their noses, not to mention innumerable bracelets and pendants. To further highlight their brilliance, they like to dress in a rich red.

It was beyond the scope of our journey to study the customs of each tribe we met. Our interest in these Gurungs was in finding the limits of their settlements. This particular village was probably one of the lowest of the tribe, as Gurungs usually live higher up in the mountains. There are several Gurung customs worth noting. One is a strange ceremony held when a child is five or six, and has his hair cut for the first time. The boy is tied to a stake with a rope round his neck as if he were a horse; his hair is cut; his mother then calls to him, and the child has to answer his mother by saying 'meow'. This ceremony has never been fully explained, and we could not find an answer to it.

What characterizes the tribal and clan organization of the Gurungs is their strong communal bonds derived from the fact that boy-girl relationships are very liberal. Not only are marriages decided according to the lover's choice, but young teenagers lead an active social life living in clubs with their own dormitories. Boys' clubs visit girls' clubs into the small hours, and club outings are frequent, while field work is performed jointly. When a girl gets married, all her club members receive small presents from the groom. Each club has a club mother or father who prepares food and keeps an eye on the young, who nevertheless have a very good time. Such a liberal custom is worth looking into, and could well be copied by other peoples! It also possibly explains why the Gurungs are among the most sociable and cheerful of the hill people of Nepal.

As we joked with the father of the three beauties standing on the beach, a man suggested that we fill our water bottles from a stream that ran down the mossy cliff on the opposite bank of the river. This water tasted so sweet to our palates, by now accustomed to crude silty river water, that it might have been an exceptionally good wine. Such was our thirst we could appreciate the different types of water we met, and for many days we kept a little of what we now drank in stock as a treat. Hardship can be the source of countless pleasures which in the normal circumstances of an easy life do not exist. Civilized man, often without knowing it, has far less opportunity for joy. In a rigorous, hard life, on the other hand, every favourable circumstance, however small, gives intense pleasure.

Leaving the Gurungs and the ferryman, we set off once more. However, we were soon to find that soaring carefree, even on an air cushion, can lead to trouble. Trouble on this occasion came in the form of the bottom falling out of my hovercraft. This was due to the vibrations of the high-velocity two-stroke engines that powered our fragile craft. Like most of our other breakdowns, it was in no way related to the hovercraft principle or to anything connected with the unusual nature of our machines, but was simply the result of their being too light to withstand the vibrations of our two motors. As I limped ashore, a naked fisherman came up to marvel at my craft's intricacy. He did not realize it was broken, and I could hardly mobilize him to help me, as he could never have seen a screw or nut in his life before. With Michael to help, I managed to turn the craft over against a prop, and got down to work. No matter how much practice I had at sitting on a sandbank slaving away in the midday sun, I could never get used to it. In an hour of hard work in the tropical heat one can lose up to 23 per cent of the volume of one's blood through perspiration. As much as five pounds of water in an hour! This I proceeded to lose as I struggled to repair my craft. I felt dizzy several times, a symptom Michael had also suffered, and which we learnt only later was a characteristic of sun stroke brought on by dehydration. I now worked with frenzy, not to say panic, for I knew that without my machine I might never be able to get back, short of a very long walk and having to abandon my craft. I had at all costs to repair it. Gone were the days when John Trueluck could fix anything for us; far away also seemed our all too brief crash-course in mechanics. How I deplored spending so much time on Latin at school and so little looking under the bonnet of a car! Michael's education, like mine, was defective, though not his pessimism, for he now remarked, 'Let us pray that the carburettors don't go wrong.' Carburettors were one thing neither of us knew anything about; their very name was mentioned only with fear when far away from our spare parts. As Michael had said, 'Those things are full of pins and needles.' Pins and needles, we well knew, were for mechanical fakirs, not for us. Luckily putting the bottom back on a hovercraft is not so complicated, and at last we were ready to go. My mechanical skill was proved a mile farther down when once again the bottom of my craft fell out – this time just a hundred yards above the booming rapids up which we had had to carry Michael's craft, the worst and most dangerous of all those we had encountered. On losing its bottom my craft also lost its cushion, and now was being swept towards the turbulent water. My heart thudded, as with paddle and full thrust throttle I tried to beat the current and make it ashore. These are some sweats that have nothing to do with tempera-ture. Inch by inch I tried to gain a beach before being smashed down the rapids. I just made it. Then, seeing Michael roar up behind me, I waved for him to come ashore and help.

Michael had seen the rapids, and understood my waving to be a sign for him to hug the left bank of the river on the way down. The left side happened to be a series of a dozen great steps perhaps four or five feet tall where the water tumbled down from one boulder to another. Down this stairway Michael now shot, trusting to what he believed were my instructions. Here for the second time that morning he came within a few inches of disaster. Like a rubber ball, his craft bounced and lurched as, picked up by the waves, it was thrown down step by step, rising and falling and spinning round, now completely out of control, and constantly in danger of being overturned

Michel Peissel demonstrates a hovercraft on the Bagmati river to General (now Field Marshal) S. Shaha, our patron in Nepal, while the Prime Minister looks on smiling. Below: the hovercraft packed up and deflated before being fitted into the King's helicopter with only an inch to spare and transported to the head of the Kali Gandaki cataracts.

The great Himalayan breach. Part of the Kali Gandaki travelled by the
expedition.

and crushed by the boulders. That Michael came out alive with
his craft still in working order was the greatest testimony to the
incredible resistance of our crafts' inflatable structure and also
to the validity of the principle of hovercraft applied to rapids.
It proved also what we had suspected all along: that our particular machines were something more than just hovercraft.
Their design associated with their rubber hull produced a true
'bouncing machine', the captive air within the bag-skirt acting
as a shock absorber capable of withstanding terrific impacts.

Having repaired my craft once again, we carried on down
the now familiar lower portion of the river, suffering nothing
more than two incidents whose interest is only retrospective.

The first of these was that, cruising over relatively still dark
water, I saw something splash off the right bow of my craft and
I noticed the rectangular whitish scales of what I believed to
be a fish, some six feet long or more. When Michael, who was
behind me, reached this spot his lift engine stalled, and since
he was unable to start it from the craft, he had to jump into
the water and swim ashore. Then, just above the junction with
the Marsyandi, my fan-belt started slipping. I dragged my craft
on to a small beach just below the towering village of Daveghat
and there spent half an hour working, then swimming to cool off.

Eventually I got into camp. It was a relief to be back safe
and sound and we celebrated the occasion with a good meal.
The first thing Bob said to us was, 'Do you know this place is
full of crocodiles?' Both Michael and I laughed at this silly joke.
Then after a while I found myself thinking, 'Crocodiles? Why
not?' But of course I could not believe it. 'I'll show you one
right away if you want,' said Bob, but I did not appreciate his
Australian humour that afternoon. We were too tired and
excited by our journey to worry about anything else. Nevertheless, Bob kept on repeating his story about a huge one just down
from the village of Daveghat the other side of the river. 'You
can see it whenever you want, it's been living there for thirty
years.'

Of course Bob was right. What is more, we were soon to
discover that we were in the heart of what might be called

Nepal's 'crocodile belt'. Between our camp and Narayanghat, eight miles downstream, the local people had counted over fifty of the reptiles – giant muggers and long-snouted gharials that grow to be twenty-four feet long! These were huge monsters, far greater than their American cousins and rivals even of the biggest African varieties.

Later we went to see the beast Bob had been shown, and there to my horror I noticed that it lay exactly three yards from where I had spent half an hour that afternoon bare-footed, swimming and working on my fan-belt. Everything now clicked into place. My 'fish' was beyond doubt the belly of a crocodile diving to get out of my way. Michael began stammering about the hours we had spent bathing or just soaking at the water's edge, not to mention our sleeping on beaches. 'If you sleep on or near a beach,' an expert on reptiles later explained, 'you should always plant stakes and join them with rope to which you attach tin cans to scare the crocodiles away,' adding horrified, 'Where did you think they lived?' Yet this friend was no coward, for he himself had collected reptiles in Nepal. 'You were,' he concluded, 'both lucky and mad.'

Lucky we certainly were; as for being mad, the truth is that we were plain ignorant, and what one is not aware of one never sees. Crocodiles and tree-trunks look much alike, and we had seen many logs on the beaches as we zoomed past. Once Bob had shown us our first crocodile we began seeing them everywhere. That spoiled our swimming and other aquatic games, to say nothing of Michael's readiness to jump overboard on every occasion!

Slightly shattered, we pored over Michael's manual on Indian reptiles. There on paper was a portrait of the brute that dozed in the sun near our camp. Michael, the guilty zoologist caught off guard, now read us the most significant passages about their habitat and customs. 'The mugger,' he read, 'is very swift and can run faster than a normal human being.' This made us laugh, because one thing we knew was that all human beings run faster than normal when chased by a crocodile.

We also learned how the muggers can live to be sixty or even one hundred years old. This explained why, as we later discovered, most of these brutes have been given names by the people near whose village they live. Wise old crocodiles are animals of habit, and live always in the same spot overlording a specific territory. Their resting-places are easily recognizable from the large caterpillar-like tracks in the sand all around. At the spot where I had readjusted my fan-belt just before reaching camp I saw that these tracks were mingled with my own.

In the heat of the day, the crocodiles lie in the water facing upstream in true crocodile fashion, with eyes just above the surface, or rather half submerged, peering at two worlds. In the water they are quick and powerful, and thrive on large fish. The gharials are particularly well equipped for such a job as they have, unlike ordinary flat-faced crocodiles, a very long beak-like snout with teeth protruding laterally, something like the snout of a gigantic saw fish. Had someone not invented the word 'crocodile' there would be no other name for them but 'dragon'. These giants are indeed the largest reptiles on earth, and beyond doubt the most frightening creepy-crawly machines ever invented.

The crocodiles' taste for fish does not deter them from eating dogs, and indeed having a snap at anything that moves. Daughters of Ganga, crocodiles are held sacred by most Hindus, and poor virgins used to be fed into their angry jaws from the temples that lined the banks of the Hooghly where Calcutta now stands. At Daveghat the Brahmins still consider them worthy of veneration, and they are not killed for that reason. 'We think we've had mechanical trouble,' Michael now commented wryly, 'but you wait till they take a snap at our machines.' This was not an impossible thought: our craft were only eight and a half feet long – one-third the length of a large gharial.

10 *A Tiger on our Track*

The subject of crocodiles led us to prepare our new plans. Having now inspected the Kali Gandaki as far north as we could go with our existing permit, we wished to travel the rest of its course right down to the Indian border through the jungles.

Our map showed that the Kali Gandaki combined with the Marsyandi below our camp and took the name of 'Narayani'. It then headed south-west for some forty miles before flowing into India. Some ten miles south of our camp, the river fanned out to form a network of branching waterways enclosing jungle-covered islands, the largest nearly eight miles long. I feared that we might easily lose our way in this maze of islands, and suggested that the first thing we should do was to set off overland to a lodge called 'Tiger Tops', located in the middle of the Chitawan game reserve. There we could leave a few jerry-cans of petrol in reserve, inquire about the rivers, and determine a few landmarks to guide us. We would then return to camp and try to make it down to Tiger Tops along the Gandaki and Rapti rivers, and eventually up a little river called the Reu that penetrated the heart of the game reserve and flowed by the lodge.

We agreed this was the best plan, and decided to start out the following day, which seemed to suit Marie-Ange who by now was bored with sitting on the riverbank. From Tiger Tops, with luck, she could find her way back to Katmandu on one of the small planes that fly to Megauli, an airstrip that had been cut out of the jungle in 1962 to fly in Queen Elizabeth and Prince Philip when they attended a great tiger and rhino shoot organized for them by the King of Nepal. Nearly one-third of the Nepalese budget was spent in building a city of tents, the airfield, and collecting 363 elephants at Megauli for the occasion. This famous hunt had been one of the grandest ever held in Nepal – that is to say, one of the most spectacular tiger shoots ever staged and beyond doubt the last such ever to be held. On three previous occasions the Nepalese had entertained British royalty with their fabled shoots. In 1886 at Chitawan the future King Edward VII had bagged twenty-three tigers, one leopard and a bear. King George V killed ten tigers, one rhino and a bear all in one day – a list which makes sad reading now that these animals are threatened with extinction. On the 1962 shoot Prince Philip, who had publicly identified himself with the cause of wild life conservation, developed a diplomatic 'infected trigger finger'. The variety of wild life in the area is demonstrated by the list of animals presented by the Nepalese to the late Duke of Windsor in 1921 after he had shot in Nepal. The animals, destined for the London Zoo, included one baby elephant, one rhino calf, two leopard cats, two Himalayan black bears, one black leopard, one tiger, one Tibetan fox, one sambar, one thar, one unicorn sheep, three musk deer, and a number of other animals besides.

We were told we could reach Megauli overland from Bharatpur, and from there carry on to Tiger Tops. We therefore decided that next morning we would get our machines in top condition and then try to secure a vehicle to take us down to the lodge to establish our petrol depot. After some difficulty, we managed to get our old truck to take us to Bharatpur, and from there a mile down the river to the sprawling town of Narayanghat. This beautiful name turned out to be that of a wretched bazaar, a frontier town of sorts that rivalled Birganj in ugliness, if not in size.

The heat was terrible and the flies swarmed in droves above the narrow filthy street of this forgotten little place stretched upon the banks of the Narayani. The day before we had been in the high, cool hills; we were now in a suffocating inferno. For hours we combed the streets in search of a jeep for hire, and were getting desperate when Bob reported having found what he called a 'taxi'. This, he said, would drive us to Tiger Tops.

The 'taxi' was an old Dodge command car sporting a bright red star on its bonnet, though whether this was Chinese or Russian we never found out. It was a surplus of surplus, and had seen many wars, not to mention a long and equally difficult civilian life. Ten steel bolts held the torn front tyre together, while the rest were bound with string. We boarded it at 2 p.m., the only passengers. At 4.30 we were still in Narayanghat, the truck having in the meantime collected twenty people and an entire domestic zoo. When at last the machine rumbled out of Narayanghat (shaking off a few passengers in the process) we began to envy Noah's Ark – for at least it floated – while now, without springs, we were bouncing painfully over a dirt track with some doubts about ever completing our journey east.

To reach Megauli we had to cross thirty-five miles of agricultural land recently cleared from the jungle and now the home of countless settlers from the hills. It took us three full hours to cover this distance, with stops every few miles to fill the leaky radiator or to unload pigs. Covered in sweat and dust, we bounced wearily on – rubbing shoulders with arrogant-looking Brahmins, greasy coolies and growling women, some with rings in their noses. The trip was made more depressing by the fact that less than ten years ago where now sprouted hideous villages of concrete, corrugated iron, and bamboo huts, there had been virgin jungle. The smiling faces of the hill people had given way to the sad, dreary eyed expression of the people of the tropics – the face of apathy bred by heat, malaria, and the particularly unpleasant social relations which seem to develop in agricultural societies living on rich lands.

The sun was setting when at last we reached Megauli and the vast rectangular airfield. Having still some ten miles to go, we coaxed the truck driver to take us right on to the lodge. This lay on the other side of the Rapti and Reu, and could be reached only by fording these rivers. We crossed the airstrip, bumped over a trail through some marshy long grass, and finally reached some sandbanks on the edge of the Rapti. The river here was wide but shallow, and the truck ploughed in with water only up to its axles. Halfway across it halted jerkily on a sandbank.

The driver clambered down and Michael and I got out to see what was the matter. Under the vehicle lay the drive shaft that had somehow fallen off into the sand. We were by now good enough mechanics to know that this would mean hours of delay. Consequently Michael and I decided we would set off alone on foot through the jungle. So, as dusk descended over Chitowan, we thrust unarmed into the heart of what is the last and greatest reserve of tigers and rhinoceros in the Asian sub-continent.

We walked in silence under the majestic trees, the track a mere double path through which a jeep could barely brush its way between the trees and tall grass. There were the cries of birds and jungle fowl all about us, the barking of jackals, and many other unidentified noises. Slowly night began to fall and we wondered anxiously how far we should have to walk. I thought about bumping into a tiger or rhino, the common obsession of anyone in a jungle, but it did not bother me as I do not believe that dreams of that sort come true.

Michael walked ahead, his brisk elegant step making me imagine an umbrella swinging back and forth from his arm. This set me brooding on the fact that by now I had begun to see behind the mask of Michael's upbringing and had started to fathom some of those feelings he would never out of 'good taste' want to reveal. It always amazes me how little one ever knows another person and, for that matter, how little one really knows oneself. I was still full of these thoughts when suddenly a bush beside me exploded with a sudden cracking of branches and ruffling of leaves. A dark form darted away – a swamp deer, I thought. My eyes followed its path as best they could through the tall grass and trees to where I had seen the shape disappear. There, twenty yards away, was a huge tiger, its hairy collar ruffled around its characteristic evil eyes, which were staring straight at me.

I rubbed my own eyes. How often in dreams had I pictured myself face to face with a tiger! Incredulously I called to Michael. 'Look there,' I said. 'A tiger' – as if pointing out a taxi.

'Where?' answered Michael, coming up to where I stood.

'Over there by the tree-trunk.'

'I can't see a thing,' Michael said in disgust.

'There to the left of that palm frond near the bush.'

I began having doubts and looked again. The thing had not moved; it looked just like a frozen tiger staring at me. I stared back, thinking it must be my imagination.

'Over there – look,' I repeated, this time less sure of myself.

Michael looked. 'Yes, I see, it's just a tree that looks like something.'

'But it looks like a tiger,' I protested.

'Don't be silly,' Michael replied, adding, 'It does look a *bit* like a tiger.'

We were about to have an argument, but by now neither of us believed that the thing was anything but a product of our imagination, for the light was fading and staring hard made everything look fuzzy. At that moment the tree-trunk got fed up with our talk and turned, presenting us with its gloriously striped flank as it majestically paced off parallel to the trail in the direction for which we were heading.

'I told you so,' I whispered, feeling faint.

Suddenly the true implication of this encounter struck us. There was a tiger on our track going our way and we had neither gun nor even a pocket-knife. It was dusk and we had disturbed his dinner – having frightened the deer he was no doubt stalking. We had to do something, but what? We now began talking in hushed tones and walking on tiptoe, unaware of how ridiculous we were, since it was pointless at this stage to make ourselves invisible.

'I heard one should speak very loudly,' I shouted to Michael, who jumped, before agreeing that there was no point in whispering once the tiger had seen us. 'They don't attack humans unless provoked,' I added to cheer myself up. Michael's pace was now a fast clip. 'Wait,' I called, 'I don't want him to snatch me from behind.'

'You know,' Michael answered, 'that is just what I was thinking – they catch the one who is behind.'

We now walked abreast of each other, every rustling leaf sending shivers down our spines. Ahead we suddenly saw the flicker of a light. Had we arrived? Sadly it was just a shack marking the entrance to the rhino reserve and housed three Nepalese chatting beside a lamp. They asked where we were going. 'To Tiger Tops,' we replied. 'Is that far?' 'A few miles,' was their vague answer. 'Are there many tigers?' we asked, hoping these men would prove our encounter a nightmare. 'Oh, yes – plenty.' On this statement we pushed off in a hurry, still haunted by the beast we had met. It took us more than an hour in the dark forest to reach the banks of another river, the Reu. Stumbling in the mud, we forded the river, exhausted and tense, and on the other side we saw some pale lights. We had reached Tiger Tops.

'You were foolish to come on foot,' was one of the first comments we received, as covered with sweat and dirt from the drive, and more dirty than from a week in the camp, we were greeted by Chuck McDougal – an American anthropologist, a friend from Katmandu, and the new manager of Tiger Tops.

We had burst into a huge circular room whose vast conical thatched roof rose fifty feet above our heads. We were in an oasis of luxury, for one wall was lined with an elegant well-stocked bar, and vast chairs extended their arms, grouped around a massive central fireplace.

'Have a drink.' We had one, then another, then a few more. We had forgotten the taste of a cool drink; ice in camp had been only a dream and now it tinkled in our glasses. We wanted to arrange for a jeep to go out and collect Bob and Marie-Ange, but while we were making arrangements two headlights appeared and the truck rumbled up.

It takes a surprisingly short time to bridge the gap between diverse circumstances. Our camp and all its problems seemed far away. We could not believe that only yesterday we had slept on an unnamed beach deep in the Mahabharat range, up a gorge we were the first to explore, and now we revelled in the luxury of Tiger Tops, a hotel built for travellers who want to have a look at the teeming wildlife of Nepal without sacrificing their comfort. We felt at once out of place and at home.

Six or seven tourists had flown in that morning from Katmandu to Megauli. Now, before the fire, they were listening attentively to a lecture on the Royal Nepalese tigers given by the resident game expert, an Indian army major. We eavesdropped, learning more about our friend in the jungle. The tiger, I discovered, originally came from central Asia, but now it is found all over the Asian continent. As they moved southwest, they grew bigger and redder – the Royal Nepalese tigers being the longest, and the original Siberian model being fatter but shorter tailed. Short tails within a species is generally indicative of a cold climate, while the colouring bears some relation to the background. In Siberia, which is snow country, tigers are nearly white. The south-east Asian tiger is the smallest. There used to be thousands of tigers in Nepal only a few years back, but there may be only a few hundred left today. The reason for this is that the jungles are being destroyed, but faster than the jungles can disappear cattle are grazing the underbrush, thus eating the fodder of the deer that the tiger eats. Tigers, we now learned, are slow breeders – litters are of one or two cubs, rarely more, and at best a tigress may rear only two litters in her lifetime, which can span up to twenty years. Of these four young, maybe only two will live to become adult. The menace of extinction is tragic, for there is no arguing that the tiger, more so than the lion, is truly the king of beasts. Agile and powerful, tigers can lift in their mouths a small buffalo weighing some five hundred pounds, while they themselves weigh only six or seven hundred pounds.

Listening to the talk, I felt full of remorse at having partaken in a tiger shoot with Boris back in 1963. How things had changed since then – alas, not to the tiger's advantage. I also recalled the late Maharajah of Sarguja, who held the world record with 1777 dead tigers to his name. Today no one would dare mention such a sinister record, yet ten years ago it was considered a valid boast (the Maharajah's son was second with half that number). As I listened, I remembered all the tiger lore that I had learned in the company of Boris – busy writing up his experiences with man-eaters.

India and Nepal without tigers would never be the same. No animal holds such an important place in the myths and lore of the country, in fact in the minds of many people in the world. This noble beast stands for so much, probably because our subconscious is still haunted by some primeval fear of wild animals. Yet he is reduced to finding refuge in a few minute enclaves, of which Chitawan is possibly the largest and finest.

'We stake young buffalo all around Tiger Tops,' the lecturer continued, 'to attract the animals and in the hope of getting them accustomed to our presence.' Tigers for the tourists, I thought cynically, yet this was in fact their only and last chance, for the more people see them and get to know and admire them the better their chances of being protected and of surviving. In fact, Tiger Tops plays a considerable role in the protection of wildlife in Nepal. In the first place, it proves that tigers can be beneficial to the local economy as a tourist attraction and, secondly, the vested interests in this trade guarantees that game protection laws will be better enforced.

There was no electricity at Tiger Tops for fear a generator might frighten the animals, but there was every other modern convenience, and we spent the night in comfortable beds in one of the two houses on stilts that stood guard around the vast circular dining-hall. As I dozed off, my head full of tigers and, in particular, the one that had stared at us, I felt a fresh anguish on recalling that tomorrow we were to return to Daveghat and attempt to hover all the way back along the rivers through the jungle.

11 *Sandstorm*

All was dark as we left Tiger Tops at 5 a.m. We waved goodbye to Marie-Ange, whose journey with us ended here. If all went well, though, we trusted we might be back by the end of the day, having blazed a new trail along the rivers.

As the sun rose we took good note of a series of low hills that rose along the southern skyline. This outline would be our only landmark when it came to finding again this isolated spot. The trip down would be the first to require navigational skill, since we had not only to find the mouths of the Rapti and the Reu but also pick our way among the islands which dotted the delta-like course of the lower Kali Gandaki where it spread out on reaching the lowlands before crossing into India. This journey would also be our first down any long stretch of water not previously tackled upstream, which meant that we had no way of judging a rapid's strength until we started to go down it, by which time it would be too late to turn back if we encountered a waterfall or excessive turbulence. I tried to comfort myself by thinking that, as the river neared the plains, there should be fewer rapids and these should be less swift. Unfortunately, as we were soon to find out, rivers are not very logical things.

Going down meant we should also have to come back up, in all a total of some eighty-five miles – no small distance through virgin territory. Ever since leaving London, I had been haunted by the idea that some trivial accident might bring our expedition to an unexpected end, while we still had a long way to go to complete the task we had set ourselves: the crossing of the great snow ranges. I frequently found myself praying that while we were at Daveghat the General in Katmandu had not forgotten our case and was sorting things out with the Prime Minister. I was so worried about the ban on our approaching the northern frontiers that I could hardly enjoy our present activities. Our entire project now depended on this matter of a permit, since our expedition would lose much of its significance if we were unable to penetrate the high northern ranges.

For three hours we bumped over the wretched track back to Bharatpur, and all the way I was assailed by these thoughts, mirrored by the depressing scenery. My only consolation was that the terrible state of the road, which would be closed to motor traffic by the least rain, served to emphasize the value of hovercraft as a future means of communication. At 10 a.m., four and a half hours after leaving Tiger Tops, we at last reached our camp at Daveghat, and found all well with Nyma and Lhakpa in control. Our three craft were on the beach as we had left them, and in the mounting heat we busied ourselves with final adjustments, repairs and refuelling. We then loaded our craft to the limit with jerrycans and our water bottles – but, to save weight, no food. This meant Tiger Tops or bust, as we certainly could not afford to spend a night on some crocodile-ridden sandbank.

We eventually set off at twelve. One behind the other, we roared down the Marsyandi, joined the Kali Gandaki, and then headed due south on the mighty combined flow of the two rivers. Although the current was swift there were no breakers on the surface, and for the first three or four miles we raced along at nearly thirty miles an hour. Narayanghat soon came in sight, its dilapidated houses backed against the riverbank, and a large crowd appeared, attracted by the noise.

Below the town we hit the first rapids, several wide sloping ramps of foamy water over which we rattled like a car running over a corrugated surface. On our right ran a long ridge of hills parallel to the river, disappearing below the horizon ahead. To our left was a steep bank, above which extended jungle and the flat alluvial plain of the Rapti, across which we had driven that morning. Every few hundred yards we ran into more shallow rapids, while the riverbanks rose half a mile apart on either side of us enclosing boulder and sand beds, the home of numerous crocodiles and the roost of aquatic birds, among which Michael spotted some black-headed ibis, with their crooked beaks, and several varieties of egret.

As we progressed a strong wind began to race up-river towards us. It got stronger and stronger, slowing us down so that we had to bunch together and crouch behind our small canopies to make headway when we were unable to hug the shelter of the riverbanks. These tricks soon proved useless, for a regular storm was coming up from the southern plains. It was the 'Loo', a famous hot wind from India which drove sand and water in our faces. Even going downhill with full throttle we made hardly any headway, so that eventually I decided to pull up for fear of our engines overheating. Standing still, we experienced the full force of the gales, and looking south we saw the entire sky blurred with great clouds of sand and flying grit. The sand of the beach was running madly through our legs while wind howled in our ears. A few dark-skinned boys soon appeared along the top of the embankment, staring at us dully. I tried to ask how far we had gone but could not make myself understood, so we decided to push off again. With engines at full blast we remained under hump, travelling only at the speed of the current, and even slower at times.

Only the shelter of high banks allowed us to gather a little speed, but as we rounded a bend we were struck once again by the full force of the wind and blinded by the sand. As we went down the fast, shallow rapids the spray was lifted from the crests of the waves and hurled in our faces, while steering became very difficult because we were advancing crabwise with little or no control over our craft. I thought it was useless to carry on like this, for the engines were bound to overheat and seize up. The horizon was by now dark with flying sand as we entered a large rapid whose waves were as big as any we had encountered. With difficulty I managed to steer clear of the largest waves, using my weight rather than the rudder to counteract the drift caused by the wind, and in this way did make some progress.

I saw Bob behind me, crouched behind his windshield. Then, as he rattled over the big rapid, his thrust propeller exploded and he drifted ashore. Michael and I pulled up a little lower down upon a beach with a few huts, and Bob came down to meet us. We discussed what we should do.

As the storm was continuing I felt it was useless to go on, for the little headway we were making hardly justified the petrol we were using and we still had far to go. After giving Bob a hand replacing his fan-blades we all took shelter in one of the huts. We noticed that we were at a ferry-crossing and that on the beach a boat was being built, axe-hewn from fine red boards of sal wood. A large crowd gathered about us and a young man came up and explained in broken English, 'I was very afraid, very afraid when I see you.' His sentiment seemed to be shared by the onlookers, who had not yet made head or tail of our monstrous machines that had roared out of the storm on to their beach.

I anxiously asked in my poor Nepalese how long such storms usually lasted, for we had been gone two hours, and the dry wind did little to alleviate the heat, although the sun barely shone through the dust-filled sky. No one could give us an answer, although we learned that this wind was a daily occurrence in the dry season. The Loo is caused by the hot expanding air of the Indian plains rushing into the cool hills. It is difficult to describe this desiccating hurricane: it would shrivel a flower in a matter of minutes.

Cowering in the hut, we felt like ancient mariners weathering a gale in some lost harbour. This storm upset all our plans, and we wondered now whether we could make it down before dark, for we still had over twenty-five miles to go along the most difficult stretch where we should have to pick a course among the islands and make certain we did not miss the low main entrance of the Rapti river. This was going to be difficult, as the river itself kept dividing and branching off only to merge again into one flow, so that we should have no means of recognizing what was a lateral branch of the main river and what was a tributary. We learned that the ferrymen never travelled up or down the river at this season, for no part is deep enough to float a boat and the water often barely covers the boulders. Unlike the river at Chatra, the Gandaki reaches the edge of the plains while still travelling at a good speed, as its wide alluvial bed below the Mahabharat range is relatively steep.

Michael and I had a slight argument about whether we should set out. Optimistically I hoped for the wind to lessen, while Michael felt that any progress was better than none. Eventually we decided to wait half an hour more, during which time the wind kept up its infernal din, while the hills to the north remained blurred.

Such were the conditions when we strode back to our craft. Thanks to the shelter of the crowd, which followed our every step, we were able to refill our fuel tanks without letting in too much sand. We then set off, hoping for the best.

After a lot of trouble for the first mile, the wind abated a little and we were able to go over hump. Ahead, the river was wide and powerful, then it split up into mere rivulets that bounded down long, even inclines around sandbanks. Soon we reached the first large islands. From our low level it became difficult to tell mainland from islands, and to make matters worse I soon found myself steering up a dead end when the branch of the river I had been following proved to be a backwater. We all stopped to look round and noticed that the wind had practically dropped. To our right stretched a huge patch of jungle which we believed to be a large island. To the left in the distance we could see the tree-crested outline of another embankment. Was this the mainland or another island? Between the two stretched a small desert of sand and gravel a mile wide, through which we felt must run the main arm of the river, though it was hidden from our view.

Looking north, we glimpsed one of the most breathtaking views we had seen. Across the horizon stretched the massive green Mahabharat range and, rising high above it, the white pinnacles of the great Himalayan range, with Annapurna and Machupuchari raising their icy pillars to a blue sky. It was a majestic sight that brought home our staggering presumption

Mount Dhaulagiri at sunrise.

Above left: monkeys were our frequent spectators in southern Nepal.
Above Right: a yak, our only rival
a means of transport in northern
Nepal. Left: a rhino in his natural
home, the elephant grass on the
banks of the Reu river.

in hoping to blaze a new trail right across the heart of this vertical continent, the greatest barrier on earth. So far, in spite of all our troubles, we had at least succeeded in crossing the first and easier half, for we were now nearly on the Indian frontier and had already driven from here across the Mahabharat range a few days previously. All that remained for us to do was carry on through the middle hill area of Nepal and then, hopefully, up the Kali Gandaki's secret route right through the great peaks via the Himalayan breach. How appealing was the snow seen from the suffocating lowlands! Our minds and bodies thirsted for it. Yet there was this ominous official decision to ban us from trying. I wondered again if we would ever be allowed to see the great peaks at close range.

In the meantime we were literally at a dead end. We started the engines, and Bob shot ahead and missed what I guessed to be the way out down a lateral arm of the river. I stopped to wave at Bob, as separation could prove dangerous on this vast river. Resuming once more, I skidded across the water, at times shooting over sandbanks, going from land to water at full speed and in the air. Suddenly Bob saw before him the beady eyes of a crocodile and its great snout. Unable to avoid it, he bounced over the monster, leaving it to ponder what had happened.

On either side of us rose flocks of birds, disturbed by the noise, as we entered an ornithologist's paradise of reeds and water. I began to think that we were probably lost when, looking east, I recognized the low characteristic skyline of hills that marked the heart of the Chitawan reserve. Hugging what I believed to be the left bank of the Kali Gandaki, we ran into a tributary, but I could not tell whether this was the Rapti or just a branch of the Gandaki. A fisherman stood on the shore so I drove up to ask him where the Rapti lay. The man pointed downstream. We carried on and soon came to a wide shallow strip of water branching off on our left. This I assumed to be the Rapti. We now sped over mud and sandbank up its shallow bed bordered on either side by dense jungle. Three or four miles upstream we ran into a herd of many cattle drinking in the river. At this spot a mud-clogged tributary branched off to

G.H.P.   M the right; this, I thought, should be the Reu. At its deepest there were only six inches of water running over weeds and branch-littered mudbanks. In the middle of one of these Michael's engine stalled, and we pulled up to help him get it started. Our craft now became very difficult to control over mud and we skidded dangerously close to lethal branches of driftwood. This reminded me of my puncture on the Muga back in Spain, which I did not want to happen again, so we advanced very slowly until we got the feel of steering over mud. On either side rose the jungle, although to our left this was interspersed with wide fields of reed-like elephant grass. There was no doubt we were in rhino country. I prayed that our engines would not die on us now, leaving us stranded in this rhino and crocodile haven. We carried on for several miles and I was beginning to worry whether we were on the right arm of the river when all of a sudden I saw the large thatched roof of the first of the buildings of Tiger Tops. We had arrived, and in no time the bank was clustered with friends. We dragged our craft up the embankment of elephant grass, and while we shook each other's hand a Japanese tourist stared amazed and un-comprehending at seeing a hovercraft for the first time in his life in what he had probably seen advertised as the most isolated corner of jungle in Nepal.

Never was a drink better earned, and we did full justice to Chuck McDougal's hospitality. We could not believe that we had left only that morning. The harrowing trip downriver and the nervous tension involved had made the day feel like a week, yet it was only four-thirty and, in spite of being delayed by the sandstorm, we had reached Tiger Tops from our camp in considerably less time than the overland drive had taken. Only one question remained unanswered: would we be able to travel back up the river the following day?

For the moment we were too happy to bother, and sat with our drinks gazing into the elephant grass on the other side of the river, where – so we were told – the last of Nepal's great one-horned rhinoceros were to be found. Dusk fell with its habitual speed as wild birds rose from the marshy riverbanks. We all retired to the vast conical central house where we were served an early dinner. The talk as usual was about tigers and rhinos. In our euphoria we speculated wildly on how hovercraft could change the area by providing a better and more efficient means of guarding the game reserve from poachers and illegal grazing.

We were about to attack a very English pudding when suddenly the screen door of the dining-hall burst open. A dark Nepalese ran into the room and went over to the bar, and a hushed phrase ran like wildfire round the room – 'There has been a kill!'

A report had come in that one of the buffaloes staked out in the jungle as tiger bait had been found dead. The tiger, everyone knew, would return by night to feed on its prey. With a little luck, we might be able to see the beast as it came back to eat. Everyone present (some seven people) got up and began to speak in whispers. Flashlights were handed out, and instructions given that we walk in silence behind the game warden, who would lead us to the top of a ridge from which, thanks to a battery-powered spotlight, we might be able to see the tiger.

In a matter of minutes we were tiptoeing through the dark, our flashlights shielded by our hands. The tension of knowing that here somewhere very close lurked a tiger was almost palpable. Once again all the fantasies conjured up by the name 'tiger' filled our minds.

Every shadow, every tree now had eyes and stripes. Slowly climbing up an embankment, we reached a little hut, a blind set upon the lip of a ravine. Down below, a few yards away, the tiger might be at its kill. We waited in silence, the shikari scanning the dark, ears alert for a tell-tale noise. We all peered through the little holes in the hut's walls in keen anticipation. At that moment our hearts leaped as there was a flash in the sky and a great crash. It was the first onslaught of a tropical storm. Suddenly it was pouring, while a lightning flash lit up the post and broken rope below us where a few hours earlier a young buffalo had been tied prior to being killed by the tiger.

In dead silence we listened to the staccato of rain upon the leaves and the damp earth as the downpour watered the parched soil. The storm was magnificent, but the tiger did not appear. In the end, disappointed, we made our way back. As consolation we were promised we should see a rhinoceros the following day.

It was ten o'clock when we returned. For us it had been a long day. Exhausted, I fell asleep to visions of sandbanks, rapids and burning sun. Secretly I longed for the eternal snows.

12 *The Heavy Brigade*

The great Indian rhinoceros is one of the mightiest beasts in the world. A prehistoric relic walking on three toes, it belongs to that rare family of animals known as 'odd-toe ungulates' and which includes the horse and ant-eaters. Like most of the great prehistoric monsters the rhinoceros is a timid beast when not provoked, and entirely herbivorous. The stretch of swampland between the Rapti rivers just in front of Tiger Tops is one of its favourite haunts. Not so long ago, these great beasts roamed about in large herds. Yet in 1958 their number in Nepal was estimated to be only 300. By 1962 that count was down to 185. The most recent census made by helicopter gives their number in Nepal as some eighty animals, while there are about half as many left in India. The great Indian rhino may well be extinct in a few years.

The reason for their disappearance is twofold. Like the deer on which tigers feed, they see their pastures reduced every year by cattle grazing on their territory, but their worst and most wicked enemies are poachers. These fine animals are the victims of lust – mainly Chinese lust – the reason being that for centuries an old wives' tale has it that their horn when ground to powder and ingested is a powerful aphrodisiac. The greatest consumers of this presumed aphrodisiac are the Chinese who, to quote Prince Philip, are 'a race whose statistics alone prove that they do not need any.' Alas, the rhino horn is still very much in demand, so much so that a native poacher in the Chitawan area will be offered 30,000 rupees (3500 dollars) for just one horn. This sum of money represents a fortune by local standards – three to four years' salary, even more. And thus the great beasts are tracked down and ruthlessly killed. The irony is that rhino horn is not a horn at all, but a protuberance of densely matted hair. As for its aphrodisiac qualities, they have yet to be proved. Such is man's greed that very soon there may not be one rhino left, and then the whole world will deplore its loss, including the impotent clients who have brought about its extinction.

In the meantime, conservationists are putting their heads together to see how to protect them. There are strict laws against cattle grazing on the reserve, but these laws have not been rigorously enforced for years. Permission has now been given to the wardens to shoot rhino poachers on sight, yet even such a drastic measure has not deterred the boldest, lured by the thought of the colossal financial reward. Complete fencing of the reserve has been suggested, but this is too costly. Besides, what fence could contain man?

At eight-thirty, five elephants lumbered on to the grounds of Tiger Tops to take us out into the jungle in search of rhinos. One by one we clambered aboard, sitting in crude howdahs, wooden railed platforms chained on to the backs of the elephants. Some of these animals were on lease from the elephant farm of the King of Nepal, which is located some twenty miles east of Tiger Tops.

It was a change to be riding elephants after driving our little machines. An elephant will go practically anywhere, even through trees, which if need be he will uproot to pass. There are only two things that an elephant cannot do. One is that he will never go into a swamp. Indeed, an elephant's fear of muddy, spongy ground is so great that if he begins to sink he will panic and even grasp his riders and shove them underfoot with his trunk. His fear is justified, for an elephant that falls into quicksand knows a most atrocious death, as he can survive for hours breathing with his trunk raised once his body is entirely submerged. The other thing an elephant cannot do is jump. Not even one inch. The particular bone structure of an elephant's legs, which are set vertically into the pelvis, something like human legs, together with the form of the ligaments of the foot and toe, do not allow them to spring upwards at all.

Thus an elephant cannot cross a ditch if it is a few inches wider than his stride (six or seven feet) and he can take no hurdles, however low. But this does not stop him from running through the thickest vegetation and manœuvring in tight spots. In Bhutan, which today has in its southern jungles the greatest concentration of pachyderms in Asia, elephants are found up to five, six and even ten thousand feet in the hills, a good proof of their agility. Elephants are generally good mountaineers – witness Hannibal's elephants crossing the Alps. An elephant also crossed the entire Himalayas from India to Lhasa – as a present to the Dalai Lama; it is now still there, in the custody of the Chinese Communists.

The soft padding under an elephant's foot is remarkably adaptable and moulds delicately to any object on which it steps. Those who believe that elephants are clumsy are greatly mistaken. An elephant is very agile, and steps softly. They are also quick – far quicker than a tiger. This has been proved many times when tigers have charged elephants. When the two fight, the elephant always wins, for before the tiger knows it he finds himself being hurled through the air to his death or crushed under the hind foot of the elephant, who can whirl round at lightning speed.

Few animals have so many odd characteristics. For one, his brains are not in his head, or at least not in what looks like his great skull, which is made only of spongy bone; the famed brains of the elephant are in fact much smaller and are set at the top of the nose. Their legendary intelligence can be doubted, although their memory is made all the more impressive by the fact that elephants can live to be a hundred, and generally live to be well over sixty, even when domesticated. The elephant also has a secret which it took zoologists years to solve, and that is where he stores water; he has a kind of water reserve that can be extracted from the mouth at need by way of the trunk. Five times in his long life he will grow new teeth (molars) at the ages of 2, 6, 9, 25 and 60. The hide is so tender that a horse-fly will draw blood, and elephants are exceedingly sensitive – the slightest cut will make them scream with pain.

Such were the beasts upon which we lumbered across the Reu river into the tall elephant grass (which elephants do not eat but in which tigers and rhinos love to seek shelter). Five abreast in a great arc, the elephants advanced, giving us an excellent view of the jungle. We soon came upon small barking deer which scattered out of sight. The size of a large dog, they get their name from the barking sound they emit. That morning we were in luck, for we also saw some spotted deer and several large swamp deer. We did not, however, see any nilgai, the tall horse-like deer very common in these parts. No wonder tigers loved Tiger Tops, with so much food on the hoof, not to mention the buffaloes staked out to attract them! Michael was delighted, but I wanted to see a rhino. Fortunately I was not alone, for with us were some Japanese, come to make a documentary film on Nepal with the Government's blessing. This decided Chuck to press on with our search. For two hours we paced slowly through the tall elephant grass until we came upon a huge heap of rhinoceros dung. A rhinoceros tends to go and relieve itself at the same place, and this orderly habit of theirs is one of their downfalls, for poachers lie in waiting near these dung heaps. When a rhino approaches the heap (backwards) it presents an easy target and is shot. In his desperate efforts to stop the poaching of rhinos, John Blower, the United Nations wildlife expert, came up with a highly original idea. He suggested jokingly that all rhinos be captured and have their horns removed and replaced by plastic ones. Such an operation sounds ridiculous, but sadly it may yet well be the only way to save these creatures from extinction.

As we rode through the jungle I reflected how animals have become things of the past. Today they are often at best only curios, bits of history destined to recall in us that ancient thrill from the time when beasts were our true rivals. To get this feeling, it is now necessary to go to such places as the Chitawan reserve, and it is perhaps significant that all over the world game reserves have replaced cultural festivals as an experience in past values, as crowds come flocking to these animal shows. The true reason why Bob and Michael and I were present with other tourists at Tiger Tops was to titillate our imaginations, to set in motion dormant terrors, to stir up a thousand years of genetic reflexes and lost cellular reactions, to reactivate our hereditary fear of wild beasts, and to recognize that we had all once shared nature on an equal footing with other living things.

The elephants came to a sudden stop. Standing on the head of his mount, a mahout pointed into the tall reedy grass. 'Rhino,' someone whispered. The elephant next to ours pawed the ground. He too knew ancestral fear. Before us, the grass swayed. Our elephants began to fidget. With great blows of a steel prodder on his head, another elephant was driven forward. We now formed a ring around the invisible rhino. I heard a grunt, then our elephant backed a few steps as out burst a furious snorting beast. Skin rumpled like armour, a grotesque skull ending in a single menacing horn, a rhino appeared. Ten thousand years of evolution and two tons of flesh standing on three toes stood before us. It charged one of the elephants, then swerved past the one we were riding before stopping short just behind it. Never before had I realized how big rhinos were. What mobility for weight, what a frightening reminder that here on earth there are other wills than our own! Having escaped the peril of the ring of elephants, the rhino now trotted off slowly, disdainfully assured of the superiority of its fearful horn, ironically his one great asset which is also the reason for his downfall.

After following another rhinoceros through the tall grass we eventually returned to Tiger Tops. It was nearly midday, and much as we should have liked to stay for ever in the comfort of the lodge we knew we had to leave, and that nearly fifty miles of turbulent water awaited us on our way back to camp. A small crowd waved when, having refuelled, we set off slowly, floating over the mud of the Reu river, gliding between the elephant grass that lined the banks where in the heat of the day rhinos and tigers were sleeping. Slowly we slid ever deeper into the Garden of Eden of lower Nepal, from the Reu into the Rapti river, before striking the great aquatic universe of the sprawling Gandaki. Here we began our laborious climb up the hundreds of rapids which we had shot down the day before. Although not very rough, these rapids were so extensive that it took all the power we had to climb against the current. Slowly we headed north towards the distant mountains, leaving behind the humid jungles. Where the Rapti had joined the Gandaki we had been within six miles from the Indian border! I prayed that soon we might be allowed to proceed north to within the same distance of Tibet.

As we travelled, we kept watching for crocodiles, and also – vainly – for another large beast, not a reptile, one of the most amazing of all animals and believed to be the most intelligent: the dolphin. Dolphins in the Himalayas over 1500 miles from the sea may sound ridiculous to those who know them exclusively as marine animals. Few people are aware that in India are found the freshwater Gangetic dolphins, close cousins of the sea dolphins. They are as large as sea dolphins and come in two varieties similar in appearance to the common dolphin, while a third variety has a flat rounded nose like that of a small whale. These dolphins can be seen far up the Ganges, and there is no reason why they should never have gone up its large tributaries such as the Kali Gandaki. In the end, though, we saw none, and it may be that they never enter the cold waters of the hills, or perhaps the water level was now too low for their great bulk.

All went well on the journey up until three hundred yards below our camp, where both my lift and thrust blades broke as the result of a bolt coming loose. When we had replaced the blades we returned to camp, our mission along the lower Gandaki having been a complete success. From the point where we had stopped north of the Mahabharat range down to Tiger Tops, we had travelled over eighty-five miles (more than half-way across Nepal), crossing at speed a rugged hill and mountain region with no roads. We had travelled this distance faster than was ever previously possible. I now felt confident that the lessons we had learned could one day be put to good use in this or other similar inaccessible areas of the world. We now knew that it was possible to travel over the turbulent rivers all the way from central Nepal to the sea, for none of the lower rivers of the great Indian plains present obstacles comparable to those we had overcome.

We rejoiced also because, thanks to our machines, we had been able to acquaint ourselves in a short time with a variety of Nepal's flora and fauna and peoples. To cover the same distance on foot would have taken very much longer. By travelling along the rivers we had also been able to witness the slow transformation of nature from the edge of the sultry plains through the deep gorges of the ravined hills. Now we wanted only to complete our plans and cross the other half of Nepal from the middle hills to beyond the great snow peaks. There we knew a whole new world awaited us – and also new dangers – icy cold, rapid waters in which to overturn could mean instant death.

Before breaking camp and returning to Katmandu we decided to spend a day exploring the Marsyandi river, up which we had proceeded only a little way the day after our arrival. So we prepared our craft again for this journey, after which we ate a large meal prepared for our return by Nyma and Lhakpa. It was a grand meal of rice, curry and chicken, which we shared with a one-armed holy man whom Bob had befriended the day Michael and I went up the Kali Gandaki. He was a strange character who spoke a few words of English and claimed to be in charge by royal consent of a holy shrine at Daveghat, and which he was enlarging to receive pilgrims and to start an ashram. We learned from him of the great market festival held every September at the confluence of the two rivers, to which come thousands of people from the hills and plains. These crowds camped, so we were told, upon the vast stony beach near where we had set up our tents. This market is one of several held at the foot of the Himalayas which provide the inhabitants of the hills with their only contact with those people of the great plains. The origins of these fairs are lost in antiquity, but they have always played a considerable part in the exchange not only of goods but of ideas, and in their dissemination throughout Central Asia.

The next morning, rising early, we prepared to travel up the

Marsyandi. We planned to travel only thirty miles upstream and if possible visit villages inhabited by the rare Bot or Maji people. We had already had the good fortune to meet at our camp two Maji women, a young girl and her stout mother, since they were employed by the Brahmins of Daveghat to tend their cattle. Both had spent a good deal of time with us, smoking our cigarettes and pestering us to be allowed to keep some of our old food and oil cans, already the envy of nearly all the local villagers. It was easy for us to forget how precious to some people are those shiny smooth little cylinders that we would throw away. The making of suitable containers is one of the major problems of primitive peoples, and these are generally their most important manufactured objects. Here at Daveghat only three types of container were known: empty calabash pods, and earthen or copper pots, both these last being expensive and heavy. Glass is nowhere found in rural Nepal, while wooden barrels or buckets are encountered only in the far north along the Tibetan border.

The Dunwar, Maji and Darai tribesmen, collectively known as Bots, live by fishing, settled in minute villages on the riverbanks, often close to Magar and Gurung communities. The Darais, who now number only some 1500, live mostly on the banks of the lower Gandaki and on the edge of the Rapti in the Chitawan reserve.

Since our arrival odd encounters had enabled us to witness the nautical skill of the Maji, in their slim, elegant dug-out canoes. What is unusual is their special way of propelling their dug-out. There will be two men, one who will sit at the stern, the other at the bow, and both let one leg dangle over the side. With their legs in rhythm like oars, they paddle or push their craft over the shallow rivers. To see these canoes 'walk' in this way is a very strange sight.

There was little doubt in our minds that the first inhabitants of these gorges were members of these three ancient river tribes. In appearance we thought they looked similar to the fishermen we had encountered at Tribeni. One of the best indications to their ancient origin and right to be called one of the aboriginal populations of Nepal is that they depend entirely on the rivers for survival and have never taken to agriculture. Another indication of their very ancient origin is the fact that they possess no linguistic link with the other tribes of known foreign origin, nor even with the indigenous Tharus of the terrain. Masters of the rivers, they have lost out today to the wealthier agricultural settlers, and their slow disappearance is no doubt a result of their failure to adapt to another, more profitable way of life. Adaptation, which is essential for survival, is also the hallmark of intelligence. Are the Bots less intelligent? It was not for us to judge.

Going up the swift Marsyandi once again, we were able to note how practice had now made us masters in the art of shooting up rapids. However, twenty miles from camp, I ran into trouble once again with the bottom structure of my craft and reluctantly had to stay behind to repair it, while Michael and Bob pushed on into the Mahabharat range. On their way they passed a large village, then penetrated deep jungle. After crossing several large rapids they came upon a community of grey langurs, tall slim monkeys with a characteristic lion-like mane of nearly black hair around their heads. Numbers of these monkeys watched while other members of the family sat unperturbed by the waterside looking like holidaymakers.

It is only recently that the noted zoologist E. P. Gee discovered in the jungles of Bhutan a new species known as the 'golden' langur, which has a gold-white coat. The most common variety of monkey in Nepal is the Rhesus monkey. These creatures have little to fear as they are considered sacred, for the monkey god, Hanuman, is one of the most famous divinities of Hinduism. The monkey's only true enemies are the numerous cats of the country. There are over nine different types of feline in Nepal, not counting the tiger, but it is rare to see any of them as they are discreet, silent, nocturnal animals. Indeed, the Nepalese civet cats are hardly larger than our own domestic pets. The most beautiful and dangerous cats are of course the leopards or panthers, some of which are black, while the biggest are the large, pale spotted snow-leopards who live in the high northern mountains where they prey on wild sheep.

Leopards are generally considered a much greater menace to man and cattle than tigers. Like tigers, they occasionally become man-eaters when lame or too old to catch other game. Because of their cunning, leopards who become man-eaters are far more dangerous and difficult to track down. They have little fear of man and often live near densely populated areas. Only fifteen years ago, Boris used to see leopards in the immediate suburbs of Katmandu, where they thrived on eating chickens and stray dogs.

Carrying on up the Marsyandi, Michael and Bob came to its junction with the Modi river, where they decided to turn back. In the meantime, surrounded by half-naked Dunwars, I repaired my craft. Then we all returned to base camp.

There we got busy making arrangements to return to Katmandu. That evening we began dismantling our craft. It was with regret that we were leaving this beautiful spot from where we had spent so many exciting hours travelling the great rivers. On the other hand, Nyma and Lhakpa were only too happy to leave; having lived most of their lives at 11,000 feet near Everest in the high, cool mountains, they had suffered more than we had from the extreme heat.

The following morning I set off towards Narayanghat on foot in search of transport. This proved difficult, for there were no trucks in sight. For hours I roamed the streets, running towards any vehicle I could see, only to discover that it was either out of order or already had a cargo.

In the meantime the deputy district commissioner was paying a visit – alas, too late – to our camp, in the hope of seeing our machines. On his way back he brought Bob and Michael, so that we spent the rest of the stifling day hunting trucks together. It was very late when we managed to lay our hands on a vehicle and persuade its driver to take us to Daveghat, where most of our equipment was loaded before nightfall.

13 *In the Year 2028*

Dawn was breaking when we rumbled away from Daveghat the next morning, leaving behind us the tropical world of the great jungles. At ten o'clock that night we drove into Katmandu, and a new phase of our journey was under way. After a day's rest, we began tackling the problem of getting our permits to proceed into the great northern ranges. Hastily I called General Surendra, believing that during our two weeks' absence he would have been able to contact the Prime Minister and straighten out matters with him personally.

My heart sank when I heard the General's pessimistic tones on the phone, and I soon gathered he had not been able to get in touch with the Prime Minister and that we were still therefore forbidden to proceed. We were requested nevertheless to send a complete report of what we had done and seen to the Government who, however unco-operative, were apparently keen to find out how our machines had operated. Not knowing by whom and for what reason our project was being stalled, we could only make wild, unproductive guesses. I felt embarrassed to bother the General further. He looked pale and disheartened and was, in fact, very ill. It seemed he could do little for us now, yet without him there was nothing we could do but wait.

The General again promised that he would see the Prime Minister, but the Prime Minister always appeared to have other matters on hand. Try as we would, we were getting nowhere, and I was now faced with the grim prospect of failure. What made matters worse was the fact that now at last we felt confident in our machines and were prepared to attack the worst rapids. With success so close at hand, it was disheartening not to be allowed for political reasons to make an attempt to cross the greater Himalayas. Several other travellers explained to us sympathetically that they too had run into similar problems about permits, but we found little solace in their tales. George Schaller, the famous American naturalist and the author of a number of important works on natural history, had been studying the various types of sheep and goat to be found in the highland areas; he told us that he had just been sent back in disgrace for straying a short distance beyond the limit of his permit. In desperation we asked at least to be able to run our craft on the Bhagmati, the river that cuts through the valley of Katmandu, and also requested permission to travel up the northern sections of the Sun Khosi and the Indrawati, two rivers which we could easily reach from Katmandu in three hours by truck along the Chinese Highway that led to Tibet. But even these permits were not forthcoming, despite promises that they might be.

The accumulation of fatigue from our journeys, now aggravated by frustrating delays, began to try our nerves. Bob was particularly restless, as he contemplated the fact that he would be obliged to return to Spain before the onset of summer. Marie-Ange, whose passion for hovercraft and interest in our project had dwindled since her stay at our camp, was pressing that she and Bob should use their time to greater advantage than by sitting around in Katmandu waiting for a permit that both of them felt we would never get. This opinion, I saw to my dismay, was shared by several people in the valley. Only the British Ambassador stood by us with advice to be patient. Unfortunately we had little patience left as we saw the monsoon drawing ever nearer – and with it the end of our project.

It was a severe blow to us when Bob announced that he was tired of waiting and was setting off for a short trek north of Katmandu with Marie-Ange, after which he planned to go to India and buy material for his boutique.

After ten more days of waiting I too began to lose heart. It was Michael, generally so pessimistic, who now came to my aid. 'We should stay and fight for the permit and finish

A frieze wall lines the ancient trade route through the Himalayas, for centuries the only access to Tibet. Below: a salt caravan coming down from Tibet.

At Tukutcha (8250 ft) our hovercraft is surrounded by admirers who have never even seen a bicycle before.

what we came to do,' he declared. And so we began a campaign to be allowed to proceed with the experiment it had originally been agreed we should carry out.

We sat down and wrote a letter to the Prime Minister outlining our intentions and stressing what we had so far accomplished and what we saw as the benefits accruing to Nepal from our project. This letter we handed over to the Prime Minister's office, yet days passed and we received no answer. Telephone calls received only evasive replies. To make matters worse, it began to rain, and not only had we no news of our permits, but we were still being refused permission to use our craft in Katmandu.

Fortunately we had several friends to comfort us, and in the back of my mind I still hoped against hope that we might eventually be allowed to proceed. Unable to face the thought that we might never be allowed to go, I decided to appeal directly to His Majesty the King of Nepal. This I did in a letter, setting out all the facts concerning our project. Here again, we received no reply.

Why? To this day we don't know for certain. Desperate, I resolved to accept defeat and leave, but Michael insisted that we persevere a little longer. In the meantime we decided to drive up the Sun Khosi along the Chinese road to the Tibetan border, to have a last look at a Nepalese river. It was a pitiful letdown to have to hire a taxi like ordinary tourists and look at the rivers from the road along their banks while our machines sat idle in the grounds of our hotel.

All the same, the journey was instructive, and took our minds off our worries. We drove out of the Katmandu valley and headed east, to a village called Dhaulaghat, where the Sun Khosi coming from Tibet and the Indrawati coming from the Helambu range meet. Here the Chinese had built a large steel bridge for their new road, the only one in Nepal to penetrate right into the high mountains. It is a fantastic route, whose extensions lead all the way to Peking via Tibet, the only link for vehicles between China and the West. The economic and historical interest of the road is considerable, but unfortunately political considerations render it useless since no foreigners are allowed to drive into China. Nevertheless, it is today physically possible to drive from Paris to Lhasa, and from there on to Peking.

The only people to use the road are those privileged Nepalese traders who have maintained shops in Lhasa where, prior to the Chinese occupation, a vast Nepalese community of merchants and artisans had thrived. Famous among these was the Newar family of Dhakwa, merchants of Marco Polo's calibre, who still traded with Tibet in such romantic goods as silks and musk. Musk is the malodorous gland of the tiny fanged musk deer, and an essential product for the perfume industry. Today musk is worth more than its weight in gold, and it seems strange that our modern Western world still needs such a seemingly odd product. In exchange for musk, the Chinese import from Nepal a great deal of sugar, grain and kerosene – goods which it is easier for them to bring from Nepal than to import overland all the way from China.

Along the road we encountered many Chinese engineers and workmen, all wearing the characteristic Mao cap and blue overalls. Driving alongside the upper section of the Sun Khosi afforded us an interesting view of how this river rises in steps from 2500 feet at Dhaulaghat to 6500 feet at the border – the lowest border between Nepal and Tibet. We estimated the first stage of some twenty miles would be relatively easy to negotiate by hovercraft. This meant that, with a good reserve of petrol, one could drive by hovercraft all the way up from Calcutta to Nepal, past Chatra and our old camp at Tribeni, then up to Dhaulaghat and beyond, to within ten miles of Tibet! The last few miles before the border were too steep for any machine, as here the water rushed down in leaps and bounds over steps some ten to thirty feet high.

At the border our taxi came to a halt where a bridge spanned the river, now reduced to a small bounding strip of foam. On the other side of the bridge stood two very martial-looking armed Chinese guards, a reminder that they had 'liberated' Tibet. For me it was a sad sight; over the past years I had witnessed the tragedy of the Tibetan people, whose way of life and ancestral culture has been destroyed in favour of an alien political system imposed by Tibet's traditional enemy – China. However beneficial Communism may be to Tibet in economic terms, however backward Tibet may have appeared by the dubious economic and technological standards of our modern world, the Chinese have no right to force their system on the Tibetans. China's invasion of Tibet in 1950 was clearly against the wishes of all Tibetans, not only of the haughty lords and rich lamas but of the simple people who constituted the 'people's associations' that in 1959 called for the expulsion of the Chinese. It is these same people who furnished the soldiers of the rebel forces that since 1950 have resisted the Chinese through guerrilla warfare. Sadly enough, far too few people know anything about the true situation in Tibet and consequently the entire world has stood by, indifferent to the country's plight. Many people believe that the Chinese were a blessing to feudal Tibet, forgetting that no nation is ready to accept military occupation by another race with an alien culture, however great may be the merits of this culture, and however good the occupiers' intentions.

Behind the Chinese guards at the frontier rose three structures in gaudy red and yellow covered in dragons in the style dear to Chinese restaurants. In a land of sober dignified architecture like Tibet these hideous buildings typified the difference between the two cultures. I turned away, and headed back to Katmandu. Not even the interesting data we gathered on the way about fishing techniques could cheer me up. I now accepted that I had gambled everything on this expedition, and had lost. My only consolation was that at Tribeni and Daveghat we had done our best, had spared no effort and run considerable danger in what had now proved an unsuccessful attempt to travel a completely new route across the world's most impressive mountains. Perhaps, I brooded, there was no longer room for adventure; Michael and I had acted throughout as private individuals, and the days of such disinterested initiative might well be over. A man today is too often judged only by what institution he represents, and we had no organization behind us. We felt alone and powerless.

If only the Prime Minister or the King had seen our machines! They could not have failed to be amazed, and might have appreciated what we had come to prove. But neither the Prime Minister's office nor the King's secretariat had paid any attention to us. Not one official, not even the General, had come to see our craft.

Patience is the virtue of the East, and I had become too Westernized. After all, we had only been waiting a little over two months for our permits, and what is two months east of Athens? Unfortunately, though, the monsoon would not wait and it was now May 24th. At best we might have three weeks' fair weather left before the rains.

'There was a call for you from General Surendra Shaha,' the receptionist of the Shankar Hotel advised me when I returned from an afternoon spent booking our tickets back to Europe the day after our visit to the Tibetan border. I immediately rang back. 'Can you give a little demonstration tomorrow?' said the voice of the General on the phone. 'Somewhere on the Bhagmati river. Make sure everything is ready, I will send my Land-Rover over at 9.30.' Without further explanation the General hung up. A demonstration for whom? I rushed with the news to Michael. 'What's the use?' Michael argued, cooling my own enthusiasm. 'Why should we put on a demonstration? We have been here for weeks and no one has even been interested enough to come and look at our machines.' That is to say, no one save Prince Basundhara, the late king's brother. I recalled his visit, and the disastrous demonstration. His Highness had stood near the craft that I had started on the lawn of the hotel. All had gone well except that when I slid off the grass (since it had not rained for some days) the entire garden of the hotel had filled with clouds of dust. An instant smokescreen had billowed round me, smothering everything and everybody. Eyes closed, I had hit a wall, bounced back and crept on to the lawn again. Ten minutes later, when the smoke cleared, Prince Basundhara was still there looking a little grey under a thick coat of dust as he choked violently, his face in his handkerchief. His Highness had, sportingly, pretended to be delighted, and we had downed several long drinks to clear our throats of dust.

The General soon rang back. 'The Prime Minister may be coming,' he announced. 'Take two machines along in case something goes wrong.' We began to panic. I recalled the Bañolas fiasco and wondered what would happen if our engines would not start. We rushed out to polish and oil and test our machines. Our hopes soared. The Prime Minister! We might now get our permits, anyway we were staying. We cancelled our reservations. Late that afternoon the General arrived in his car and took us out to inspect the site of the demonstration. We drove west of Katmandu down to the Bhagmati. At this time of year the river was practically dry, a series of wide sandbanks enclosing a weed-ridden central channel. There was just enough water to demonstrate the amphibious qualities of the machine, while a side stream would allow us to show how precisely the hovercraft could be steered.

'All set,' Michael said calmly as we went to bed. Those two words kept me awake all night.

Saturday, May 26th, of the year 2028, was a fine day, one we will never forget. If the Nepalese year 2028 is the equivalent of our year 1972, our Saturday has also to be reworked and is Sunday in Nepal. All the shops were closed and the offices empty, so that large crowds roamed the streets in a festive mood as we honked our way through the town, two of our hovercraft, fully inflated, swaying upon the roof of our car and Land-Rover.

We drove slowly past sacred cows, coolies and groups of gaily dressed women, swerving to avoid small children as we worked our way down to the river. We crossed it, then turned left towards Kiritpur, the town of the 'cut noses', at the foot of which sprawl the new buildings of Katmandu's first university. It was ten o'clock when we reached the appointed spot. The sun beat down through the cool morning air. When we arrived the riverbanks were deserted, save for little clusters of vultures hobbling around the carcases of dead dogs and the bloated remains of a sheep.

Perspiring and nervous, we carried our craft down to a strip of sand on the water's edge. While doing so, I noticed that one of the craft had a puncture and, to the accompaniment of a sinister little whistling sound, was slowly losing air. We reckoned, nevertheless, that if we pumped it up just before setting off we could still use the machine.

Anxiously we paced up and down the beach beside our craft. Already we had attracted a small crowd of passers-by. Just to make sure everything was all right, we decided to try the engines. It was a good thing we did, for as I pulled at the cord of the first one the starter-rope, which we had carefully checked the preceding day, snapped. We replaced the cord – a tricky operation involving an oily ungovernable spring – and then started the other machine. Again, the same thing happened. It was sabotage, we felt, as we replaced the rope with our last spare cord.

At half-past ten no one had yet appeared. I felt as if on the eve of an examination, for there was no possible doubt that the entire future and success of our enterprise depended on this demonstration. Or so at least we naïvely believed, for we thought the Prime Minister would have either to give us a permit or an explanation.

We had agreed that I should pilot the craft, while Michael explained its finer points and underlined our objectives and ambitions to the Prime Minister. We were discussing all this between ourselves when the General's car pulled up and out strode our patron, looking pale. This was despite the flowered hat on his head, a traditional Nepalese cap, but which, instead of being black, was spattered with elaborate pink and blue flowery designs. We had so far been given no details of who would actually be present at the demonstration and, seeing the General alone, we feared that it might have been called off. But he confirmed that all was well, stating evasively that there would be some Cabinet members, several Ministers, and probably the Prime Minister. We thought we understood that possibly the King might come; there would certainly be a representative from the palace.

All this information thrust upon us at the last minute only succeeded in making us more nervous as we stood foolishly beside our machines, one of which was still hissing as if to mock us with its leak.

After our demonstrations at Bañolas, on the Seine, and then down St James's Place, I thought I had acquired some proficiency at them, but now I felt more nervous than when facing the worst rapid. As by magic, the crowd on the bank had grown to hundreds. Looking up, we saw a smartly dressed officer emerging with several aides from a car. Then, stomping down the road, came a detachment of some two hundred men, five abreast in khaki drills and red berets. These were the police – possibly the entire force of the valley.

Their arrival suddenly lent an official air to the whole affair, as they took up positions along the banks and started ordering the crowd about. More cars began to drive up, from which alighted plump officials with sari-clad wives. One of them was introduced as the Transport Minister, another as his secretary – soon we lost count of names. These people milled about our machines, making odd comments. The leak unfortunately did not pass unnoticed, and one woman raised the cry, 'It has a puncture!' Everybody nosed in; punctures anybody could understand, while for most the principle of our machines remained obscure.

I looked at our little darlings with mingled pride and anxiety, fearing that they were planning some ghastly breakdown. I felt a great urge to call the whole thing off, but the police now seemed to have us ringed in properly – there was no escape. The sun beat down with full force, we were perspiring heavily, everyone was fidgety as we stood waiting, waiting. By eleven-thirty there was still no sign of the Prime Minister. In the meantime General Surendra Shaha introduced me to a gentleman who announced that in his office he had a permit ready to allow us to go up the Sun Khosi and Indrawati rivers. This pleased us to a certain extent, but we could not help fearing that this might be all, and that the permit we wanted, which would allow us to proceed to the high altitudes up the Kali Gandaki, had been finally refused. We immediately expressed our fears to the General, but he again became mysteriously evasive. Once more we stressed the point that, from a purely technical point of view, it was essential that we try our craft at high altitudes. No one, we said, had ever taken hovercraft as high as we planned to take ours, and this might reveal new aspects of it operationally that calculations alone had not shown up. 'If hovercraft were ever to be used in Nepal commercially it was essential that the principle be tested in altitude,' we pointed out. The General sympathized but turned away, for at that moment the car with the Prime Minister, Mr Giri, arrived.

Six foot tall, for size alone Mr Giri deserves to be the leader of the Nepalese Cabinet. His youthful, elegant figure and kind features nevertheless betrayed little of his thoughts. Michael and I showed him our machines, ran through our brief account of the principle on which they operated, and then let him have a peep under our skirts. He did not seem impressed, and I had to agree that, lying side by side before such a large crowd, they looked a little silly, like two land-locked rubber dinghies.

Having finished my word of explanation I wanted to proceed with the demonstration, but the Prime Minister asked us to wait a little longer. Were we expecting another visitor, the King? We waited another fifteen minutes, by which time the entire bank on one side of the river was black with onlookers: Tibetan monks, Newar shopkeepers, Gurungs from the hills, representatives of every tribe of the country, casual passers-by attracted by the first onlookers. No one, I felt certain, really knew what it was all about.

No one came, and the Prime Minister eventually waved for us to begin. My hands trembled as I grasped the starter cord, while Michael pumped a little air into the leaky hull. One pull, two pulls, the thrust engine turned and started; then, to my relief, the lift engine also rolled over. I sat in the pilot's seat and pushed down the throttle. The roar of the motors floated above the river, while wind from the propellers sent the ladies' saris flying as I slithered down the sandbank and over the water across the gravel bed.

With what I hoped was graceful mastery, I went through all the tricks of hovering over sand, mud, gravel, water, weeds and grass, up small embankments, then down close against the shore where the Prime Minister and Michael stood. As I passed, I saw the General waving frantically, lifting his hands to the sky. Seeing our machines for the first time, he expected them to float a yard or more right up in the air. Michael had to explain, to his disappointment, that we were already on an air cushion above the ground. In the meantime I skidded all over the Bhagmati, praying that none of the propellers would break and leave me to wade ashore ankle-deep in mud.

Eventually I pulled in. The Prime Minister complimented me on the show, asked a few questions, then clambered up the bank and disappeared.

Behind him went the Cabinet Ministers and the secretaries, the General and the other officials. The police formed ranks and marched off, the crowd slunk away and, before we knew it, we were alone by the river with a few stragglers.

'Well!' I said, quite pleased.

'Well what?' echoed Michael.

'Well nothing.'

We had not been able to broach the subject of permits. We had been given no clues as to our future. We were no better off than before.

'At least we can travel the Indrawati and Sun Khosi,' I remarked, disheartened.

'So what? You can drive up the Sun Khosi on the Chinese road,' snapped Michael.

'Well the Indrawati is no doubt more interesting, as there is no road along its bank,' I argued, while remembering that it only rose to 3500 feet. Nevertheless, I thought, it would be worth hovering up, as this would give us a close look at a river of inner Nepal that crossed the central section of the land we had not yet travelled. Along this river we could get within twenty miles of Tibet and consequently demonstrate how nearly all the country up the Indrawati/Sun Khosi river network could be crossed. 'What good will that do us?' Michael remarked sourly once again. 'We're not here to sell hovercraft. In fact, we have no link whatsoever with the business.'

14 *Buddha's Birthday*

The more I argued with Michael the more I became convinced that there was only one objective we must try and achieve, and that was our original one of crossing the Himalayan range up the Kali Gandaki. There, and there alone, we could prove to all that hovercraft could indeed open up a new era of transport in mountain terrain. 'Imagine penetrating where only yaks can tread,' I pleaded.

In the meantime we resolved to go for a short run up the Indrawati. When we came back something might have come through, and we would still receive our permits, though I secretly feared that all that would arrive in our absence was the monsoon. Nevertheless, we decided to be off the next day. In fact, we could not leave until the day after, as the Government had yet to cut through some red tape and designate a police officer to accompany us.

Finally, on May 28th, at 6 a.m., we left Katmandu with our hovercraft in working order upon the roofs of two cars. The police officer beside us hugged our permit and declared that he would stay at Dhaulaghat and wait for us there.

Soon we passed Bhadgaon, one of the ancient royal cities of the valley with its beautiful square dominated by a remarkable five-tiered pagoda. We then drove through Banepa along the wide Chinese road. I recalled how, on my first expedition in 1959, Banepa had been the end of the trail for jeeps and that it was here I had assembled our porters for the seventeen-day trek to Sherpa country at the foot of Everest. From Banepa it had taken me two days to reach Dhaulaghat, the little village we would now reach in under two hours. Driving down towards the village, I could see the bright red hills along which I had toiled on foot. How different everything seemed, seen from the comfort of a vehicle! Today in the West, the car comes in for so much criticism that we forget what a marvel it is. There is no doubt that fast locomotion is one of man's greatest achievements. I had now no qualms about introducing a new means of transport to isolated areas for, from the standpoint of the common man, transport is the stepping stone to progress. Properly developed, hovercraft will at least have the advantage of not disfiguring the environment. No roads or highways are necessary to scar the earth, as these machines will pass through scenic beauty without leaving so much as a trail on the water.

We unloaded our vehicles beneath the huge, ugly steel bridge built for the Chinese road. This journey was to differ from our preceding trips in that we would travel as self-contained units, with our food, fuel, tents and cameras all on board.

The area we were to cross was typical of central Nepal – a land of steep eroded hills bordering the deep valleys of rivers running south from the snow slopes of the great Himalayas. Each hill, despite its slope, is cultivated in well laid out terraces. The art of building terraces on the most improbable mountains is one in which the Nepalese are great masters.

Central Nepal, the strip included between the Mahabharat range and the great Himalayan range, is inhabited according to altitude by a cross-section of all the land's inhabitants. Thus Sherpas of Tibetan stock inhabit the regions about 8000 feet, while beneath them in the west are the martial Magars and Gurungs, in the east Rais and Limbus, while in central Nepal are the Tamangs. Tamangs were particularly numerous around Dhaulaghat, living close to odd Brahmins settled by the rivers. Our drive up the Indrawati was to introduce us to these Tamangs and their neat villages of oval or rectangular two-storey houses clustered upon high ground overlooking the rivers.

As we toyed with our engines on the beach of the Indrawati, a man beside us was busy casting a butterfly net into the river. His graceful movements reminded me of the fishermen of

Mexico, and recalled how few are the basic techniques invented by man and how they impose all over the world the same rhythms, the same smooth movements.

The Indrawati is particularly rich in fish, mostly *asa*, a type of Himalayan trout. These were caught in various ways: with circular weighted butterfly nets, with other nets looped to poles, with hook and bait, and even with lassoos, a noose set at the end of a fishing rod which is cast out to catch the fish around their gills. To lassoo a fish requires much more skill than the strange technique of poisoning them, which we also encountered. Fish are poisoned, or rather drugged, by placing certain leaves which we were unable to identify in the shallows, weighted down by stones so that they do not float away. Fish that swim beneath these leaves fall asleep and float up to the surface. This ingenious method is hardly sporting but, as a peasant once remarked to me, 'You can't eat sport.'

In Nepal alone 120 different varieties of fish from twenty-one families have been recorded. One of these, the *Macrogratus aculeatus*, more simply known as the *bam*, breeds in the ocean like eels, which proves that, long before us, nature had already developed a means of penetration into the Himalayas by the rivers. In Nepal small dried fish are often found in many rural markets, yet there is no doubt a better place for fish in Nepalese diets of the future. Plans are under way for introducing new varieties of fish which can be bred in the minute pools found throughout the country.

Unlike the wild rivers up which we had been travelling, the Indrawati's banks were lined with well cared for terraced fields, above which perched small villages whose thatched houses looked inviting and comfortable.

Nepalese rural architecture reflects the variety of the land's inhabitants, their occupations and the available building materials, and since our arrival we had seen a great variety of homes. First there were the wooden houses on stilts of the jungle-dwelling Tharus that proclaimed the presence of tigers and the fear of wild animals. Higher up, we had found the wooden one-storey squat stockade houses of the lower Magars.

Proceeding north, we now encountered two-storey houses of clay, some with thatched roofs, others with stone slabs, or even, around Katmandu, small baked tiles. If we were allowed farther north, we would encounter the sturdy stone homes of the mountain peoples with roofs of split pine shingles; while beyond the mountain ranges are the flat-roofed Tibetan-style houses. Not only do these structures reflect the material lives of their inhabitants, but their architecture also reveals many of their religious beliefs.

For example, all the windows of traditional Newar houses have to be entirely closed by wooden lattices, as these are believed to stop evil spirits entering. Other houses have intricate hearths that represent the inhabitants' conception of the world. In general, the hearth, the true heart of a house, is the residence of the household divinities. Doors also have their particular significance. The terminology used to describe elements of a house is frequently of ancient origin and recalls customs or beliefs often forgotten by the inhabitants themselves. Even corners are important, as it is there that demons lurk. There are also certain things one can and cannot do in a house. The Sherpas believe that to whistle in a house is evil, while the Newars do not like anyone to die in their houses, so they turn the dying outside on mats. Special talismen are buried under doorsteps or objects set above doors to protect houses from evil spirits; while in some parts walls are demolished to remove the body of the dead, then repaired so that the spirit cannot return and haunt the survivors. It would take a lifetime to study all these beliefs. I myself had made a detailed investigation of these features in the houses of the northern Tibetan-speaking areas, the high hill regions to which I longed to return.

Leaving Dhaulaghat, we proceeded slowly upstream. The river bed was very wide but the flow of the water was small for the season. Despite the altitude, we again suffered from the heat because the river beds, enclosed by mountains, become like ovens. As luck would have it, 1972 was one of the hottest years the Indian subcontinent had had for decades. On returning to Katmandu we learned that in the Terrai area and the adjoining plains of Bihar hundreds of people were dying daily of heat-stroke. So far we had stood up all right, thanks, no doubt, to our frequent baths (crocodiles or no crocodiles).

The Indrawati rose in a series of terraced steps linked by more swift shallow rapids per mile than any other river we had yet travelled, although none of these rapids were particularly rough as there was not enough water to cause large turbulence. Nevertheless, these rapids were to give us plenty of trouble, and our journey up the Indrawati was to prove the most disastrous yet.

To begin with, a ferrous oxide present in the sandbanks got into our engines in the form of little magnetic balls and clogged our spark plugs. This caused our engines to stall and meant constant cleaning. The magnetic dust delayed me for so long on one occasion that I lost track of Michael. When I tried to catch up with him I found that I was so heavily laden with gear that on every other rapid my bow would dig in and I would be thrown back. This involved several attempts at each rapid before finally making it.

Twelve miles from Dhanlaghat I found Michael, who had stopped on the bank. I pulled up, shut off my engine, and asked what was the matter. Michael was laughing. I wondered why.

'You'll never guess what's wrong with my machine,' he said, smiling. 'I've lost my rudder.'

'Your rudder? How could that happen?'

And indeed there was his craft without a rudder, and Michael had no idea when or where it had come off. We could repair some things and limp along without others, but the rudder, needless to say, was vital.

How it had come off we could not guess, as it was firmly attached by eight screws. This mishap, like nearly all the others we had had, could only be blamed on vibration. The vibrations had nothing to do with the hovercraft principle or indeed with the engineer's design, but were simply the result of using two-stroke engines. These are notorious for their vibrations because of their speed and the fact that, having only one cylinder, there is no opposing force to balance them. With two engines per craft, this problem of vibration, familiar to all motor cyclists, was twice as bad. As waves can wear down a cliff by their constant lapping, vibrations would work miracles – or rather disasters, snapping the strongest steel rod, spinning and un-screwing the smallest bolt, cracking the best wood, eroding the most resistant rubber fabric, and even in extreme cases causing the loss of one's rudder.

We felt foolish as we paced up and down the river looking for the rudder – a large, rectangular aluminium affair. We looked and looked, but could not find it. The joke was wearing a little thin when some local people came down and we tried to explain what we were looking for. Soon we had a small bunch of assistants wading in the river at our side. One of these, no doubt a keen fisherman, strayed far downstream where he let out a shout and soon waved above his head our missing treasure.

This we soon screwed back on, and up we went. Step after step, level after level, we climbed in loops and bends into a beautiful landscape leading straight towards the great moun-tains that rose to some 18,000 feet ahead of us. A couple of nasty rapids with obstructing boulders gave us a little trouble, but otherwise all went well until, travelling at considerable speed, I failed to see a sudden turn and my craft side-slipped and crashed at full speed into a steep bank of rocks. I was bumped around and cut my leg as my craft ground to an abrupt halt. Revving up the engines, I disentangled myself and pro-ceeded a few yards without trouble to where the river forked. I was riding over boulders up a strip only three yards wide when Michael drew ahead of me and disappeared out of sight. I now noticed I was making little headway and eventually began losing ground, so I pulled in to the bank to find out what was the matter. My skirt, I now saw, was ripped wide open with an L-shaped gash some four yards long. This was the first serious tear we had had. Confidently I believed I could repair it in a few minutes with a miracle glue we had brought from England, but to my dismay I found I had left the glue behind

One of the 29 cave cities recorded and found by Michel Peissel in Mustang. It is still a mystery who built these gigantic skyscrapers in which each unit was linked to the next by exposed passageways. Below: an ancient fortress, one of the chain that guards the trade route to Tibet.

Michael Alexander prepares
climb up to inspect a ca
dwelling high above the K
Gandaki, and points out a co
necting passage in these ma
made prehistoric dwellings.

or in Michael's craft. This left only needle and thread. I had no choice but to get down to work.

I have never made a dress or turned up a hem or even done any embroidery. I always thought it sissy stuff, better left to girls. I now began to regret bitterly not having learned sewing at school instead of riding. Certainly sewing requires as much skill and is both more useful and more dangerous and character-forming. I admired the stoicism of those who go in for needle-work, as my left hand suffered countless lethal jabs handed out by my right hand which did not know what the other was doing. Dripping in blood, my angry left hand grabbed the needle and took its revenge on my right. Only then did it come home to me that both were mine and hurt like mad.

Four yards is a long distance when traversed stitch by stitch with clumsy, bleeding fingers. The sun on my head did not help, nor did the suffocating crowd that babbled and commented on my lack of skill, breathing down my neck and shutting off the oxygen I badly needed. For as usual, alerted by the unexpected sound of our engines, people had come pouring down the hills and waded over to where I crouched, fighting a losing battle on my long march down the tear.

Eventually, after three-quarters of an hour, I stood up. I had only progressed some twenty inches, twenty inches of stitches that would have made a monkey laugh. My spectators, craning their necks, laughed also when they saw my handiwork. I was getting irritated, so I thrust my needle and thread into the hand of an onlooker. To my surprise, he grabbed it and got down to work with nimble fingers. I had picked a tailor.

A young boy then went over to his house, and soon I had two volunteers sewing away like mad while I hung around trying to explain they must be extremely careful not to let their needles slip and puncture the craft.

It was a good hour and a half before they were through and I was set to go. Of Michael, not a sound. I gave a present to the tailors, waved goodbye to my friends, and shot off. The beauty of the great sloping hills dying at the water's edge in successive buttresses made me forget my self-inflicted wounds as I now raced after Michael. I carried on bend after bend, but still could not find him. I had been travelling some time when magnetic dust once more cut off my engine. I cleaned the spark plugs, started off, stalled again, and had to restart the whole operation. We had been up since six, and it was now four-thirty, I was exhausted, and the heat was unbearable. Dis-heartened, I sat down by my machine to rest on a rocky island between two branches of the river. In front of me rose the houses of a beautiful little ochre-coloured village shaded by tall trees, while around bubbled water.

It was such a beautiful spot that I was soon lost in reverie. Then I heard a shout. Getting up, I saw Michael drifting down-stream – a pathetic sight if ever I saw one. There he was, haggard and wet, kneeling in his craft which looked a total wreck with planks sticking out in odd directions. One side was submerged (no doubt punctured), while Michael, who had lost his paddle, tried to steer a course away from the rocks with the plywood support of his smashed canopy. What on earth had happened? I wondered, as I raced to the shore. Michael shouted for me to hang on as he was swept past. I grabbed his wretched craft and he jumped out.

'Well?' I found myself saying in Michael's fashion, hoping to hear a sad tale of remorse about some ghastly mistake.

'You should have seen it, it was fantastic,' Michael said unexpectedly.

'Fantastic – what do you mean?' I said angrily, pointing to the craft.

'Well, I mean spectacular. You see, it was like this.'

And he told me his story. Michael had ascended the river without trouble to a point where he hit very rough water on a bend. Here his lift engine suddenly stopped. Immediately his craft was swept backwards down the rapid and the rushing water lifted it and jammed the hull vertically between two rocks. Michael fell out and scrambled ashore, but the craft, now obstructing the current, became submerged and the force of the water broke the canopy, sweeping the paddle away and eventually puncturing the hull. The fantastic spectacle I should have seen, according to Michael, was the aesthetic aspect of this crash. I appreciated that a photograph might have been some small consolation, but I could find nothing for Michael to be proud of in all this, although I did congratulate him on still being alive.

On my saying this, Michael turned pale, sat down and declared he was feeling dizzy. I immediately diagnosed the onset of sunstroke and got him to drink and rest. By now I was not feeling too well either. Seven hours in the sun was having its effect on both of us, but we had to get back to work. Twenty miles separated us from our point of departure and we had to repair the craft all the faster because Michael's engines were full of water and could not be left in that state.

I think a monument to our courage and perseverance under stress would be in order at this point, and under the monument should be buried the man who invented the first machine. From that day on, I have always looked with respect at any mechanic I meet, having plumbed the depths of what makes up the delight of those who dedicate their lives to men's steel children. I now recalled Michael's famous first words – 'I can't think of anything more boring than crossing the Himalayas in a hovercraft.' How right Michael's caution had been! And yet – was 'boring' the right word? We sat and laughed at each other.

However hard we tried, we could not get Michael's lift engine to start again; it seemed that water had damaged the electrical system. We gave up, desperate and exhausted. Salvation suddenly came in the form of a little one-eyed man in rags who waded across from the village the other side of the river, carrying a pot and a flat copper soup plate. In the pot was a yellow pasty mush: 'chang' – local beer. This saved us from despair and changed our spirits. Taking a bit of mush, the man placed it on a copper plate, added river water, and then set about stirring it with a little wooden stick he rolled between the palms of his hands. By mixing the water and the fermented corn mush, in a minute we were drinking the best local beer we had yet tasted. We drank one, two and three plates, with the instant effect that our morale soared, while the horizon shifted and blurred. In this happy state it took me some time to grasp that the tom-toms I heard echoing in the valley were not just in my head. We now learned that this auspicious day was Buddha's birthday, and the Tamang villagers were celebrating the occasion. We decided to relax a little and forget our driving ambition in enjoying a glorious sunset, the distant sound of singing voices and the cool breeze rising from the river.

Michael's clothes and sleeping-bag were all soaking wet, and so were our biscuits, yet we had not eaten since morning. We opened a warm tin of meat, but soon abandoned it in disgust. We had been so absorbed in our struggle with our craft and the river that we had not fully appreciated how exhausted we were. Michael was still unwell, and I now also felt faint. Both of us fell asleep on the gravel shortly after sundown, tucking our heads under the shelter of our small tent. I was busy dreaming when someone shook my arm. I woke up with a jolt to see two men peering at us. These, I discovered, had waded across the river to our island, carrying two warm hard-boiled eggs and a compound of salt and red peppers which they proceeded to give us. Half asleep, we gobbled the eggs, thanked the villagers, gave them presents, and then fell back exhausted, although it was only nine-thirty.

Michael was soon snoring away, but I could sleep no more. A full moon rose in eerie whiteness above the hills and threw a sheen of silver upon the river. All was still save the ripples of water, the distant bark of a wild dog, and the occasional sound of singing voices that drifted from the village to where we lay, on fading waves carried by a slight breeze.

When we awoke next morning a small crowd was already standing around our machines. They were all Tamangs, we discovered, a tribe that, like the Magars, the Gurungs, the Limbu and the Rais, claims to be of Tibetan origin. Although the Tamang language differs from the Tibetan more than the Magar language, their religion and customs are much closer to those of Tibet than are those of the other four tribes. The name 'Tamang' is believed to derive from the Tibetan words *ta* (horse) and *mang* (many), and legend has it that originally the Tamang were horse-traders from Tibet. Today they number over half a million, which makes them one of the largest tribal groups of Nepal.

A sturdy, honest race, the Tamangs make good soldiers, although they are not as numerous as the members of the other tribes within the various Gurkha regiments. No doubt this is because the Tamangs are very industrious and can survive without having to seek employment as mercenaries in the Gurkha brigades as other tribes do. To join the British Army Gurkha brigades has been for the past 150 years one of the few available means of survival for many young landless Nepalese of the poorer tribes. At the age of 18 or 19, young men would join for periods of 10–15 years, then return with enough money to take a wife, buy a field, and live the rest of their lives as relatively prosperous farmers. What is remarkable is that these soldiers, many of whom travelled the world, lived in Hong Kong, Singapore or Britain and fought in France, Burma, Libya, Germany and many other lands, apparently forget their entire military past on returning to Nepal and revert to their traditional way of life. Many forget the few words of English they have learned. They also forget the neon lights of Singapore, its skyscrapers and buildings, in order to lead, in the seclusion of their narrow valleys, a life identical with that of their ancestors.

Here is proof of the strength of tribal tradition and the power of conformism. Nevertheless, it is impossible to estimate the good many of these ex-Gurkha soldiers have done to their home villages, some bringing back new types of seeds, while others – mostly ex-officers – frequently become village headmen or self-appointed schoolteachers or engineers, building on their return the much needed bridge or irrigation canals for their community.

The Tamang, in spite of their long isolation from Tibet, still practise Lamaism, although in a much altered form. It consists mainly in keeping Tibetan religious texts and decorating with Tibetan divinities their few small chapels. The Tamang are divided into many sub-tribes; one of which is called 'lama' and whose members are all considered priests. The Gurung tribes also have clan names derived from Tibetan titles that used to be attributed to a specific profession, and these clans consider this profession's attributes as a hereditary privilege.

This tendency to render hereditary what was originally a profession requiring special training is quite common. In time the name alone remains, while the skills or even the meaning of the name is lost. We have a similar phenomenon in Europe where family names frequently recall a particular profession: Smith the blacksmith, Miller or Tanner. The study of these names and of certain traditions can throw light on the organization and activities of societies that have long disappeared, while frequently, as with certain Nepalese tribes, the people alive today are far less advanced than their ancestors.

Too often, anthropologists study a race or tribe in the general belief that societies through the ages tend to develop new and better social systems, not realizing that many are in fact mere fossilized distortions of what were once well-organized, more sophisticated societies. Possibly new light will be thrown on the history and development of man if a greater effort were made to find in a so-called primitive society traces of the more advanced society from which it may have been an offshoot, rather than regarding the existing level of a culture as a direct reflection of years of positive development. This is true of many Tibeto-Burmese hill tribes of Nepal and south-east Asia, and might also apply to the Indians of North and South America, whose present culture could well be the remnants of a superior but vanished civilization. Anthropology should be used, like archaeology, to reconstruct from surviving fragments the refined cultures of the past. Such an approach might reveal traces of highly sophisticated civilizations whose existence we do not yet even suspect.

A particularly interesting aspect of Tamang life is their custom of young men marrying much older women (generally

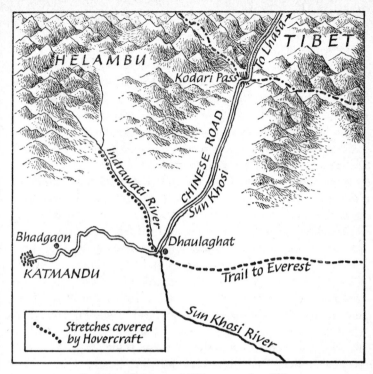

Indrawati River and Chinese road to Tibet

widows) – a custom which used to have an analogy in the European Middle Ages. Old men marry young girls, who when they are rich widows marry young men, who in turn marry young girls when they get older. Anthropologists have argued that in a society where women frequently die in childbirth and where life expectancy is generally low, practically everyone marries twice. This is a sort of vertical polyandry and polygamy, for everyone eventually has two or more wives or husbands. Medical advances in our modern world have so reduced the chances of a man or woman being widowed at an early age, and thus having several husbands or wives, that this may partly account for the number of divorces. Monogamy may not prove to be a valid institution for a long-living people.

Cutting through the crowd assembled near our machines, we got down to work again in a desperate last attempt to get Michael's hovercraft to start. In the end we had to admit it was beyond repair, and so I decided to push on alone. Eventually I came out on to a long stretch where the river widened considerably. Later, it narrowed again before dividing in two just where it began a nearly vertical ascent up the great Helambu range. On reaching the end of this wide stretch, I stopped. There was no point in trying to carry on. According to my map, I was some eighteen miles only, as the crow flies, from the Tibetan border, eighteen miles that my craft could never hope to travel, as the river petered out into a mere rivulet. Recalling Michael stranded on his sandbank, I turned about, and headed back downstream. After shooting four or five rapids, I suddenly swung round a bend a little too fast and I found myself heading straight for a rock standing five feet high in midstream. There was nothing I could do to avoid it and I braced myself for the inevitable crash. At full speed, my craft went into the rock, then to my surprise rose in the air, bouncing right over it, flying in a great arc back to the water like some missile projected from a cannon. Hanging on for dear life, I came down with a bump, followed by an explosion as my thrust engine fan-blades broke, scattering their sharp slivers of green plastic all over me. I was now without means of control and hovered in small circles above the foaming water, while being dragged slowly down in spirals towards a cliff against which the current rushed before rebounding in a great arc on to another rock.

Glancing back, I noticed that my lift engine was still running, thus saving me from falling into the current, but that on its protective grille was a piece of broken blade. Immediately I leaned back and grabbed the blade, as it was about to fall into the lift-fan, which would then have been broken too. Whether it was a jolt from the rapids or the haste of my movement I do not know, but as I put my index finger on the shattered blade the lift propeller, spinning round at full speed, caught the tip of my finger and cut it clean off. I felt something like an electric shock, and withdrew my hand. In a matter of seconds it was covered in blood. I howled in pain and panicked as the craft bounced wildly out of control over another rapid. Putting my finger to my mouth, I was wondering what to do when the lift-blades broke with a terrible bang and my craft suddenly fell into the water. I was now like a leaf upon the flood being swept straight on to another rock. I reached for my paddle but could not find it, so I grabbed the plywood canopy support to push the craft away from the rocks. I then attempted to avoid the next embankment, towards which I was rushing at dizzy speed. My finger hurt terribly, I had blood all over me, but I had to keep on paddling to avoid the banks. I was in a complete mess, as at any moment I felt I might faint or the hovercraft be overturned. Yet there was no point in making for the shore, for I somehow had to get back to Michael. I swept down another rapid, after which the current slowed and for a few minutes I floated gently. I took the opportunity to inspect my finger. In one neat blow the very tip had been severed, shearing off part of my finger-nail as well. The descent was a nightmare; in pain and in constant fear of overturning, I was carried down rapid after rapid at the will of the river.

Decidedly the gods of the river were against us. It was with no small relief that I sighted Michael, who came out to grasp my craft as I floated by. Scrambling out, I felt weak and had to lie down. I was too exhausted to think, yet in my mind one thought beat constantly: we had to travel back down, but how? Michael's craft was beyond repair, while I could not move my hand; and we further discovered that my lift cables were broken and we had no spares with us. There was only one thing to do, and that was to try and float all the way down to Dhaulaghat. I loathed the idea, recalling how I had nearly drowned when we had tried to float down the Arun. But we had no other choice, as we could not leave our craft behind.

It would be wise for the prestige of our project if I did not describe the return. We looked like a defeated armada as we pushed our broken craft into the current while keeping our fingers crossed, I with one of mine in my mouth. To add to our miseries, my craft had a puncture, so I had to keep on jerking the pump to keep afloat between bouts with the paddle. In all, it took us four and a half hours in the burning sun to float down to Dhaulaghat. For most of this time I was in great pain, and I was often obliged to grab the paddle for fear of worse punishment. Altogether the journey was so ghastly that, whenever the current swept Michael's boat close to mine, we could only laugh at our predicament. We did not laugh long, as we promptly got caught in a whirlpool and for several minutes our craft would spin round and round.

Halfway down, Michael, who was behind me, got caught in a second whirlpool so powerful that it took him fully twenty minutes to break free. To do this he had to attach a rope to the hovercraft, then jump into the water, swirl around in it, and finally grab a rock. He was then able to haul his craft out of the circling water by means of the rope he had attached to it.

At long last we sighted the Chinese bridge up ahead and knew we had arrived. If ever a journey was a nightmare this had been one, but we were so thankful to have made it back that we forgot all our troubles. Feeling faint from stress and sun, we abandoned our craft and stumbled to a shack beside the bridge, where we ordered rice alcohol and downed three glasses, together with five boiled eggs and floods of tepid water. Despite the refreshment we were too weak to go back in the heat to collect our craft and had to hire four coolies to drag them up to the edge of the road. Against all expectations, the two cars we had arranged to have come and fetch us arrived on time and our sorry-looking machines were loaded on their roofs and we were soon speeding back to Katmandu.

15 *By Royal Appointment*

Our journey up the Indrawati, if eventful, had done little for our morale or for our physical state. We had enjoyed the journey through the central hills of Nepal, but we were still as far as ever from our ultimate goal. With the two craft smashed, my finger out of order, and both of us tired beyond belief, we felt we would never get the permit we so dearly wanted. We had been under way now for three full months, three months of constant physical effort in the most gruelling of climates and aggravated by mental strain. I feared we could not carry on much longer like this. The sky was becoming increasingly cloudy and a damp heat hung above Katmandu. It was characteristic pre-monsoon weather: the rains could break any day.

Reluctantly we made up our minds to leave Nepal. This decision cost me a great deal, but it had to be taken, for now, even if we got permission, by the time we flew or drove our craft to western Nepal and transported them by truck to the Kali Gandaki it would be too late. Once on the river, we should still have to take our machines up the great cataracts as far as Lete, a long and difficult operation.

Exhausted and disheartened, I braced myself to face having to return and admit that we had only been able to cross half of the Himalayan range and had never been higher than 5000 feet – we who had left with such cocky assurance, declaring to the press that we planned to reach 10,000 feet and cross the entire Himalayas from the Indian plains to beyond Annapurna.

I telephoned the General to advise him of our departure. He was sympathetic but confirmed that he had been unable to secure the permits. Then, having expressed polite regret, the General asked if we could give another small demonstration of our machines on a road and over rice fields. 'What for?' was Michael's indignant response when I told him of the General's unexpected request. 'They have had three months to look at our machines, we have already demonstrated them to the Prime Minister and the Cabinet, we have received no permit, no acknowledgment whatsoever of our efforts and endeavours, or even of our reports sent to the Government. Yet we have complied with all the Government requirements. We were invited here and then refused permission to do what we had planned, and now after all this we are supposed to lay on another show!' I agreed with Michael that this was stretching things but, as I tried to calm him, I discovered that deep down inside me I had not lost all hope. If they want another demonstration, I thought, then they are interested in our project at last. But the thought was swept away by the knowledge that the monsoon would never wait, it was too late, we had to go back, it was all over. Our project had been a partial failure.

Reluctantly, I nevertheless agreed to the last demonstration. Together with the General, I reconnoitred the country in search of a trial ground. My heart was heavy, and the General, I noticed, was no longer his jovial self. He apologized for all the delays; it was not his fault, he explained, the whole matter was too complex, he could not tell me why we had been banned from the hills but he promised to try yet again. I was unable to find out what the Prime Minister had thought of our demonstration or even what the General had thought himself.

I had been driven by now to the conclusion that I must have some personal enemy in the Government; someone who might have taken objection to something I had written in one of my two books on Nepal. The moment one sets anything down in black and white, one becomes the voiceless victim of all those who might disagree, without being able either to explain or answer. I had of course nothing on my conscience unless it was that I had told the truth, and some truths are perhaps better left untold. Later, I discovered that my recalling Mustang's ancient Tibetan origins and status as an independent kingdom before its annexation by Nepal was considered unfavourable to Nepal's efforts to unite the country. Others told me that I should not have mentioned the Tibetan crisis and the continuing struggle of the Tibetan freedom-fighters, who are not yet reconciled to seeing their land occupied by China. Perhaps this was why we were not allowed into the mountains; I did not know for sure, and these reasons hardly seemed plausible since our present project, which had been approved by the Government, was in no way related to my past journeys. This I had already spelled out both in my letter to the King and in the letter I had sent to the Prime Minister.

From his car the General pointed out a stretch of the Chinese road and asked, 'Could your machine climb up this?' 'Yes,' I answered, thinking, 'What's the use, anyway?' The General's chauffeur then sped off down a dirt road to the gatehouse of what is known as the King's Game Reserve, a vast walled park on the outskirts of Katmandu. We entered the reserve, which is stocked with captive deer and said to harbour several leopards. The General took me to a very steep, narrow lane that clambered up one of the hills in the park. 'Will your machine go up this?' 'No,' I had to reply, as the slope was far too steep.

The General then drove me to the edge of a rice field that sprawled against the great stone and brick wall of the reserve. 'Could you go over these fields?' Beneath me was a series of low terraces flooded with water in which grew rice some twelve inches high. 'Yes, that would be no problem, but the lift-fan will probably cut or knock down the rice stalks into the water.' 'That is no problem,' said the General. 'We will pay the farmer compensation.' That sentence struck me as unusual. Who was *we*? The army? The Government? Or the General himself?

As we returned, the General began to explain. 'I had lost all hope,' he admitted, 'but now I think you may get your permit. I think you will be allowed to go into the hills, but is there a river other than the Kali Gandaki you could use? How about Rara Lake near Jumla, which is 10,000 feet above sea-level? You could carry out your altitude tests there.'

We had already thought of the lake as an alternative, but it was far west of Nepal and would be very difficult, if not impossible, to reach. Anyway, travelling on a lake was of no great interest, as we had come to study river ecology and drive our craft up fast mountain rapids. Moreover, Rara Lake was on the southern flanks of the great Himalayas, while what we wanted to do was to cross the range.

'I will call you,' said the General as he left me at the hotel. Once again, Michael and I were left to speculate on whether we would be allowed to go, or if we should give up.

Having decided that morning to return, we felt that we did not care to go to Rara Lake and that we were interested only in the Kali Gandaki. There, and there alone, could we complete what we had come to do. But anyway it was too late as there was the problem of getting to the rivers in time. Thinking it over, Michael had an idea. 'The only possible means of still carrying out our plans and making a success of our journey before the monsoon,' he suggested, 'is to hire a helicopter and pack one of our craft into it.' If we could land, for example, at the head of the great cataracts of the Kali Gandaki, we should save both the time spent in reaching the river and the portaging of the craft up the falls, and this might yet allow us to beat the monsoon. If we could find a helicopter, and if our machines, or at least one of them, would fit inside, we could then get to the river in the minimum time and begin fighting our way up through the Himalayan breach. It all sounded easy, but there were many ifs. First, there were only two large helicopters in Katmandu; one belonged to the King, the other belonged to the army. There was no reason to think that either would lend us their precious machines, as the Government so far had given us no facilities whatsoever. In any case, we still had not got the permits. Yet I could not help hoping, so I called the General and suggested Michael's idea about helicopters. As usual the General's answer was vague, but he was not entirely negative. That night, for the second time, we cancelled our return reservations.

The following day the General called to say that we were to be ready for the new demonstration at 4 p.m. on June 1st. He did not explain for whom and for what the demonstration was being planned, but he repeated that we might yet get the permit. Might? We had heard that word a little too often. Nevertheless we busily repaired our three craft. That night we went to the Yak and Yeti, where Boris treated us to an excellent meal. The whole of Katmandu's European colony, we felt, was aware of our failure to achieve our main objective, and everyone at the restaurant seemed to eye us knowingly.

The foreigners living in the valley were an odd lot, for the most part newly arrived civil servants working for national or international aid. They were a breed of what Michael called 'new colonials', dedicated people, less arrogant than their predecessors but also less glamorous, though possessed of that same chauvinism which required them to find or establish the identical amenities to which they had been accustomed back home. Most of the wives of these civil servants spent their time attempting to set up commissaries to cater to their favourite taste in breakfast cereal, and their main conversation seemed to be how to operate electrical appliances on the town's rather unreliable network.

Slowly foreigners were making Katmandu into a white man's world in which the natives were required to cater to Western tastes. In a few years a new breed of Nepalese had sprung up, taking to Western clothes, Western music, and even Western food. Katmandu would soon become a pseudo-Western town quite unrelated to the country, its culture and its historical destiny. It was sad to see the irresistible attraction the more trivial aspects of our society have for the élites of Asian countries, and how little attraction they feel for the sturdier values of our culture. All our flashy mechanical gadgets find a ready public, and every Western middle-class snobbery is faithfully reproduced. It is all the more regrettable that this mania should have struck Katmandu, the capital of one of the very few countries which was never a colony, and a city once the centre of a rich culture which had little cause to envy our own.

The invasion of Katmandu by tourists, hippies and foreign 'experts' had slowly broken the close links that used to unite the few European pioneers with the Nepalese. These, it seemed, had been made to feel culturally inferior, whereas before the privileged few Europeans in Katmandu tried to understand and adopt everything Nepalese. Slowly, the inhabitants of the capital were losing their pride in the town's charm, and soon Katmandu would be just another hybrid oriental city. In the course of our stay we had made a few friends, and these were now our strongest support. They reminded us that the year had been a tragic one for many other expeditions, that two of those to Mount Everest had failed, while a Korean party had lost thirteen members in an avalanche, and several Japanese climbers had also died. Other parties had also had their permits refused. It seemed that we would just join a long list of failures.

We had practically lost all hope when, the following day, June 1st, we drove over at four o'clock to the General's house with one of our hovercraft. To our surprise, we found him taking a rest, and we had to wait while he got ready for the demonstration. We then drove over to the game reserve, but stopped short of its gate by a bridge over a dry river, on either side of which stretched the rice fields. This was not the exact place the General had shown me before. I remarked on this, but he said it did not matter and that I should try out the craft here. Strangely, there was no one present except the General and two friends we had asked to come along. This all seemed very odd. In fact, this whole second demonstration was suspect. Without further witnesses, I sped around the dry river bed, then on to the rice fields, where the craft operated in a spectacular manner, bouncing from one level to another over the little earthen *levées* surrounding the flooded fields. To my surprise, the lift fan did not blow down one blade of rice. Nobody would have to pay compensation to the farmers over whose fields I now cavorted.

Eventually I stopped, and the General said casually it was all right and that we could load the craft back on to the jeep. When we had done this, two military vehicles arrived with smart-looking soldiers. They were too late. Why, I wondered, had we not waited for them? I suggested we put on another

Source of the Kali Gandaki on the Tibetan border. In the distance, the Annapurna range, the rarely seen north face of the Himalayas. Below: Tibetan villagers from the headwaters of the Kali Gandaki.

Above: a hunter rejoicing in his capture of a snow leopard, the finest of high Himalayan animals. Below right: alpine flowers near Tukutcha.

demonstration, but the General only repeated it was all right. The mystery of the whole affair was now even greater. The General then announced unexpectedly, 'You will have the permit to go to the Kali Gandaki tonight. I will also see whether we can arrange something about a helicopter!'

I could have shouted with joy, but I was too puzzled and hardly dared to believe what I had heard. It was only two weeks later that the mystery of this demonstration was solved – or, rather, that we guessed what it was all about, and even to this day we are not certain.

Apparently our prior demonstration before the Prime Minister had stirred up considerable comment in the valley. The King, informed through the Prime Minister or one of his private representatives sent to watch us, had expressed a wish to see our little machines for himself. In the game reserve was a royal bungalow; if we hovered beneath it, the King could have a look at our craft without officially coming to see them. The last-minute change of plan was probably because in the end the King had not been able to come, so we had just been asked to try them anyway. There seemed little doubt, however, that it was the King himself who gave instructions that we be permitted to travel up the Kali Gandaki.

That evening the General gave us the longed-for papers that allowed us to proceed right into the Himalayas to within two miles of the border of Nepal's restricted northern area. With understandable joy we busily got to work tackling the many technical problems the journey would involve. To begin with, we contacted the King's senior helicopter expert, a Frenchman who was in Nepal to train pilots, as the two helicopters were jet-propelled French-built Alouettes. These craft can carry seven people, but we did not know whether our bulky machines would fit in to them, nor whether we would be allowed to carry petrol. We learned that we could take a few jerrycans, on condition that we had them with us in the front seats, so that 'in case of an accident you can throw them out of the door.' In case of an accident? We then learned that flying a helicopter in the Himalayas is at best a risky proposition, the reason being that if the engine stalls in high mountains there is often not sufficient altitude above land to make a safe crash-landing. We learned that under normal flying conditions helicopters usually try to fly at three to four thousand feet at least, so that in case of engine trouble they can drop from a sufficient height to give the rotors enough speed to break the fall just before striking the ground.

As luck would have it, the army helicopter was under repair, so this left the one belonging to the King. The General advised us we could use it, but of course at our expense (300 dollars an hour), which meant in fact 600 dollars an hour, as we should have to pay for the return flight. According to our estimates, it would take us nearly two hours to reach our destination, Lete, the village at the head of the cataracts.

Back at the hotel we pored over our maps once again, looking at our proposed route from Lete through the great Himalayan breach between Annapurna and Dhaulagiri. Our permit would allow us to travel as far as Marpha, a village just behind the great ranges.

Although we should have preferred to travel all the way up the Kali Gandaki from where we had left off beyond the Mahabharat range, we had to agree that by flying to the head of the cataracts we were only missing out the relatively easy portion where the river ran from west to east, seeking the passage through the Mahabharat range up which we had travelled. In any case, we had no choice but to use the helicopter, as the monsoon could break any day.

I regretted that we could not go all the way north from Marpha to Mustang, but this was only to be expected as the area remains restricted to foreigners. Only three Europeans had been allowed there since my journey in 1964: a UN official, an expert in airfields, Mr George Lothian, and a German scholar who unfortunately had died in Mustang of intestinal trouble. The time factor also limited our planned investigation of the mysterious cave cities that line the upper Kali Gandaki, although we could hope to visit a few en route. These cave cities had first been noted by Tony Hagen, the first European to travel up to Mustang. He believed these caves to be the remnants of old monasteries or mines. Peter Aufschnaiter, the companion of Henrich Harrer who spent seven years in Tibet, also sighted more of these mysterious cave cities. In the course of my expedition to Mustang, I had found twenty-nine such sites, several of great size, many carved into cliffs 300 feet above the valley floor. It was a total mystery who had built and inhabited these cave dwellings, since neither the monastery or the mine theory stood up under examination. My earlier investigation of their origin had thrown little true light on the subject, except that I had found out that none of the ancient historical records written in Tibetan mentions these caves, so that they appear to have been abandoned long before the thirteenth century.

Prior to our leaving, Professor Purna Harsha of the Department of Archaeology and Anthropology of the Nepalese Government came over to see us. We discussed the subject of the caves as he recalled the communication I had made to his department in 1965, when I first recorded their existence and tried to attract attention to them. He informed me that it was the intention of the Nepalese Government to work on their identification in the near future. He, like me, felt that they might lead to very significant discoveries about the prehistoric populations of Nepal. I could not help recalling how the discovery of similar looking ancient caves in northern China at the beginning of this century had produced such a wealth of manuscripts and paintings of the fourth and fifth centuries A.D. We hoped that with the long-awaited permit we might now be able to solve some of the elements of the cave mystery. In the meantime we had other problems to solve, for after being dropped by the helicopter we should be on our own as never before – seven days' walk from the nearest airstrip, hundreds of miles from a mechanic. We should have to be entirely self-sufficient, yet we could only take along a minimum of spare parts. The size of the helicopter meant we could only take one craft at best, assuming it would fit in at all – and of this we were not yet certain. This meant that one of us would have to proceed on foot, a grim prospect that could not be helped. In the end we decided to take along a spare engine and a light assortment of other parts. More than ever before, we would have to rely on our newly acquired mechanical skills, and I still had my finger in plaster.

As we could not helicopter back to Katmandu, we had to plan provisions in advance for the long return trek on foot down the cataracts and over the two ranges that separated the Kali Gandaki valley from Pokhara, where we were to catch a plane back to Katmandu. Apart from these minor considerations, there were three crucial, unanswerable questions. How long would the monsoon withhold its rains? How would our craft operate at such high altitudes? What would the rivers be like?

The maximum height we could reach according to our permit was 9000 feet. Never before had hovercraft been at such heights. The air at this altitude would be much lighter and our engines would lose one-third of their power, yet gravity would remain practically the same. Would our engines manage to produce enough air-cushion pressure? All the ratios of air flow and air pressures would be changed, and although mathematical calculations could predict most of these factors, the future was to prove that between theory and practice there is often room for error.

But all these varying problems were insignificant compared to the most vital of all. Would our craft fit into the helicopter? Measurements of the solid fibreglass base plates of our machines compared to those of the helicopter showed that in theory we had less than one inch to spare! The only way of knowing for certain was to try. Anxiously we headed for the airport with craft 002, which we then dismantled. It took great skill to squeeze it in, but in it went.

At long last everything was ready. We were to leave Katmandu at 5.30 a.m. on Saturday, June 7th. At 6.30 on Friday evening a telephone call announced that we could not take off until Sunday. We lost all heart, neither Michael nor I believing we would ever leave.

We spent Saturday by the swimming pool of Katmandu's most luxurious hotel. Neither of us enjoyed a minute of it, as our minds were already on the upper course of the Kali Gandaki and our eyes turned towards the cloudy sky.

Once again we went over the check list of tools, spare parts, and petrol. Everything seemed well, and we retired to bed early. It was dawn when we rose. A taxi was waiting and we rumbled out of the hotel grounds observing that a few menacing clouds were floating in the sky. This was the moment for which we had yearned for so long and our empty stomachs twitched with excitement. Everyone was asleep in the valley, including the stray dogs, as we drove to the airport.

When we reached the airport, attendants were already busy taking canvas covers off the rotors. One by one, each item of our equipment was weighed. The hovercraft hull, its thrust unit, our jerrycans, the spare engine, the food, our gear. This last now included a whole new assortment of clothes, as we should be entering cold country and could no longer travel in bathing suits and life-jackets. Instead we should need our fur hats, waterproof trousers and parkas, rubber mud-sloshers, and deep-sea diving shoes.

The pilot, a young Nepalese, came forward, a little pessimistic about the weather. 'We can only tell from the air if it is possible to make it up the cataracts,' he remarked. 'It is up to you to show me where you want to be landed.'

One by one our bits and pieces were loaded into the helicopter and strapped to the rear seat. Despite our protests, our jerrycans of petrol were loaded right against the craft's engine. What if they leaked? In the end all was ready. The pilot climbed in and we followed. Surely this was the first time a helicopter had ever carried a hovercraft, and this one of the strangest missions ever flown by the King's helicopter.

The doors were closed, the engine began to whine. Very slowly the giant rotors started to turn, then whirled madly above our heads. We crept down the runway, then suddenly rose like a dragonfly, the ground beneath us getting smaller and smaller. The sun had just begun to graze the sleepy valley of Katmandu over which we now hung suspended. In a great arc, we swept over the Singa Durbar, one of the world's largest palaces built by a member of the Rana family to house his 1500 concubines and now the seat of government offices. Then, slowly, Katmandu glided out of sight, and we slipped away from the valley between two mountains, bouncing above hills dotted with small villages.

Nervously I scanned the sky; here and there were little white cloud puffs – would we make it through? The helicopter's characteristic beating noise echoed overhead, while we floated as if suspended from a string. To our right we soon saw the massive wall of the great ranges rising far above us, blocking the horizon to the north. The rays of the early morning sun carved dark shadows on the peaks, the true gods of Nepal that separate the entire Indian subcontinent from Tibet – Tibet, the homeland of most of the tribes we had encountered and the source of all the rivers up which we had battled. Behind these jagged crests, high on desert plains, lies an entirely different world and culture from that of the rest of Asia. For the Tibetans, contrary to general belief, are a quite separate race. They speak an entirely different language from the other great languages of Asia. Tibetan is the root of the Tibeto-Burmese languages, shared only by the hill tribes of Nepal, Bhutan, Burma and south-east Asia. It is not related to Indo-European languages, nor to Turko-Mongolian, nor even to the Chinese languages. Tibetans in this respect form a race on their own.

Too many Europeans have come to believe that Tibetans are a mild people, a race of meditative sages lost in contemplation in their lofty monasteries. This erroneous idea stems from the fact that in the West too much attention has been given to Tibetan monks and their fascinating religion, and not enough to the common people. The true martial character of the Tibetans is hidden behind their religious front. Indeed, the entire history of the Tibetan Lamaist Church and the reason for its near-total domination over the land springs from the warlike nature of the inhabitants: these people could only be led by priests who preached peace. Oddly enough, warrior races, whether Christian or Moslems, often combine aggressive-ness with a strong faith. In fact, aggressiveness and piety seem to be linked all over the world. Christians have fought some of the greatest wars, and Moslems have conquered some of the greatest empires. Likewise the Tibetans had for generations done battle with the world around them. Only in recent times have they laid down their arms, and not entirely even now. The trail of water we were about to travel would take us into a land not only of lamas but of fortresses, for the upper Kali Gandaki is flanked by dozens of medieval castles guarding the holy gates to Tibet.

Half an hour after leaving Katmandu we flew over the little village of Gurkha. Its brick palace, erected by the first Gurkha kings, stood upon its rocky pinnacle, a reminder that it is often the initiative of one man that changes the destinies of nations. Next, as we advanced towards Pokhara, a town two hundred miles west of Katmandu that has only recently been linked to the capital by road and whose airfield was for many years the only one in the interior of Nepal, we saw to our right the entire Annapurna range filling the bubble of the cockpit. On our left, we caught sight of the golden strip of the Kali Gandaki as it streamed along the northern face of the Mahabharat range. We could now look down on the green summits of this range that we had crossed from Daveghat and see at the same time to our right the snow range we now planned to traverse. From the air we saw once again between the two ranges the central portion of the river that we had not had time to travel.

After he had flown over the three lakes that dot the Pokhara valley, the pilot turned to ask me to show him the way. Like a map beneath me, I saw familiar valleys and hills. In a few minutes our little machine was fluttering only a few hundred feet above the rhododendron-covered crests of Gora Pani, the pass that leads into the Kali Gandaki gorge. To our left, high above us, towered the white snowfields of Machupuchari, the fishtail peak whose spectacular rocket-like summit shades Pokhara. Looking at this tormented waste of ice and snow, I admired the courage and ability of our friend Colonel Roberts, who was the first person to scale this peak and also that of Annapurna 2.

We had little time to meditate. Beneath us appeared the Kali Gandaki. We hovered above it just where it emerged from its cataracts at Tarto Pani, then went up its deep gorge following the cataracts of white and grey water as they plunged from cliff to cliff down a devilish staircase. The pilot asked me to point out where I wanted to land. We were heading now into the massive wall of the Annapurna and Dhaulaghiri ranges and could hardly believe that somewhere near lay the great Himalayan breach. Looking at the foaming water and the incredible mass of mountains above us, I began to wonder if we were not a little naïve to think we could ever cut through all this on our fragile machines. Suddenly I spotted a shaky wooden bridge marking the summit of the cataracts. It must be Lete. We came down and I saw where the river levelled out above the falls. 'There!' I pointed, as the helicopter came down and hovered above the grey stone bed of the river. Quickly I searched for a flat piece of land near the river from which we could launch our craft. I spotted a minute field projecting from a cliff above the water. The field looked flat and empty. I pointed it out to the pilot. The land came up towards us as, lightly swaying, we came down. Ten feet, five feet, three feet, the wheels touched ground, the engine cut out, the blades rotated slower and slower, and finally the pilot released the door. I nudged Michael. We had arrived.

16 *The Grandest Canyon*

As we climbed down we were immediately struck by the cold air and the sound of birds singing in the early sun. It was 8.30 a.m., a chilly spring morning, one half of the valley was steeped in shade, pine trees towered around us, and the river rushed past even faster than I had anticipated at the edge of the field on which we had landed. We were now at 7000 feet in an entirely new world. Every noise echoed against the monumental mountains that rose 18,000 feet on either side of us, up to the snow-covered peaks.

A heavy scent of pine needles was in the air, mingled with the smell of earth as the dew evaporated in the early-morning sun. There was not a soul in sight, although on the other side of the river half a mile away stood a few houses at the foot of an almost vertical slope. We eventually heard shouts and saw a lone rider galloping towards us up the far bank of the river. It was a fairy-tale sight, and we understood at last that we had hit the romantic Himalayan world of the great ranges. It was hard to believe this was the same body of water as that where the crocodiles lazed farther south. The rider tried unsuccessfully to ford the Gandaki, and so darted off downstream to cross it by the wooden bridge at the head of the first cataract. On our bank other men came running towards us. One of them, a Tibetan, was wearing a dark red homespun cloak; the others were draped in yellow woollen jackets. For them, no doubt, this was a great event, the first time a helicopter had landed there. Perhaps they thought it was the King, for his father had often used helicopters to pay unexpected visits to the far corners of his kingdom. A small crowd gathered at a respectful distance, as we busied ourselves unlashing our gear.

In the meantime the pilot refuelled the helicopter from a jerrycan for the return flight. We were still dazed from the flight when he came over to shake hands and wish us good luck. We thanked him profusely. Then the crowd backed, the rotors whirled then gathered speed, stones and blades of grass went flying as the great dragonfly rose slowly, hung high above our heads, then whirled about and disappeared to the chatter of its rotor. A strange silence set in as we stood alone beside our gear, surrounded by a strange group of people who eyed us with smiling, friendly faces.

'It's up to us now,' I heard Michael saying. The crowd was jabbering away shrilly as we made a tour of inspection of the area in which we had been dumped. The field projected into the river, which looked cold and menacing and much swifter than I had anticipated. I was glad we were warmly clothed, and extracted from our bags my skin-diver's boots, ankle-length foam rubber slippers that we had been told would keep our feet warm. This was a vital precaution as the water was near freezing-point as it ran down from the snowfields and glaciers directly overhead. To fall in here would mean nearly instant death – a numbing pain that would lead to paralysis and drowning.

As the river skirted the minute field entirely, we should have to lower the hovercraft directly into the water. This would be difficult for, if we slipped and let go, it could get carried away. Eventually we found a shallow spot on the far side of the field where there was little current, and we decided to put it in there.

We now set about assembling our machine. To the crowd's amazement, they saw our hull grow as we pumped it up. We then fitted in the floorboards and tackle, bolting in the thrust engine and ducts before fitting the rudder and connecting the cables. How many times had we performed this operation? We were well schooled and knew every bolt and screw, yet this time we were unusually careful, as the entire success of our mission could depend on a single little bolt. As we worked I felt increasingly nervous. What I could see of the river was one continuous rapid and, although there were not too many large breakers, the surface was nowhere still. Looking upstream, I could see about a mile away the point where the river disappeared between two pine-covered buttresses that rose right up to the snowfields. This was the mouth of the great Himalayan breach, the entrance to the world's deepest canyon. Through this breach ran one of the few trails linking the Indian subcontinent with Tibet – possibly one of the most ancient trails since it was the principal road for the salt gathered since antiquity from the shores of the lakes of the central Tibetan Highlands, salt – more even than gold – having always been man's most sought-after commodity.

The view downstream was less comforting. Eight hundred yards away the river took its first plunge down the cataracts. To stall here and be swept down out of control would mean instant death. It was a nightmare we had both already experienced in dreams. By starting out'so close to the head of the cataracts we were taking a great risk.

Michael turned over our engines for a trial run on the field. This was a crucial moment, for now at last we should be able to discover the effects of altitude on our craft. We knew that our engines would have lost a good deal of power. Would there be enough left to fight up one long continuous rapid? Everything appeared normal; the cushion inflated fully, although the carburettors had to be adjusted to take in more of the light, cold air.

The time had come to set off. We decided that I should travel up the breach first, Michael following on foot with spare fuel, parts and other equipment that several porters recruited from the crowd would carry up. The trail through the gorge hugged a ledge above the river from which Michael would scan the water to make sure I was not stranded or in trouble. If all went well we were to meet halfway through the breach some fifteen miles upstream at Tukutcha, the largest village of the area and capital of the Thakalis, a tribe of some 6000 souls who inhabit the banks of the Kali Gandaki from the foot of the cataracts up to the village.

The Thakalis are today the true kings of the Kali Gandaki,

since they now control the lucrative salt trade from Tibet. Those who are not traders are innkeepers along the trade route. In ancient times the salt trade was controlled by Tibetan lords who ruled over two dozen fortresses, the ruins of which still tower along the riverbanks north of Tukutcha.

The Tibetan-speaking rulers of Mustang overlorded the most powerful of these strongholds until the end of the eighteenth century, when after many battles they became vassals of the western Nepalese kingdom of Jumla. When, a few years later, in 1796, the kingdom of Jumla fell under the domination of the Gurkha kings, the *rgyal-po* of Mustang (*rgyal-po* means 'victorious one' and is the title of Tibetan kings) became a vassal of the Nepalese king, who conferred on him the title of 'rajah', which he holds to this day.

The rajahs of Mustang continued to rule their isolated land, taxing the lucrative salt trade, until in 1876 some Thakali merchants, aided by the Nepalese Rana Maharajah, were able to deprive the rulers of Mustang of their monopoly. From that date the Thakalis have prospered – at the expense of Mustang, whose impoverished peasants continue to handle the transport of salt but no longer for their or their ruler's profit.

Already at Daveghat the Kali Gandaki had been held sacred. I was now about to travel up its holiest section. The Himalayan breach is famous not only as a trade route but is known all over the Indian continent as the fount of all Salegraim – the source of 'sacred stones'.

The sacred stones are fossils of ammonites, an ancient sea snail, and are believed to be spontaneous representations of the Hindu and Buddhist wheel of life; they are found in the river bed where the Himalayas meet the Tibetan plateau north of Tukutcha and not far from the holy shrine of Muktinath, whose fame rivals or complements that of the sacred stones. This shrine is mentioned in the most ancient of Buddhist and Hindu texts. In Tibetan, the shrine is called *Chu-mig-rgat-tsa-gye*, 'the 108 springs'. In spite of this name, its fame derives not from the 108 water spouts that receive the flow of a stream issuing from the shrine, but from its miraculous flaming water, burning rocks and earth. These natural fires have been a marvel for centuries, an object of mystery and devotion. They are actually due to a leak of natural gas that escapes through the water and the surrounding earth and into the shrine.

Praying that all would go well, I jumped into the river. My feet sank in the wet sand while the icy water swirled above my knees. Thanks to my diving boots the cold lessened after a while, and to my amazement my feet actually became warm. Without these boots I could not have stood the water for more than two minutes, and then only with considerable pain. Helped by members of the crowd, Michael slowly lowered the craft down to me. As it flopped into the water I dragged it on to a low nearby sandbank.

Some people are never afraid, but I was shaking as I stood on the edge of the great river, measuring at water level the force of its icy flow as it hurtled down like one long endless rapid. Looking up at the trees and the vertical rock slopes rising more than three miles to the partly invisible snowfields, I felt weak at the knees, while the thought of the cataracts below made me feel worse. I wondered at my folly and prayed for protection as I started the engines and headed out into the river. The current immediately began to swing me round slowly, then my heart swung upside down as '002' suddenly dug in sideways and was swept downstream towards the cataracts! I pushed the throttle full on and was crawling slowly sideways towards the bank when fortunately I ran aground on a low rock.

My lift engine was not developing enough power. I fiddled with the carburettor to try and obtain a higher speed, and then set off again. This time, very slowly, I managed to travel against the current for a few hundred yards, testing the various controls. I noticed that the slightest turbulence would make my craft dig in as again I swung round and pulled inshore. There was nothing I could do about the lack of power. I should have to fight my way up as best I could. I waved to Michael and set off for good.

It was 9.30 a.m. Spattered by freezing spray, slowly gaining momentum, I headed up-river, balancing myself carefully so as not to aggravate the machine's tendency to dig in. Squinting through the spray, oblivious of the icy water running down my neck, I sped into the first bend of the river and out of sight. Ahead the river narrowed between two columns of rock, the bases of the world's most staggering buttresses that rose vertically to support the mighty peaks. I was now entering the great breach. Dwarfed to the dimensions of an insect, filled with awe and loneliness, I carried on up the river. Soon I was locked in on all sides and could see no exit ahead. At any moment I feared I might run into some impassable stretch, but the river continued as before, swift yet relatively smooth, as its bed here was lined with small flat pebbles. Then I hit several foam-crested waves in quick succession, which reduced my speed to a near standstill. Leaning forward, I tried to help my craft along, but when I looked at the steep sides of the rocky canyon I noticed I was losing ground, so I slowly edged sideways towards the cliff where the water was less turbulent. With the engine howling I managed to regain enough forward speed to battle through the rough water. Minutes dragged into hours. Looking behind me, I realized that nobody was following me this time and that, whatever happened, there would be no witness.

Along this stretch the trade route was obliged to climb out of sight over the steep cliff hugging the mountains. As I rounded another bend, the river widened and to my left I saw the broad gravel bed of a stream that rushed down to join the river. Looking up, I could see this stream had its source in a glacier, from which it fell in great leaps and bounds a hundred feet at a time. Not surprisingly the water was freezing, for this tributary gushed straight from under blue ice that I could clearly see in the cold light air.

The river again narrowed, and again I swept into a bend where I hit dangerous turbulence. I managed to squeeze past by hugging the bank, part of my craft floating over stones. However, I then hit a rock, and the craft, swinging inland, ground to a halt. I had to get out, drag it a few yards, then jump in, only to get caught again on a small boulder. It seemed that my skirt was not rising to the proper height. There was nothing I could do but climb out again, haul my craft off the obstruction, and try once more. This time I slid back into the river and, giving the throttle all I could, managed to gain enough forward momentum to fight the current.

It was only later that I fully understood what was causing the craft to hover so low off the ground. In their calculations the engineers had overlooked that while at high altitudes the weight of the craft remained the same and therefore so did the air pressure needed to lift it, the pressure inside the bag of the skirt that enclosed the air cushion varied because the propeller could not force enough of the thinner air through the skirt intake hole. Thus my skirt could not inflate sufficiently to encase the air cushion, which resulted in lowering my clearance height to a few inches. Consequently I was much more subject to the drag of the water as it rasped against the hull or that of the smallest rock to hit my understructure, both of which could slow me down or even stop me if I was not going fast enough.

Rounding another bend, I saw that the river bed widened out until it filled the entire valley floor with alluvial stones between the flanks of the gorge that rose over two whole miles above me. I was now entering the lower end of a wide corridor some ten miles long, at the head of which stood Tukutcha. The sun at last reached the river bed, which in parts was nearly 800 yards wide and looked like a bone-white gash across the mountains. This gravel stretch was steeply inclined, and the river rushed down it, switching from side to side and occasionally breaking up into several branches before uniting again.

Many of the stones littering the river were too large for me to hover over, so I was obliged to stick to the water. At one point the flow narrowed to a violent rapid crashing against the sheer sides of a rock cliff, high in which I caught sight of a groove: the trade route. I had to make several attempts on this stretch before getting through, as the river bore down on me in one continuous rush. Finally I reached the even, sloping bed of what must have been the floor of the lake built up before the river overflowed the Himalayas many millions of years ago.

By my reckoning I was now passing between the summit of Dhaulaghiri and Annapurna. So far so good, I thought – just as my craft crashed again on to some stones. For ten minutes I struggled to slide off, jumping in and out and soaked from head to foot and blue with cold. In my mind one thought beat insistently: I must get through, I *must*! With every yard I was nearing my goal, drawing closer to the point ahead where Tukutcha stood, just before the wide bed of the river narrowed and swung round several curves through more gorges before eventually emerging on the other side of the Himalayas.

To left and right I now saw several villages perched on flat narrow ledges between the river bed and the steep rock cliffs. Then, a few miles away, to my right, I spotted the rectangular mass of a monastery on a rocky outcrop. This I knew was Narshang, the first Tibetan Buddhist monastery on our route, the southern limit of a long chain of monasteries that runs all the way to Lhasa, the holy epicentre of the new world I was penetrating. Already I was aware of the change as I left behind the southern slopes of the Himalayas. I was edging my way on to the Tibetan plateau, and the cliffs on either side began to reveal the first traces of sediments foreign to the rest of Nepal. I was nearing the geological line that marks the head-on collision of the floating continents that had caused the Himalayas to rise, throwing up from the bowels of the earth all the elements of our planet in what must have been the greatest collision of all time.

The vegetation was also changing rapidly as we slowly fell behind the Himalayan rain shadow. The pines were thinning out and the grass was becoming rare and looked burned and dry. On reaching the monastery I pulled up on to the gravel and slid to a halt. I was trembling with cold, dripping water from head to foot, yet happy. For all these months I had dreamed of the moment when I could land my craft at the foot of such a monastery; now this moment had come. Above me loomed the rectangular, massive, whitewashed structure, its flat roof rimmed with ochre paint, the four corners supporting

A young nobleman from Mustang. Below: a noblewoman from Mustang with her child.

North of Annapurna, the Kali Gandaki runs through a desert zone reminiscent of Arizona. Below: the Kali Gandaki flowing through the Himalayan breach.

prayer flags fluttering in the morning breeze – a breeze that I knew would soon turn into a howling gale as the terrible winds that arose each day rushed up through the Himalayan breach.

As I looked at the monastery I saw a crowd of some three hundred people lining the far banks, while on my side several figures made their way over the gravel bed towards me. Extracting my camera from a waterproof bag, I took photographs of the crowd. Here more than anywhere else the hovercraft caused a great commotion. Few, if any of these people had ever seen a machine of any kind, apart from an occasional helicopter overhead. I recalled the reactions of one of my friends in Mustang when he had seen his first engine-powered craft (a helicopter). He had believed it to be a man waving his arm above his head and shouting, for nothing would allow him to imagine that what moved and made noise could be neither animal nor human. More amazing, though, had been my friend's reaction when he saw the helicopter at close range when it landed. 'Then,' he told me, 'I knew it was only a fascinating combination of elements and chemicals, and I felt we must be as stupid as cows to be incapable of doing anything so clever.'

A few hours later I learned what the people at the monastery thought on hearing and seeing my machine. Their answer was in a way deceptive but equally logical. They just thought I was a helicopter gone wrong! To them, helicopters are now synonymous with all machines, since they are the only ones they know. So I was not taken for a god or a dragon, just for an odd sort of helicopter – a thing far less impressive.

I left the monastery after a few minutes, knowing I could stop here on the return journey to inspect the monastery in detail and the beautiful flat-roofed village houses that lined the trade route.

I still had a good way to travel and feared the wind might make steering difficult, so I sped off again up the great causeway of stone through the very heart of the Himalayas. To my left I passed another monastery tucked against a cliff which I immediately noted was cut by the openings of dozens of little caves. This was one of the first cliff abodes of the upper Kali Gandaki.

We would investigate these and others, I hoped, as I carried on fighting the current. At long last, ahead of me, the first houses of Tukutcha came into view.

Roaring up, I reached the foot of the village, looking for a low section in the bank up which I could climb. I had to go past most of the village before finding what I was looking for: a flat grassy field sloping gently down to the water's edge. Turning across the river, I rushed up the bank, carried on for a few yards, and came to a stop. Getting out, I felt like hugging myself as little tinkles of congratulations echoed in my head. I had made it to Tukutcha.

Dozens of children rushed towards me, followed by the entire population of some six hundred people, including beggars and monks. An ill-assorted crowd soon surrounded me, caravaners and traders, peasants and herdsmen, an old woman spinning a prayer wheel in her hand, and a man sporting a very Western-looking shirt and a brand new umbrella. The entire town crowded around me and my machine, talking excitedly yet somewhat intimidated. To them I must have seemed a mad scarecrow or a monster in my soaking wet baggy orange trousers and my pale blue anorak blowing in the strong wind that rushed up the gorge, making the prayer flags chatter on their tall poles planted on the top of every roof and in the grass beside the river. I too began to chatter, my body numb with cold and exhaustion. Shivering, I could stand the cold no longer and had to push my way back to the craft and perform a sort of striptease in public as I extracted from my bag a dry shirt.

Nearly all Thakalis speak Nepalese and Tibetan, together with their own language, so I surprised everyone by asking point-blank in Tibetan whether there was a house where I might get arak, as what I now needed most was a drink. It must have seemed as if a Martian had landed in Wales and, on stepping out of his module, had begun speaking Welsh! In a few seconds everyone was smiling and laughing and asking amazed questions. How was it that I spoke Tibetan, and from where had I come?

I realized that, even if I had beaten all speed records between

Lete and Tukutcha, I had actually woken up that morning in Katmandu. It had certainly been a strenuous and unusual marathon that had transported me in a few hours from Katmandu to Tukutcha via helicopter and hovercraft. On foot, the journey takes twenty-four days, enough time to get acclimatized to the altitude and the change in climate. I was now at 8500 feet, and felt weak and exhausted.

A young man who I learned was a schoolteacher suggested I came to his house. With the crowd following, and children carrying my bags and cameras, I made for the town – a rather pompous word to describe Tukutcha, yet, as the principal trading centre of this portion of the Himalayas and the meeting point of all caravans, it is something more than a village, even if its 600-odd inhabitants and its one hundred houses do not truly deserve the title. The most opulent settlement in the area, its houses are all magnificent stone structures with flat roofs built to a typically Tibetan plan. Following the schoolteacher, I entered one of these, passing under an archway into a wide flagstoned yard bordered on three sides with stables and warehouses in which were stacked yak-hide bags full of salt and yak-wool sacks of wheat. We then proceeded through a second archway and up several steps into another neat stone-flagged yard bordered by two-storeyed buildings. On the ground floor were the kitchens and larders; on the first floor, living-rooms and bedrooms. These enclosed yards were flooded with sun and completely sheltered from the howling wind that was now reaching its usual daily gale force. I felt secure and well in this house away from the bustle of the street, as my host's beautiful wife came out with a glass of barley alcohol which I downed in a hurry while stripping naked under a towel, listening to the young lady's sympathetic comments on how cold I looked.

I then lay down upon the warm flagstones, gazing up at the pale blue sky fringed on either side directly above me by magnificent spires of snow, one of which was Tukutcha peak which dominates the village – a near vertical over a mile high.

Listening to the wind and the tinkle of the bells of the horses in the stables, I was overwhelmed with joy. At last I had reached that universe which I so much loved, that cold rugged world of the High Himalayas. All the anxiety that had been present in my mind over the past year vanished; I felt as if relieved of a heavy burden. I knew that now we had only seven miles to go to reach our ultimate destination, the village of Marpha, which marked the northern exit of the great Himalayan breach. I could see that victory was near at hand.

Only now did I perceive how weary I was from all these months of accumulated tension. Not until that very morning had I known for sure that we would be allowed to proceed north. Yet now I was listening to the echo of drums coming from the local monastery, the jangle of bells as a caravan clattered down the main streets of Tukutcha, that trade artery that until today had been the only access to this remote village.

17 *Through the Gates*

While I thawed my bones and meditated, I recalled that
Michael was toiling up the gorge on foot. After all these months
of fighting by my side to gain permission to cross the breach I
could well imagine his disappointment and appreciate his un-
selfishness in agreeing to go on foot. We had settled that the
next day we would take turns to complete the run through the
great Himalayan chain, after which Michael would drive back
down so that he too could share the thrills of the journey.

I now set off to meet him, walking through the village along
the flag-stoned caravan trail lined with the sturdy houses of the
great salt merchants. On the way, I passed the town's three
small monasteries and several long prayer walls, piles of stone
slabs on which were carved the sacred words *O mani padme hum*
– the holy sentence that punctuates every step of the pilgrims'
and merchants' journeys across the Tibetan highlands. This
sentence is also scattered to the wind by the prayer flags and
offered to the gods through the prayer wheels that young and
old spin endlessly for the good of their souls.

South of the village I crossed a wooden bridge spanning a
tributary stream of icy water that plunged down from the
vertical sides of the gorge. Such rivulets as these composed the
force of the great river as it charged to the plains. This same
water would in a few days cool the crocodiles, breed the frogs
and wet the hot sandbanks of the lower river; it would flood the
rice fields of the great Indian plains, and ultimately meet the
sea in the Gulf of Bengal. Rivers, like men, have souls; they
are the basic form of life, the first mineral movement that
triggers off all those other chemical exchanges that eventually
unite to form human life.

After about an hour's walking, I met Michael as he was clambering down stone steps that clung to the sheer sides of the gorge. In spite of the howling wind, it was hot as the sun burned down through the high thin air. Turning back towards Tukutcha, we stopped to visit the monastery I had seen against the great cliff marked with caves. It was so designed that all its cells cowered around a central assembly hall.

The Thakalis had originally been converted to Buddhism in the thirteenth and fourteenth centuries by monks from Tibet, among whom was the great reformer Ngorchen Kinga of the Sakya sect, who had set up a flourishing community in Mustang in 1447. Prior to this, local inhabitants had worshipped the magical spirits of land and water according to ancient shamanistic rites, many of which still survive today. Before becoming a stronghold of Buddhism, the entire Himalayas was once the home of Bon, a religion of ancient magical practices that has lent Tibetan Buddhism its particular character. We learned that the Thakalis are today breaking away from Lamism of their ancestors, because as traders they have been quick to understand the advantages to be derived from joining the Hindu religion. Some of their most influential leaders, who have become prosperous businessmen in the world outside their home valley, are attempting to obtain for the Thakali people a high rank in the Hindu caste system, based on the false claim that there is a link between Thakalis and the warrior caste of Thakuris, and this effort to join the Hindu caste structure is all too symptomatic of the power of the Hindu social system, based on hereditary privilege.

The few Buddhist monasteries of the Thakali area are now for the most part run by Tibetan refugee monks. The influx of refugees has produced a certain revival of Buddhism in the area and restored the lost sense of pride and identity among the inhabitants of northern Nepal who were originally mainly Tibetan in custom, language and religion. Possibly in a few years' time there may be a reversal of the trend that has tempted such people as the Thakalis away from their culture.

This whole subject is now one of acute importance to Nepal,

where the introduction of progress and the spread of the power and influence of the central administration is counterbalanced by political awareness among the once isolated hill tribes. In their attempt to impose Hindu religion and Hindu thought, the people who rule Katmandu run the risk of reviving tribalism through miscalculating how deeply rooted is the sentiment of identity among individual tribes. Even today, in Europe, regional traditions and languages survive and thrive, and militant minority groups are still fighting the modern tendency to abolish individuality among the members of one nation. The Himalayan breach has become the new frontier where the two great religions and social systems of Asia are fighting a silent battle, a battle which may soon cast a shadow over beautiful Nepal.

Michael and I attempted to climb into some of the caves above the monastery. The transformation of some of these cave dwellings into cells for monks is the origin of the belief that these cliff cities might originally have been nothing more than ancient convents. This theory seems improbable. In the first place, there are far more cave sites, some with over 200 rooms, than there could ever have been monks and monasteries in the upper Kali Gandaki area. Secondly, the biographies of great monks who came to preach in Mustang and along the upper Kali Gandaki in the fourteenth and fifteenth centuries give us a clear account of how many monasteries there were in the area, most of which still exist. Their lists do not take into account the 30-odd great cave settlements, even though five monasteries are settled at the foot or indeed inside some of the caves. Lastly, the transformations these caves underwent whenever monks settled in them seems to indicate that the monks were re-employing an existing locale for a different purpose, rather than the original one for which these cliff cities had been laboriously carved from the cliffs.

Neither in books nor in legends is there any mention of these cave sites, and when asked who built them, the local people are at a loss to answer, stating either that they are former monasteries or the abodes of eagles and spirits.

On returning to Tukutcha, we had some rice and curried meat, then set out to investigate more cliff dwellings, but these proved unimpressive and revealed no clues about their former occupation. We were obliged to limit our investigations to the lesser caves near Tukutcha and two others located farther south near Larjung. Those caves we could examine continued to reveal no clues of their origin, although we were able to note the unusual Maya-type arches in the passageways that led from one cave to another. Each room was linked to the others by interior corridors, as in those far more spectacular cliff dwellings I had seen north of Tukutcha. The individual rooms were spread out in horizontal rows with up to ten different levels or storeys, yet some of those I had recorded had their lowest level some two to three hundred feet above the valley floors.

What could have driven these people to go to such pains to find seclusion? Who were their foes? The lack of evidence of terraced cultivation in the areas near many of these caves suggests that their early occupants were not agriculturalists. On the other hand, their concentration over a small area and their lofty location seems to exclude their occupants having been herdsmen. Could these strongholds have been the homes of merchant communities that controlled the ancient salt trade, or were they the refuge of some persecuted tribes in desperate need of shelter? We could not tell. One theory is that these caves were mines, but this is contradicted by the fact that the caves are haphazardly built in varying geological formations, and their various levels do not follow the geological strata of the rock or sediments of the cliffs. However, there are in the vicinity of Muktinath certain mines which were worked until the seventeenth century. Our best conclusion was that these caves were probably inhabited for only part of the year by people who lived primarily to the north on the rich Tibetan grazing lands where certain travellers had recorded encountering many similar cave dwellings. There are indications that originally the inhabitants of central Asia frequently lived in caves when not digging their homes out of the flat open plains. It is also possible

The deepest scar on the earth's surface: the Himalayan Grand Canyon, whose walls rise 15,000 ft for a distance of three miles.

Left: a woman who looks a hundred recites her Buddhist rosary. Below: turquoise from the banks of the Kali Gandaki adorn this woman from Mustang.

This turbulent tributary of the Sun Khosi was beyond us. Below: the great Himalayan breach looking south. Wide angle lens reduces the apparent size of Mount Dhaulagiri (right). At 27,000 ft it is the seventh highest peak in the world.

Journey's end. Michael Alexander and Michel Peissel.

that these caves had a religious use as shelters for pilgrims, not of the Lamaist Church but of the early Buddhists in the fourth and fifth centuries, although one would expect them to be mentioned in the ancient manuscripts of Chinese pilgrims. This would then link them with the similar-looking cave dwellings found in Afghanistan, Sinkiang and China, so that the cave sites of the upper Kali Gandaki might close a vast loop of early Buddhist settlements encircling Tibet, then a country of 'pagan savages'. What is certain is that this region had a very ancient and busy past.

In spite of our endeavours the great cave sites of the upper Kali Gandaki remain one of the great unsolved enigmas of the Himalayas. One day it is to be hoped the Nepalese Government will accede to my now long-standing campaign to allow scholars to carry out a detailed investigation of these sites. This would necessarily involve considerable equipment to penetrate into the highest and most inaccessible caves, which are those most likely to yield artefacts, the more accessible caves having been sacked and despoiled of their contents over the years. My only hope is that, by finding many of these caves and raising the issue of their importance and origin, I may have contributed to solving one of the mysteries of the early history of the Himalayas, a history which was no doubt as complex and exciting as the present.

Scrambling down the caves above Tukutcha, Michael and I set off for a walk a few miles up the river. We noted how the vegetation on the steep banks was rapidly becoming scarcer. The pines did not grow much beyond Tukutcha, being replaced by the tormented scraggy forms of twisted junipers, the most rugged of Himalayan trees.

Tomorrow we hoped to enter at last the dry edge of the tundra zones in the rain shadow of the great range. Unfortunately we should not be able to go much farther north and so reach the higher regions and Mustang, where the first majestic fortresses line the banks of the river north of Jomoson (which means frontier fort in Tibetan). So far as the river beyond Jomoson was concerned, I could fall back on my memories and notes of when I had travelled to Mustang and lived there for three months in 1964. I knew how slowly the river bed ascended up a broad, slightly sloping valley to the edge of the Tibetan plains, cutting its way through majestic red and yellow cliffs eroded by the howling winds into fantastic pillars and imaginary castles; then, after passing the monastery and fort of Tsarang, the river narrowed to become a rivulet that ran through the eastern district of Mustang before turning west to end, or rather begin, in the swamp fields at the foot of an unnamed 22,000-foot peak that dominated the summer residence of Jigme Dorje Trandul, the twenty-fifth King of Lo, the Raja of Mustang.

On returning to Tukutcha we encountered a caravan making its way north carrying grain collected from Pokhara (seven days away) and led by muleteers from Mustang whom I was able to surprise by my knowledge of their remote land. We were exhausted when we got back, and soon fell asleep.

It was freezing cold when we got up the next morning at 5 a.m. Out in the yards of the house all was still except for the tinkle of the bells of the horses feeding in the stables.

This was the day we had so long looked forward to – the day on which we planned to carry on up the river to the exit of the great Himalayan breach at Marpha, emerging to the north of Annapurna and Dhaulaghiri, on the far side of that seemingly impassable barrier of eternal snow that had constantly barred our horizon to the north and which we had gazed on in awe from the hot jungles on the edges of the Reu river.

Our teeth were chattering from cold and excitement as we made our way down to our craft. Its much battered hull recalled the troubles we had seen, the spills and accidents, but also our escapes and how, with a machine weighing only 185 lbs, and with two small motors developing only 12 horsepower, we had succeeded in defying the laws of gravity to conquer untamed forces. Our machine had provided more than transport, more than mere sport, it had given us the chance to contemplate

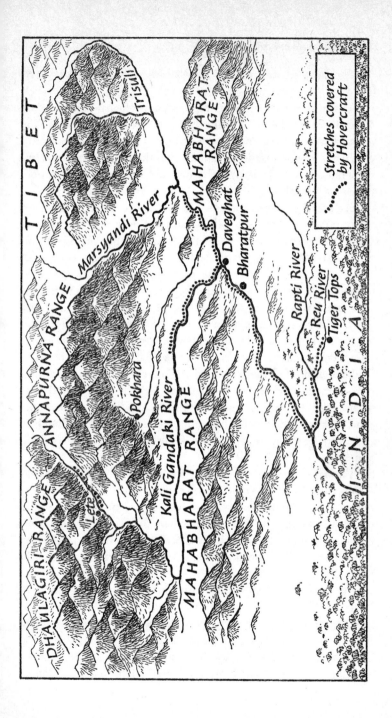

vistas of the greatest natural beauty hitherto unseen by Western man.

As we were about to start the engine we heard behind us the deep throb of drums echoing from the local monasteries. The monks were awakening to a new day. The tinkle of bells and the whistling of a muleteer announced the departure of the first caravans. It was June 9th, the day and the moment this book begins by recalling.

Six small children in rags came down to stare at us, there were no other witnesses. Michael turned over the engines. I sat down and drove the craft off the field into the turbulent cold grey water. Slowly I progressed north, picking my way up the wide gravel bed between the great peaks. My altimeter read 8700 feet. I was now climbing steeply up one endless rapid, but because I was carrying no load I kept on making steady headway. The river soon narrowed and the gravel bed disappeared as the turbulent waters lapped both banks. Rounding a bend, I slipped behind the shoulders of one of the main buttresses of Nilgiri and of Tukutcha peak. The current was becoming stronger, and on either side of me jagged rocks edged with foam warned me to keep to midstream. Two more bends and I was through the breach. Five miles from Tukutcha I could at last look south at the Himalayas. I had crossed the range.

The river had narrowed, and the current's speed increased. Only with difficulty could I stop my craft from digging in, and I felt the progressive loss of power. I was now nearing 9000 feet and making little headway, when ahead of me I saw trees surrounding an oasis of whitewashed houses, those of Marpha, the first truly Tibetan village of the north face of the Himalayas.

Just as I neared the village and the point beyond which we were forbidden to go, a large wave seized my bow and swung me round, driving me dangerously close to the rocks along the banks. I pulled back into midstream and managed to make a little headway for a few hundred yards until the river widened a little and filled with large boulders. I felt that I no longer had the motor power necessary to carry on among these without undue risks. A spill here could be fatal, since there was no-where I could shoot up the embankment to land. Looking north, I could see in the distance the cliffs where the river cut through the soft alluvial deposit of the Tibetan plateau. I was looking upon the edge of the desert wastes on the roof of the world. Before me was forbidden territory. Having achieved our objective of crossing the range and gone to the limit of our permits, I decided that it was time to pull round and return to Michael.

An hour later Michael in turn sped up the river out of sight behind the great range. When he returned we ceremoniously shook hands. Our mission was over. Both of us had reached the altitude of 8750 feet and had crossed the Himalayas.

Although the monsoon had not yet broken it could be expected any day, and we were soon on our way back. Michael drove the craft down through the breach as far as Larjung, where a howling headwind obliged him to stop. We then decided to dismantle our craft and leave the much-battered hull of '002' behind as we could not carry it all the way down to Pokhara. We donated the hull to the village schoolmaster and since have learned that it sits upon the flat roof of a house, a strange relic of our passing. Each day its thrust fan turns in the gale-force winds that rush up the breach to unite in one breath India and Tibet – a reminder that our enterprise had throughout been a journey on air.

During our trek back, over seventy miles of rugged mountain trails, I had ample time to reflect on our project and all we had been through. Our three craft had totalled 1200 miles on nine different rivers, through gorges never travelled before, and up rapids too numerous to count. We had, it is true, been prevented from travelling the full course up the Kali Gandaki, and of the caves we were leaving unsolved nearly as many mysteries as we had found. But I had accomplished at long last my dream of reaching the fringes of Tibet, not as in the past on foot up a trail, but as a navigator on nature's own highways. Against all odds, we had triumphed. I recognized that perhaps everyone had been right, perhaps we were a little mad to have gone through all this trouble just to prove a point. But *we* had been right too, for we had proved that our idea had been a good one. One *could* cross the Himalayas by boat. And in the process we had discovered an entirely new Himalayan world, one whose history is written on water.

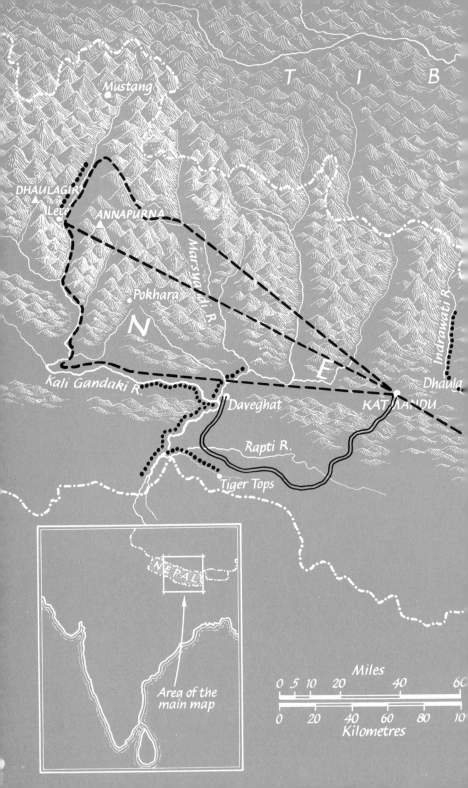

TIB

Mustang

DHAULAGIR

Leg

ANNAPURNA

Marsyandi R.

Pokhara

N

Kali Gandaki R.

Daveghat

E

KAT MANDU

Indrawati R.

Dhaula

Rapti R.

Tiger Tops

NEPAL

Area of the
main map

Miles

0 5 10   20   40   60

0   20   40   60   80   10
Kilometres